Conversations with William Faulkner

Literary Conversations Series

Peggy Whitman Prenshaw
General Editor

Conversations
with William Faulkner

Edited by
M. Thomas Inge

University Press of Mississippi
Jackson

http://www.upress.state.ms.us

Copyright © 1999 by University Press of Mississippi
All rights reserved
Manufactured in the United States of America

02 01 00 99   4 3 2 1

The paper in this book meets the guidelines for permanence and durability of the Committee
on Production Guidelines for Book Longevity of the Council on Library Resources.

Library of Congress Cataloging-in-Publication Data to come

Conversations with William Faulkner / edited by M. Thomas Inge.
        p.   cm.—(Literary conversations series)
    Includes index.
    ISBN 1-57806-135-0 (cloth : alk. paper).—ISBN 1-57806-136-9
(paper : alk. paper)
    1. Faulkner, William, 1897–1962—Interviews.   2. Novelists,
American—20th century—Interviews.   3. Southern States—
Intellectual life—20th century.   4. Fiction—Authorship.
I. Inge, M. Thomas.   II. Series.
PS3511.A86Z7593   1999
813'.52—dc21
    [b]   98-45375
                                                  CIP

British Library Cataloging-in-Publication Data available

Books by William Faulkner

The Marble Faun. Boston: The Four Seas Company, 1925.
Soldiers' Pay. New York: Boni & Liveright, 1926.
Mosquitoes. New York: Boni and Liveright, 1927.
Sartoris. New York: Harcourt, Brace and Company, 1929.
The Sound and the Fury. New York: Jonathan Cape and Harrison Smith, 1929.
As I Lay Dying. New York: Jonathan Cape and Harrison Smith, 1930.
Sanctuary. New York: Jonathan Cape and Harrison Smith, 1931.
These 13. New York: Jonathan Cape and Harrison Smith, 1931.
Idyll in the Desert. New York: Random House, 1931.
Salmagundi. Milwaukee: The Casanova Press, 1932.
Miss Zilphia Gant. Dallas: The Book Club of Texas, 1932.
Light in August. New York: Harrison Smith and Robert Haas, 1932.
A Green Bough. New York: Harrison Smith and Robert Haas, 1933.
Doctor Martino and Other Stories. New York: Harrison Smith and Robert Haas, 1934.
Pylon. New York: Harrison Smith and Robert Haas, 1935.
Absalom, Absalom! New York: Random House, 1936.
The Unvanquished. New York: Random House, 1938.
The Wild Palms. New York: Random House, 1939.
The Hamlet. New York: Random House, 1940.
Go Down, Moses and Other Stories. New York: Random House, 1942.
The Portable Faulkner. New York: Viking Press, 1946.
The Sound and the Fury and *As I Lay Dying.* New York: Modern Library/Random House, 1946.
Intruder in the Dust. New York: Random House, 1948.
Knight's Gambit. New York: Random House, 1949.
Collected Stories. New York: Random House, 1950.
Notes on a Horsethief. Greenville, Miss.: The Levee Press, 1950.
Requiem for a Nun. New York: Random House, 1951.
Mirrors of Chartres Street. Minneapolis: Faulkner Studies, 1953.
The Faulkner Reader. New York: Random House, 1954.
A Fable. New York: Random House, 1954.
Big Woods. New York: Random House, 1955.
The Town. New York: Random House, 1957.
New Orleans Sketches. New Brunswick, New Jersey: Rutgers University Press, 1958.
Three Famous Short Novels. New York: Vintage Books/Random House, 1958.
The Mansion. New York: Random House, 1959.
Selected Short Stories. New York: Modern Library/Random House, 1962.
The Reivers: A Reminiscence. New York: Random House, 1962.

Contents

Introduction

William Faulkner was famous for his refusal to accede easily to that hallmark of true fame, the interview. More often than not, he simply refused such requests outright, as when he responded by letter to Webster Schott in 1950:

> Sorry but no. Am violently opposed to interviews and publicity. What I write is in public domain of course and the writer has no right to dictate. But I hold that his private life in his own, to be—the privacy—defended. Sorry, and thank you for the courtesy of your letter.[1]

Given this stance and his characteristic rudeness in this regard, it is surprising that he actually gave as many interviews as he did.

At least three collections have appeared previous to this one. Selections from thirty-six group conferences and interviews held at the University of Virginia in 1957 and 1958 were edited by Frederick L. Gwynn and Joseph L. Blotner in *Faulkner in the University* (Charlottesville: University Press of Virginia, 1959); transcripts of four interview sessions held at West Point in 1962 appeared in *Faulkner at West Point*, edited by Joseph L. Fant, III, and Robert Ashley (New York: Random House, 1964) and are reprinted in this volume; and James B. Meriwether and Michael Millgate gathered twenty-eight mainly from American newspapers and periodicals and fifteen additional transcripts of sessions from Japan in *Lion in the Garden: Interviews with William Faulkner, 1926–1962* (New York: Random House, 1968).

At least another fifty interviews and reports of meetings with Faulkner are known to exist, and forty of the most interesting and useful have been collected in this volume. Few of them take the traditional form of the question and answer format. Rather they are articles and essays which typically report on a visit or period of time spent with Faulkner in which they describe the author and the setting but contain as well quotations of statements he made. In many ways they tend to be more engaging than the traditional interview in that they also describe Faulkner physically, report on things he did and attitudes he adopted, and give a fuller sense of the man and his personality. Several were written reflecting on a life-time acquaintance with the man or having seen him at different points in his life. Thus read collectively, one comes away with a vivid picture of Faulkner in all his genuine wit, occasional personal warmth, and more often perverse cantankerousness.

These conversations range in time from 1916, when Ben Wasson encountered a young Chaplinesque bohemian Faulkner, wearing "baggy, gray flannel trousers, a rather shabby tweed jacket and heavy brown brogans," to 1961 when *Life* reporter Elliott Chaze intruded on an irritated Faulkner of unaffected "quiet strength" pecking away at the typewriter on what must have been pages of his last novel *The Reivers*. Wasson found in the eighteen year-old budding poet already the "rare ability to dramatize himself interestingly," and so did the many journalists and interviewers to come.

Several, like novelist Hamilton Basso, noted his "beautiful manners, his soft speech and controlled intensity," and his French translator, Maurice Edgar Coindreau, found him "not talkative, I admit, but always courteous, somewhat ceremonious." Robert Cantwell thought he had a "slightly military self-conscious bearing," while Stephen Longstreet wrote that he had "the look of a shy wary man, yet with a patrician elegance." Several thought he epitomized in appearance and manner the Southern gentleman, or as Laurence Stallings put it, the "perfect civil war face" of "a confederate brigadier." Only Longstreet and Stallings dared to attempt to reproduce Faulkner's dialect, with phrases like "branch wattah," "a hundred yeahs from now," or "Could I buy yo' a drink?"

There are numerous examples too of the rude Faulkner, turning away dignitary and young student alike from his door, being obnoxious at a party or dinner, or acting unnecessarily disrespectful, as when he sent word to the eminent poet John Ciardi, by way of Nancy Hale, in response to a request that he autograph his two volumes of poetry for Ciardi, "Tell the gentleman I have given up the world of literature for the world of fox hunting." More than one aspiring interviewer never got close enough even to experience a rejection or rude retort. Columnist Joe Hyams wrote a piece in 1959 on advice he received on "How to Meet William Faulkner" and then demonstrated how none of it worked when he visited Oxford, Mississippi. While basically a non-interview, it is reprinted here as an example of what some writers endured in their efforts to corner the elusive author.

Readers can observe here Faulkner the great fabricator at work, spinning tall tales about adventures he never had or things he wished he had done. To Stallings in 1932 he recited in full detail the famous lie about how during World War I, after only two hours of instruction, he flew into combat over

France in a dog fight with German planes, crashed, and broke his legs. For Roark Bradford, he spun out a marvelous yarn about how an opossum was treed on his farm by several yelping dogs, two yowling cats, and a horse— silent because "It just isn't in the nature of a horse to whinny when he trees a possum."

In this category may well belong the stories about his capacity for drinking and the influence of liquor on his writing. Anthony Buttitta described Faulkner in 1932 as working at a table with "a jug of fresh water and a fruit jar of moonshine on the floor beside him which he sipped whenever he took a notion," and Faulkner told Coindreau a few years later that he always wrote at night and kept his "whiskey within reach." Faulkner seemed to delight in the accusation that his difficult works were the muddled results of an alcoholic stupor. Hamilton Basso's simple reply to this was, "I would only point out that the large body of his work, with its infinite variety and complexity, could not have been produced by a crock." This is not to suggest, though, that he did not have his personal problems with what several have concluded was alcoholism, nor that he privately undervalued his work. The latter was reflected in one special moment witnessed by his editor Robert N. Linscott: "One day at my farm in The Berkshires he astonished me by running his finger along a shelf full of his books and saying, 'Not a bad monument for a man to leave behind him.' "

If he encouraged some lies about himself, he also spent time debunking others. Several times here he corrects the story about how in Hollywood he told his boss he was going home to work and then went all the way home to Oxford. It is interesting to compare the accurate versions he told over time, each with fuller details, but none of which he admitted was as good as the original tale created by his Hollywood friends. Another famous incident can be explored here more completely than ever before with three versions of his interviews with student classes held at the University of Mississippi in 1947. His comments on other American writers were leaked to the press and caused some controversy, especially when Ernest Hemingway heard what Faulkner said about his work. Hemingway never quite forgave him, and Faulkner felt called upon to clarify his statements more than once over the years. Such events only served to solidify Faulkner's aversion to interviews.

The reader will find in these pages Faulkner's thoughts on any number of other topics. Although strongly opposed to racism and segregation, his comments reveal a paternalistic and gradualist stand on integration. Despite what Hollywood did with its adaptations of his novels in his lifetime, he maintained a deep respect for many Hollywood producers and their products and counted among his favorite films *Citizen Kane, The Magnificent Ambersons,* and *High Noon.* Throughout the conversations are comments on his favorite books and authors, the sources of his fiction, advice to beginning writers, the nature of the publishing industry, the situation of modern literature, the importance of education, and the state of civilization and society. A clear line can be traced from his early stance as mainly a writer and craftsman to his becoming, after the Nobel Prize, a spokesman for various political and social agenda. In sum, they add an engaging body of materials to the existing *oeuvre* on Faulkner's life and career.

The interviews are arranged in the order of when they were conducted, or when the authors first met Faulkner, rather than the order of publication. Obvious typographical errors have been silently corrected, and the uses of italics for book titles and quotation marks for short works have been regularized. Sub-titles supplied by editors have been deleted. Otherwise the texts appear as first published without annotation or revision. Contradictory versions of the same story or repetitious material have been maintained as a useful and revealing part of the historic record. Errors in the articles have not been noted, but a chronology is included as a check against biographical misinformation. Readers must discern for themselves the source of any misstatements on Faulkner's part—for reasons of humor, politeness, privacy, or intentional exaggeration.

It can also be informative to compare these encounters and interviews with other versions of the same occasions. For example, Ben Wasson provided a slightly different account of his first meeting with Faulkner in 1916 in his book *Count No 'Count: Flashbacks to Faulkner* (University Press of Mississippi, 1983). The several articles from Virginia newspapers in 1957 and 1958 can be compared with the abridged transcripts for these same interview sessions collected in Gwynn and Blotner's *Faulkner in the University,* pages 11–16, 147–51, 209–27, 279–80, and 285–86. Rather than duplicate each other, they tend to be complementary in that they include different selections of quotations. A fourth account of Faulkner's controversial classroom comments at the University of Mississippi in 1947 can be found in the Meriwether and Millgate volume *Lion in the Garden,* pages 52–58. Time, memory, and the imperfections of transcription often provide different and interesting results, but in these instances comparison suggests that we have the spirit, if not always the exact letter, of what Faulkner said.

I appreciate the continued support of Randolph-Macon College in my scholarship, especially the good will and material support of past President Ladell Payne, the current President Roger H. Martin, and Provost Jerome H. Garris. Student assistant Corrie E. Ward and faculty secretaries Nina Wells and Susan G. Timberlake provided invaluable assistance. This one is for Donária, an unexpected and undeserved but gratefully welcomed pleasure in my life.

MTI
August 1998

Note

1. Cited in Webster Schott's review of *The Faulkner Reader*, Kansas City *Star*, July 24, 1954, page 14, and reprinted in M. Thomas Inge, ed., *William Faulkner: The Contemporary Reviews* (New York: Cambridge University Press, 1995), pp. 361–63.

Chronology

1897   William Cuthbert Falkner, the first of four sons, born to Maud Butler and Murry Cuthbert Falkner, on September 25 in New Albany, Mississippi.

1898   Family moves to Ripley, Mississippi.

1902   Family moves to Oxford, the seat of the University of Mississippi.

1914   Meets Phil Stone, friend and mentor, and begins to read seriously under his tutelage and to write poetry.

1918   Enlists in the British Royal Air Force in Canada under the last name "Faulkner," begins training, but is discharged before graduating at the conclusion of World War I.

1919   Registered as special student at the University of Mississippi, publishes first poem in August 6 issue of *New Republic* and first story, "Landing in Luck," in *The Mississippian* student newspaper in November under the new spelling of "Faulkner."

1921   Visits with Stark Young in New York, works in a bookstore, and returns home in December to become postmaster at the university post office.

1924   Resigns as postmaster after an official reprimand for neglect in the performance of his duties, a good deal of his time having been spent reading and writing poems, stories, and criticism. Publishes his first book, *The Marble Faun*, a cycle of pastoral poems in December.

1925   Moves to New Orleans to join a circle of writers led by Sherwood Anderson and contributes essays, poems, and stories to the New Orleans *Times-Picayune* newspaper and *The Double Dealer* magazine. Travels to Italy, Switzerland, France, and England from July through December.

1926   Publishes his first novel *Soldiers' Pay* February 25 with the recommendation of Sherwood Anderson.

1927   *Mosquitoes* published April 30.

1929   *Sartoris* (a revised and condensed version of *Flags in the Dust*) pub-
       lished January 31. Marries his recently divorced childhood sweetheart
       Estelle Oldham on June 20. *The Sound and the Fury* published Octo-
       ber 7.

1930   "A Rose for Emily" published in the April issue of *Forum*, the first
       short story to appear in a national magazine. Purchases his home
       Rowan Oak in April. *As I Lay Dying* published October 6.

1931   A daughter named Alabama is born prematurely on January 9 and
       dies after nine days. *Sanctuary* published February 9. *These 13*, his
       first collection of stories, published September 21. Attends a Southern
       Writers Conference in Charlottesville at the University of Virginia in
       October. *Idyll in the Desert* published in December.

1932   Does his first film work in Hollywood in May and befriends producer
       John Hawks. Co-authors script based on his own story "Turn About"
       for film released as *Today We Live*. Second poetry volume, *A Green
       Bough*, published April 20. Daughter Jill born June 24. *Light in Au-
       gust* published October 6.

1934   *Dr. Martino and Other Stories* published April 16.

1935   *Pylon* published March 25. In Hollywood in December, begins a rela-
       tionship with Meta Doherty Carpenter.

1936   *Absalom, Absalom!* published October 6.

1938   *The Unvanquished* published February 15.

1939   *The Wild Palms* published January 19. Elected to National Institute of
       Arts and Letters.

1940   *The Hamlet* published April 1.

1942   *Go Down, Moses, and Other Stories* published May 11.

1944   Works on scripts for films by Howard Hawks released as *To Have and
       Have Not* and *The Big Sleep*.

1946   *The Portable Faulkner*, edited by Malcolm Cowley, published April
       29. Combined edition of *The Sound and the Fury* (with the "Comp-
       son" appendix) and *As I Lay Dying* published in October.

1948   *Intruder in the Dust* published September 27. Elected to the American
       Academy of Arts and Letters.

1949   Begins a relationship with the young writer Joan Williams in August. *Knight's Gambit* published November 27.

1950   Receives William Dean Howells Medal for Fiction from the American Academy. *Collected Stories* published August 2. Awarded the Nobel Prize for Literature for 1949 in Stockholm on December 10, where he meets Else Jonsson.

1951   *Notes on a Horse Thief* published February 10. *Collected Stories* given the National Book Award for Fiction. Travels to England and France in April. *Requiem for a Nun* published October 2. Awarded an appointment in the Legion of Honor of the Republic of France.

1953   Works in Paris with Howard Hawks on the film script for *Land of the Pharoahs* and meets Jean Stein.

1954   Continues his stay in Europe and Egypt. *The Faulkner Reader* published April 1. *A Fable* published August 2. Attends a writers conference in São Paulo, Brazil, and travels to Peru in August for the State Department.

1955   *A Fable* receives the National Book Award for Fiction and the Pulitzer Prize. Visits Japan, the Philippines, and Europe for the State Department. *Big Woods* published October 14.

1957   Becomes writer in residence at the University of Virginia for the spring semester. Travels to Greece for the State Department. *The Town* published May 1.

1958   Returns for second spring term as writer in residence at the University of Virginia.

1959   Purchases home in Charlottesville, Virginia, in August. *The Mansion* published November 13.

1961   Visits Venezuela for the State Department and receives the Order of Andrés Bello.

1962   Lectures at the U. S. Military Academy at West Point in April. Receives the Gold Medal for Fiction from the National Institute of Arts and Letters. *The Reivers* published June 4. Dies of heart attack on July 6 at a sanitarium in Byhalia, Mississippi, and is buried on July 7 in Oxford.

Conversations with William Faulkner

The Time Has Come

Ben Wasson / 1916

From *Delta Democrat-Times* (Greenville, Mississippi), July 15, 1962.
Reprinted by permission.

It was early Autumn, 1916, but now in 1962 it doesn't seem so very long ago. . . .

We were both young then. William Faulkner was eighteen and I was sixteen. Accompanied by a newly made college friend, I was crossing the small, circular campus of Ole Miss, feeling myself to be old and worldly-wise having become a Freshman in college. My friend was a Senior and this gave me a special sense of sophistication. Coming towards us, under the just beginning to be scarlet and yellow trees, was a small, slight fellow. He was wearing a pair of baggy, gray flannel trousers, a rather shabby tweed jacket and heavy, brown brogans, the like of [with] which I was unfamiliar.

"This is Bill Faulkner," my friend said.

William Faulkner nodded to me, a quick nod, his eyes very brown and somewhat almond shaped and very penetrating. His nose was quite aquiline and he sported a small, neatly trimmed moustache which struck me as quite worldly and daring.

William Faulkner and my friend talked for awhile as I stood to one side and listened. I noted that Faulkner, as soft-spoken words came from [his] thin, straight mouth, pulled a handkerchief intermittently from the sleeve of his coat. He saw me observing this and said: "The British wear handkerchiefs in their jacket sleeves. I prefer the sartorial usage, also."

Then he turned back to my friend and continued to discuss a new book he was reading—by someone I had never heard of—A. E. Housman. I listened, entranced, already bedazzled by his first remark to me.

Even though it was early Autumn, the world then seemed mostly green. Everything was so alive, so vital, and now I had met a fellow-man who was green with fresh thoughts, full of a love for creative things. Other than Miss Carrie Stern, a beloved teacher, I had never known anyone who loved poetry enough to be so bold as to quote it.

As my friend and William Faulkner concluded their conversation, I told him with over-flowing politeness that I was glad to meet him. He turned to me and his eyes held amusement: "Ah," he said, "we seem to have a young Sir Galahad on a rocking horse come to our college campus."

Then he left us, going his way across campus, pausing a moment to light a straight-stemmed pipe which he had been holding as he conversed, then continued in an opposite direction.

He must have sensed that early Autumn day that I was eager about poetry because he, in kindly fashion, soon looked me up, a lowly freshman. At any rate that first meeting was the beginning of many others in many places and over many years that was filled with talks of books—novels, poetry, philosophy. He was, unknown to himself, a mentor to a youth hungry for such talk.

Often he would invite me to accompany him to a friend's house where there was a "victrola" and a collection of classical records. These occasions would be at night and William Faulkner would select a record, place it on the turn table and extinguish the lights in order: "To hear music with no distraction—even light," he said, "can be too much distraction when music is being played."

So we listened to much music, mostly Beethoven symphonies. "Listen to those horns of triumph and joy crying their golden sounds in a great twilight of sorrow," he said.

There are other memories I hold of William Faulkner throughout the years in many places when I saw him move from verse to universe and grow into the giant figure he came to be, but these are the earliest. And I think they show that, even then when he was young, he possessed an innate kindness and gentleness and a rare ability to dramatize himself interestingly.

More importantly though, he gave to another eager youth an understanding of the power and glory of words.

William Faulkner: Man and Writer
Hamilton Basso / 1925

From *Saturday Review of Literature*, 45 (July 28, 1962), p. 11–14.

Some while ago, I saw a picture of William Faulkner standing on what I think must have been the portico of the library of the University of Virginia. His hair had gone all white, as had his moustache, and he looked remarkably handsome. "Well," I thought, "the Little Confederate has really grown up."

I meant no disrespect. I was exercising the right of shared experience. My thoughts, which soon moved on to other things, were tinged not so much with affection, although affection was not absent, as with a recollection of times past, in the middle 1920s, when I met Faulkner for the first time.

If I never much hankered after Paris during the expatriate years, it was because, in the New Orleans of that era, I had Paris in my own back yard. It was my privilege to be on companionable terms, not only with Faulkner, but with all those who made the French Quarter a sort of Creole version of the Left Bank. We weren't a literary clique, we weren't a movement, and God knows we weren't a school. What held us together was simply mutual friendliness and good will.

Our Royal Personage was Sherwood Anderson. He was then living in New Orleans and at the height of his reputation. We owed him much. All of us were young enough to profit by example, and Anderson's example, leaving aside the example of the dedicated artist, was basically that of benevolence. What he had, he shared. What was his to give, he gave—his time, his patience, his attention, and, rather like a canopy spread over all of these, the hospitality of his house. Almost every Saturday night he and his wife, the former Elizabeth Prall, had some of us to dinner. It was on one of these occasions that Faulkner and I were introduced to each other. He was then twenty-seven.

I wish I could remember the details of the evening, but I can't. I recall that we talked about the South—Faulkner's South: the world of Oxford, Mississippi, that he was later to transform into his own special world of Yoknapatawpha County—but what I best recollect are his beautiful manners, his soft speech, his controlled intensity, and his astonishing capacity for hard drink. Let us get this latter talent over with immediately. Faulkner drank. We have

3

heard many stories and probably will soon be hearing many more. I would only point out that the large body of his work, with its infinite variety and complexity, could not have been produced by a crock, and that, even in his deepest cups, he never lost for the briefest second his courtesy and consideration for others, or failed to remain himself.

Faulkner and I never spent much time together. There were seven years between us, more of a gap then than later, and while I have no more modesty than the next man, I was bound, having just turned twenty and still enrolled at Tulane University, to wonder occasionally if I had not been admitted into the ball park by mistake. Sometimes, however, we would meet on the streets, and a few of these chance encounters led to our taking a walk on the wharves.

It would be agreeable to say that we talked about art, or meaning, or the meaning of meaning, but this was a different act entirely. Compared to the modern young men who come so splendidly armored from classes in English literature and creative writing, we were both ill-educated; myself more so than Faulkner, who had been reading enormously on his own. What we talked about were the far-off places vessels tied up at the wharves brought to mind; our recent forays into the world of books (Faulkner had got past Verlaine, Eliot, Pound, and Joyce, while I was just stumbling on Conrad and Melville); and, inevitably, the South.

Yet even the South was not the bond it might have been. My South—New Orleans and its immediate environs, the swamp-and-bayou country directly south and west—was not Faulkner's. Mine was Mediterranean, Catholic, and, in such families as my own, still essentially European. Faulkner's South was much less diluted, *sui generis,* Anglo-Saxon, Protestant, and, as it were, more landlocked, turned inward upon itself. Our conversation, then, was in effect about two different worlds. It was not until I left New Orleans and went to live elsewhere in the South that I began to understand what Faulkner was trying to get at—in specifically Southern terms, I mean—and I think it is interesting that his one truly negligible book, the early novel *Mosquitoes,* has New Orleans as its locale.

My closest tie to Faulkner came out of a wholly different realm. There was then in New Orleans a gang of barn-storming aviators who called themselves "The Gates Flying Circus." They flew decrepit Wright Whirlwinds stuck together God knows how. Although I was still at Tulane, as I have said, I was also doing some space-rate journalism on the side for the *Times-Picayune;* and the city editor, having decided that the Flying Circus was worth a feature, apparently decided, too, that, as the least expensive of his hirelings, I was the most expendable. I soared into the air for the first time in my life, was introduced to a dazzling series of tricks that at first scared the daylights out of me, and struck up a friendship with the several daring fellows, who—which may have been in the back of my city editor's mind all the time—soon got themselves killed. However, they and their planes held together long enough for me to venture up with them five or six times more, purely in the line of pleasure, and for Faulkner, who was a bit hipped on the subject of flying anyway, to become an almost constant companion, and to get the substance of the experience that later went into his novel *Pylon*. (I understand that the Literary Puritans object to this sort of thing, and hold that a writer's work should be examined without reference to the field of his personal experience, but wouldn't hop-scotch or tiddly-winks be more fun?) Anyhow, it was the Gates Flying Circus that provided Faulkner and me with our strongest bond. Nobody *else* in our crowd had gone looping-the-loop in a bucket seat and open cockpit over the Mississippi River.

Just how long Faulkner lived in New Orleans I don't remember—long enough to write his first novel, *Soldier's Pay*, which Sherwood Anderson helped to get published by Liveright (the flying circus of publishing), and also, I think, *Mosquitoes*. He joined in some of our play—there was a fine game of tag one night across the steeply angled roofs of a narrow block of the Quarter—but already, unknown to the rest of us, he was caught up in his vision of Yoknapatawpha County and working most industriously.

This part of Faulkner's story has already been put together with much care and detail by Carvel Collins in his Introduction to his edition of *William Faulkner: New Orleans Sketches*, a collection of pieces that Faulkner wrote for *The Double-Dealer*, a "little" magazine of unusual merit, published in New Orleans—some of the other contributors to *The Double-Dealer* were Ernest Hemingway, Sherwood Anderson, Ezra Pound, Hart Crane, John Crowe Ransom, Allen Tate, Edmund Wilson, and Thornton Wilder—and for the Sunday feature section of the New Orleans *Times-Picayune*. In his Introduction, Mr. Collins shows how these stories and sketches foreshadowed many of the themes that were to enrich his later work. It is easy to see now, thanks to Mr. Collins's patient effort, that Yoknapatawpha County, Faulkner's mythical kingdom, first began to take shape in his ground-floor apartment in Orleans Alley, a little one-block street that runs through from Jackson Square to Royal Street.

Faulkner left New Orleans in 1926. In the years that followed I saw him only twice again. I am not too good about dates, and I've never kept a notebook that amounts to anything, but the first of these encounters was in New York City in the summer of 1929, shortly before the publication of the first of the Yoknapatawpha novels, *Sartoris*.

By that time I had left the university for a reporter's job on the long since defunct New Orleans *Tribune*, a morning paper, and then, after a spell on the *Times-Picayune*, had gone to work for an advertising agency, also in New Orleans, an episode later terminated by my complete and even appalling lack of ability as a copywriter.

I go into these details only to explain what I was doing in New York City in the summer of 1929. The agency sent me. Just what business it was that caused me to be riding one of the trains on the old Third Avenue Elevated I no longer have the vaguest idea. But there I was, and there, in the same coach, was Faulkner. We hadn't seen each other in three years. New York was then a strange, foreign country to me, as in many ways it still is; and I think it has been proven by the record that Faulkner was never really at home anywhere except in Oxford, Mississippi.

We were glad to see each other, very glad, but I believe that some of the gladness was that of two provincials, each deeply committed to his own place and sharing a set of memories, who find themselves in the large, unfamiliar city. I remember myself impulsively saying, "Good Lord, the Little Confederate," and Faulkner's quick grin; and the upshot was that we rode to the end of the line together, and then back again to where Faulkner had to get off.

He was in an easy mood during our trip. He told me something about *Sartoris* and that he had found what he thought was a good publisher who believed in him. I wished him good luck when we parted, and he wished me good luck. The 1929 crash came and then the rest of it, and, while Faulkner continued to write and publish, he fell into that long period of neglect when, at one stage, all of his work was out of print, a partial oblivion from which he was rescued by that most sensible, perceptive, and helpful critic, Malcolm Cowley.

The Faulkner commentary has now reached staggering proportions. It was Cowley, however, in his introduction to the *Faulkner Portable* he edited for Viking, who first got at the whole sweep and panorama of Yoknapatawpha County and made apparent, for the first time, what Faulkner had been up to. Sometimes I have wondered if Faulkner didn't himself find Cowley's Introduction, which can be seen as a sort of surveying job of Yoknapatawpha County, more than ordinarily useful. I don't think that even his warmest admirers would want to claim that Faulkner was a careful writer—in the way, for example, that Proust was a careful writer. One of the astonishments of Proust is how expertly everything is fitted and joined: one of the astonishments of Faulkner is how it isn't. But then, in strict novelistic terms—such terms as may again be applied to Proust—Faulkner, as Cowley was able to see, was less the novelist and more the bardic poet.

Let me seem to be arrogant for a moment. There are a few things in the South that, as far as intellectual comprehension is concerned, I "know" almost as well as anybody. So when I read Faulkner (not that I have read everything; far from it) I begin, so to speak, from the inside looking out. But then something happens. What I "know" begins to lose its hold. It fades and grows dim. And soon, instead of being on the inside looking out, I am on the outside looking in. It wasn't the South that Faulkner was writing about: it was his vision of the South; and, beyond that vision, although always a part of it, his vision of the world. Those who read him as a "realistic" novelist might just as well read Dante as a Baedeker to the nether regions, and Milton as a Michelin going in the opposite direction.

Beginning with Cowley's portable, Faulkner's reputation began its steady climb upward. He became with Ernest Hemingway our most widely read and most highly admired writer throughout the world, and, like Hemingway, was awarded a Nobel Prize. Without making a point of it, we kept in touch. I would get an occasional message via some Oxford, Mississippi, connections I had acquired through a sister's marriage (one of the things the South is is a bundle of fishhooks), and I would send an occasional message back. Once he wrote me a note, extending a standing invitation to visit, but I never took up the invitation.

And so things continued along until one noontime a few years ago, when we happened to run into each other in the downstairs lobby of his present publishers, Random House, on Madison Avenue. Thirty years had passed since our little excursion on the Third Avenue Elevated. We looked at each other, noting what the decades had done. I said, "Well, now," and Faulkner said, "Good morning to you, sir"; and then, in full sight of a small audience, we rather formally embraced.

Under the circumstances, then, I am not the one to attempt any kind of evaluation. I think there are flaws in his work, bad flaws at times, and I think he was a very great writer. I often lose my way in his pages, and quite as often don't altogether understand what is written on them, and I think he is as original a genius as this country has produced. Time as always will be the judge. I believe that time will be on his side. And meanwhile, as it was in the beginning, is now, and forever shall be, the weighers and assayers, the self-appointed anointers all, will assume time's province.

Somewhere I have read something to the effect that a dissection of Faulkner's work is the greatest task that faces twentieth-century criticism. Well, maybe so. I suppose the feast is too tempting to be foresworn. And has not his Nobel Prize speech—"I believe that man will not merely endure: he will prevail. He is immortal, not because he alone among creatures has an inexhaustible voice but because he has a soul, a spirit capable of compassion and sacrifice and endurance"—has not this utterance already been waved aside as a piece of empty rhetoric? This sort of thing isn't *done* nowadays. Who wants to be a square?

But it can't be had both ways. For what Faulkner said in Stockholm was in essence what he had been saying ever since the vision of Yoknapatawpha County first loomed up before him in Orleans Alley in New Orleans. The violence and terror is there, and the sickening horror—cannot anyone understand the chill it brought to the man, that of the horror he was the most horrified?—yet running deeper than that, a constantly recurring theme, was the belief that man, capable of sacrifice and compassion and endurance, possessed of his soul, would by his soul prevail. I am aware of the complexity of his work, but to me the important thing is really quite simple. William Faulkner was a Christian gentleman. May his soul rest in peace.

William Faulkner: That Writin'
Man of Oxford

Anthony Buttitta / 1931

From *Saturday Review of Literature*, 18 (May 21, 1938), p. 6–8. Reprinted by permission.

If you ever go to Oxford, Mississippi, and William Faulkner feels like showing you the sights, you won't understand his language unless you've read most of his books, for Oxford is the Jefferson of his many tales and he has attributed to some of its places and landmarks various characters and events of his own invention. Were you to start off with Faulkner in the old, quiet court square, with its relics of long porches and balconies of the old South, this is about what he'd say:

"The same courthouse where Temple Drake testified. Christmas did his killing in that old house. Lena Grove's baby was born there, too. There's Bayard Sartoris's bank which Byron Snopes robbed. Benbow's place. The house where old Bayard died. Christmas was killed up there. John Sartoris's statue and effigy so he could watch his railroad. That's the railroad Colonel Sartoris built. Across the road is Reverend Hightower's place. Up that road near the river Wash Jones killed Sutpen. . . ."

But that is not all you'd see if he felt like walking you a piece toward what he calls Frenchman's Bend. He usually takes it slow, quiet, absorbed in himself. You get the feeling that he is working out the macabre details of his next chapter. He may even tell you a story, outlandish and incoherent, and if you question him for an explanation you won't get any satisfaction. He goes right on telling the story in his own way. If by accident he returns to it a few days later, you may get the clue that explains everything. Otherwise, it remains a mystery forever.

"That's the bridge that washed away. Made it tough for Anse and his sons so they couldn't cross with Addie's body. Up that way a piece is where Snopes got his start in business. That's the old Frenchman's place where Popeye killed Tommy. . . ." Bill goes on, talking in all seriousness, for Jefferson is his world and he knows every foot of it. Fortunately, he has set it down on paper to simplify the geographical puzzle. He did it two years ago for

Harrison Smith, his publisher at the time, and the map now appears in the back of *Absalom, Absalom!* Faulkner considers himself the "sole owner and proprietor" of Jefferson.

No one in Oxford has yet disputed his claim, since few of its citizens have read his books. He can recall only four local "fans" who read everything of his that reaches print—a doctor, a lawyer, a professor, and his mother, Mrs. Maud Butler Faulkner. To the remaining four or five thousand Oxford people, excluding the student body and faculty of the University of Mississippi, he is a writer taken for granted. To the village folk that hang around the square, he is a curiosity. They call him "that writin' man of Oxford."

According to one source, William Faulkner (originally Falkner, and still so listed in *Who's Who*) was born in New Albany, Miss., on September 25, 1897, and, according to another, in Ripley, twenty-five miles away, in October of the same year. Both towns are near Oxford, to which his family moved during his early childhood. His father, Murry (T. or C.) Falkner, was business manager of the University of Mississippi, and was connected with the railroad, running from Oxford to Memphis, which is mentioned in *Sartoris* and more recently in *The Unvanquished*. This railroad was built by Bill's grandfather, John W. T. Falkner, an Assistant United States District Attorney, and his great-grandfather, Colonel William C. Falkner, who served in the Mexican War, at Harper's Ferry, and in the Civil War.

Colonel Falkner, by the way, was also one of the most popular romantic novelists of his time, the author of *The White Rose of Memphis*, a sentimental novel written in the best lily-laced, magnolia-decked tradition of the old South, which, up to its 35th edition in 1909, had sold more than 160,000 copies. This figure is 60,000 more copies than the total sale of Bill's works to date.

The parallel with the Sartoris family, which has been pointed out elsewhere, becomes more striking when we learn that Colonel Falkner was shot to death by R. J. Thurmond on November 5, 1889, the day he was elected to the legislature in Ripley. In the closing chapter of *The Unvanquished*, which was originally the short story, "An Odor of Verbena," Col. John Sartoris is killed in a pistol duel with Ben Redmond, with whom he had built the railroad."

William Faulkner entered the University of Mississippi as a special student at sixteen. He was a "slave" of Swinburne at the time. "Whatever it was in Swinburne," he said later, "it completely satisfied me and filled my inner life." Two years later, he dropped out to join the Canadian Flying Corps and was transferred to Oxford, England, where he was in training as a non-commissioned officer for more than a year. He spent his spare time taking courses at Oxford and reading in the University library. It was there that he started to read and study the Elizabethan poets, whom he still likes for their "beautiful awareness, power, and masculinity." He became a lieutenant in the British Royal Air Force, was sent to France as an observer, crashed twice and was once injured, and remained abroad until after the Armistice. Following his return from France, he enrolled officially in the University of Mississippi, and remained there from 1919 to 1921. Later he entered on a series of odd jobs ranging from painting roofs to acting as University postmaster. He left his imprint on many of the University rooftops, but he is best remembered for the days when as University postmaster he sat behind the grating, reading his favorite poets. On many occasions he closed the window ahead of scheduled time and wrote poetry while the students howled for their mail. He was ultimately fired.

During his first few writing years Faulkner devoted himself to poetry and a few short stories. He made his first appearance with a six-stanza poem, "Portrait," which was published in the June, 1922, number of *The Double-Dealer Magazine*. In 1924 a collection of his pastoral poetry appeared in a privately published collection, *The Marble Faun*. Very little is known of this work other than that Faulkner sold most of the edition to a bookstore for about ten cents a copy. After the success of *Sanctuary*, I heard, it was sold for as high as fifty dollars a copy. By that time the author had only one copy for his own library.

About this time, while Faulkner was painting rooftops at the University, Stark Young, another Mississippian, came to Oxford. At Young's suggestion Bill went to New York, and after a while he landed a job behind the book counter at Lord & Taylor. This was his last attempt to deal directly with the public. Fired for incompetence and lack of interest, he returned once more to Oxford. For the next year he worked as a carpenter, doing a great deal of farming, fishing, and hunting on the side. Eventually he saved enough money to take him to New Orleans, where he shared an apartment with Sherwood Anderson. He did a series of lush features on the local scenery for the New Orleans newspapers and wrote poems and articles for the *Double-Dealer*.

Faulkner's first two novels, *Soldiers' Pay* and *Mosquitoes*, came out of New Orleans. They were followed by *Sartoris* and *The Sound and the Fury*. These four novels involved two changes of publishers, and Faulkner, discouraged by their sales, began to think in terms of writing for money. In his introduction to the Modern Library edition of *Sanctuary*, he tells how he chose what he thought was the "right answer" to "current trends," and "invented the most horrific tale I could imagine." He tells also how *Sanctuary* went on the shelf temporarily: how he wrote *As I Lay Dying* while he was working on the night shift in a power plant; and how, after the latter novel, published in 1930, brought him his first critical success, he rewrote *Sanctuary*—"trying to make out of it something which would not shame *The Sound and the Fury* and *As I Lay Dying* too much."

With the publication of the rewritten *Sanctuary* in the summer of 1931, the general reading public discovered Faulkner for the first time. His work was in demand everywhere, and the short stories that had been turned down now brought him hundreds of dollars apiece from the popular and literary magazines. Random House brought out a limited edition of *Idyll in the Desert* in the same year: two other limited editions followed; overnight Faulkner's name became important in the book collector's stock exchange. And his publishing troubles were over. He came to New York that fall to autograph the limited edition of his *Idyll in the Desert*, and on his arrival, various alert publishers descended upon him with promises of advance royalties and long-termed contracts. His telephone at the Algonquin kept ringing, but he was enjoying a little private drinking and couldn't be bothered. In any case he was determined to stick with Hal Smith, who had seen him through after Liveright and Harcourt, Brace had dropped him.

On his way back from New York, Faulkner stopped off for a few days at Chapel Hill, N. C., at the invitation of *Contempo*—the little magazine Milt Abernathy and I were editing at the time. During most of his visit he stayed in bed, resting and drinking an occasional spot, even eating his meals in bed. He did venture out after three days, and we took him to a movie at Durham, twelve miles away; but the movie irritated him, and as soon as we were comfortably seated, he was ready to go. "Don't want to hear talk," he said. "Would rather talk myself. Let's go out and talk." He started talking the moment we got outside; he told us of his new book, *Light in August*, the manuscript of which he had brought to Chapel Hill; and later he recited, over and over, a poem by James Joyce. It was during this visit that we took him to Phillips Russell's class in creative literature at the University. The lecture was on the importance of form, and at the close, in response to an invitation for his own views on the subject, Faulkner rose to his feet and declared that during his entire writing career, he had never given the subject of form a single thought.

In January, 1932, when I was on a visit to Louisiana, I received a letter from Faulkner in his very fine, cryptic handwriting, asking me to stop over to see him. "I will warn you," he wrote, "that I am trying to finish my novel, and so I am going to let you entertain yourself during the forenoons. But in the afternoons and evenings we can get together."

In many more ways than I had expected, Bill turned out to be something of a conventional Southern host. He went out of his way to see that I was comfortable, apologizing for the dilapidated appearance of his big, two-story plantation house which is over a hundred years old. At the time, it needed a fresh coat of paint pretty badly; the plaster was cracked on the walls and ceilings, the wainscoting was streaked and dry with age. A year later, when Bill had cashed in on his first Hollywood contract, the house was done over, and it is now one of the most modern in that section of Mississippi.

Bill's workshop was in quite a mess when I was there. His writing table was littered with long proof sheets of *Light in August*, books, papers, letters, and a tall waterglass. The glass came in handy, for Bill occasionally took a good, stiff drink of native corn whisky. A big, halfopened wooden box full of bound manuscripts was on the floor in the middle of the room. Looking through it, I discovered original and carbon copies of his earlier novels. On the mantel over the fireplace, I remember seeing copies of his books, from *The Marble Faun* to his latest, *Sanctuary*, between two small bookends. Hunting and fishing togs hung on pegs in the right wall, with rifles and reeds nearby. Alongside his writing table was a large cardboard file in which over a hundred short stories—many rejected and paperclip-stained—waited to be pulled out, edited, retyped, and mailed to the magazines.

I was fascinated by the manner in which Bill wrote on the right hand half of legal-sized white bond, reserving the other side for later corrections. In order to get the cryptic effect that is so individual of his handwriting, Bill uses a very fine hard point on a fountain pen and scrapes it up and down the paper, in short, well controlled movements. The result is something which few people can decipher; and it is said that only Bill and Louise Bonino, who was with Hal Smith for many years and is now at Random House, are capable of "translating" a complete Faulkner novel.

During the war Bill became a pretty good pilot and he wasn't satisfied until he had bought a plane. That came about with Hollywood gold, too, following the publication of *Light in August*. In the spring of 1934, he flew up to New York to take Smith for a little ride—back to Oxford! Flying was in his system and he eventually had to write a novel about it. A year later, he completed

Pylon, the novel about a group of barnstorming flyers in a New Orleans Fair. Some time after its publication, his younger brother crashed the plane and was killed. His death was a pretty hard blow to Bill, and he has since given up flying.

But he has another hobby now: working for the films. He goes to Hollywood a few months out of the year, and he enjoys the technical aspects of production. At first he didn't like working for pictures since his Hollywood experiences weren't different from those of many other established writers. He sat around for days and weeks, collecting his checks. He was annoyed by inactivity. Subsequently, however, he has worked on a number of film assignments, including an adaptation of *Sanctuary*, released as *The Case of Temple Drake*. His next Hollywood chore may be the adaptation of *The Unvanquished* for M-G-M.

Another interest that is giving Bill a satisfaction he had never known before is his four-year-old boy Joe. The youngster means a great deal to him. His wife Estelle has two children, Sister and Malcolm, both in their teens, by a former marriage, but Joe is his only child.

Bill is a small, thin fellow, weak looking but sturdily built. He has small black eyes that rarely look into those of other people. His hair is black, lightly streaked with grey. He is slow and hesitant in his manner and speech. Asked if he'd like to do this or that, his usual reply is: "Don't care if I do." He is a shy, sensitive, and unsocial person in many respects, but on occasions when he feels free to talk, he has a ready wit and imagination for inventing the most outlandish tales. Most of the time, however, he prefers to retire within himself, for he is definitely not a man of action. In *The Unvanquished* he gives us a personal clue: "Those who can, do, but those who cannot and suffer because they can't, write about it."

This book indicates that Faulkner may be through with horrific tales of brutality and lust, morons and degenerates. Having won a reputation with *As I Lay Dying* and an audience with *Sanctuary*, he has now turned to more significant themes and characters of the South. With *The Unvanquished*, definitely in that direction, it is good news to hear that Faulkner is working on a complete book about the Snopes family, which has made a slight but favorable appearance in some of his earlier novels.

A Memoir of Faulkner in the Early Days of His Fame

Anthony Buttitta / 1931

From San Francisco *Chronicle*, July 15, 1962, This World Section, p. 20. Reprinted by permission.

William Faulkner came to Chapel Hill, N.C., on a two-week visit one late fall day in 1931, carrying a small valise and a little canvas bag. The bag contained the manuscript of *Light in August*, written in his tiny cryptic handwriting which only his publisher's secretary could decipher. He was running away from New York and all the hullabaloo that was being made over him, following the success of his gothic thriller *Sanctuary*. Publishers who had turned him down on previous books were flashing contracts in his face. It made Bill dizzy. He fled south at the invitation of the editors of *Contempo*, and on the advice of his loyal publisher, Hal Smith, of Harrison Smith & Jonathan Cape.

Bill stayed with us the second floor of a Chapel Hill office building which housed the office of the magazine and our Intimate Bookshop. He had a room to himself, where he rested and slept, guzzled bootleg corn whisky and talked of himself and his work. After a week of this, he jumped up one day and said, "I want out." We had a barber come in and shave him. We pressed his suit for him, and in no time Bill was the immaculate little dandy that earned him the title of "The Count" in his native Oxford, Miss.

Halloween Night he asked us to take him to Durham. We followed some dressed up kids. We went into a movie, at his suggestion. Bill listened five minutes and said, "Let's go outside. Too much talking. I want to talk." He did and we listened. Back in Chapel Hill Professor Phillips Russell asked him to speak to his writing class at the university. Bill accepted like a true Southern gentleman. There he was asked questions about his writing, characters, forms, etc. His memorable statement:

"Form? What form? You write and you write and if it's good, it has a form of its own. If it's not, there's no such thing. It happens."

Since we were publishing a literary magazine, we asked Bill to give us a chapter or scene from *Light in August*. While he had been sleeping, we tried to decipher the script, but we made no headway. We told him so. He laughed. Bill told us not to worry, he had stacks of rejected manuscripts, stories and poems yellowing in his files down in Oxford. When I told him I planned to visit my folks in Louisiana that Christmas, he invited me to stay with him in his rundown mansion and go through his files and take whatever we wanted. This was more than we had hoped for from the new literary light of our day.

For two weeks I stayed with Bill at his shabby Oxford mansion. I went through his files, dug out poems, short stories for our All Faulkner edition of *Contempo*. I watched Bill at work at his big, broad table, piled with scripts, a jug of fresh water, and a fruit jar of moonshine on the floor beside him which he sipped whenever he took a notion. He worked silently; tediously he wrote in that tiny handwriting on the right two-thirds of the page.

Also on the desk was a small, portable phonograph which he had wound by hand to play his favorite record *Rhapsody in Blue*. He said he wore out three recordings of it during the writing of *Sanctuary* as it set the rhythm and jazzy tone of this weird tale.

The room was dilapidated like the rest of the house. The wainscoting was a sorry sight, the plaster was peeling, mounds of it were on the floor near to his cabinets which contained hundreds of short stories that had yellowed with each rejection. Since he became successful, he simply edited and shipped them out to be published throughout the world. Of this Bill said "I couldn't give them away those days when I wrote them. Nobody wanted them. Now I get letters from the magazines asking for them. All I do is read them over, have them retyped and ship them out. And they're paying thousands of dollars for them."

One night after dinner we sat by the fireplace. His wife, Estelle, was there and she kept wanting Bill to learn to dance. She loved to dance. But Bill only wanted to talk. He started telling stories. All we could do was listen. He could spin a yarn with the directness of a born storyteller. Estelle said Bill had just gotten his third wire from Hollywood begging him to write his own ticket. She wanted to go. She eventually won. But at the time Bill said "You're only looking for a good time. I don't want to go. I want to stay here. This is the place I know. This is the only place I can write about."

One afternoon Bill took me for a walk into his world, the world he dreamed up and wrote about most of his life; his incredible fictional county of Yokna-patawpha, Miss., which is the surrounding area of Oxford, Miss. He pointed to a stream. "That's where the folks dropped the coffin in *As I Lay Dying*." We walked toward a road around a bend, he pointed: "That's where Lena

Grove started on her fur piece to Alabama, looking for the father of her child." Then we stopped before an old barn: "That's where Popeye came to life. Over there, Frenchman's Creek, is where Christmas hid for awhile from those white folks that were after him." Christmas was one of the central characters in *Light in August* which was still in Bill's handwriting.

Weeks after I returned to Chapel Hill and our All-Faulkner issue of *Contempo* was the talk of the literary world for printing ten of his poems, we received a wire from Bill asking about a missing page from his manuscript. We couldn't find it. We wired him back. Another wire came from Bill, this time a frantic one, pleading that he had to have it since there was no way he could possibly reconstruct the missing page. We wired him the same story. We don't know if Bill ever did find it. But knowing how Bill wrote, with no set plan but from his inner self, it is possible that *Light in August* may have seen the light of day without that page—and this could have added a bit more to mystify readers and critics of his many works.

The Faulkner I Knew

Maurice Edgar Coindreau / 1931

From *The Time of William Faulkner: A French View of Modern American Fiction* (Columbia: University of South Carolina Press, 1971), p. 91–102. Reprinted by permission.

If he were still among us, it surely would not occur to me to reflect on the relationship that linked me, over a period of thirty years, with William Faulkner. His role in my career as a translator had become so important, he had become such a part of my life that I no longer asked myself questions about him. If I studied his work with my eyes as wide open as possible, I accepted the man with my eyes closed and was no more concerned than he himself over the things that might be said about him. But he is dead and already his image is becoming blurred. Some who did not know him attempt to describe him by using their imaginations. Television viewers were favored, I understand, with comments on his oddities. The day after his death one could see the words *imbecile* and *genius* coupled in many a newspaper, not without perfidious intent. Let us not discuss the errors that were spread everywhere. In a single article I learned first that he was born in Oxford. That is not true. In the early years of his career, it was said that Ripley was his birthplace, and for a long time I believed that assertion, attested to by the blurb for *As I Lay Dying* (1930). He was born in New Albany, Mississippi. I learned also that his wife had died the year before, whereas she actually closed his eyes and attended the funeral, bowed beneath a large black hat, as shown by a very fine photograph published in *Life* (July 20, 1962). I learned something even more astonishing. The author of that very instructive article, because he had not exchanged more than a few words with Faulkner while accompanying him on a battlefield, concluded that the novelist never talked with anyone. To strengthen the point, he wrote: "M. E. Coindreau, who translated Faulkner's first novels, scarcely got more than two sentences out of him in twenty years: 'How are you?' and 'So long.' "[1] Here we are no longer concerned with a factual error, something which can always be excused, but with a gratuitous assertion, a pure fabrication of a kind that gives the most false and unjust

---

[1] Since I have not found the article in question, the phrasing in English is mine.

view of Faulkner's character. The same cordiality which he showed me at our first interview, in 1931 (for our relations lasted thirty years instead of twenty), prevailed also at the last dinner we had together, in 1959. Meanwhile, there had been various meetings, and I had always found him consistent with himself: not talkative, I admit, but always courteous, somewhat ceremonious, never giving me what I did not expect of him, but nevertheless surprising me at times by spontaneously telling me what I wanted to know but would not have dared to inquire about.

I am entirely aware that he did not show himself to everyone in the same light. There were several Faulkners. I will simply talk about the one I knew.

Having read, during the winter of 1931, not only *Sanctuary* (which came out in February) but also the five novels which preceded it and whose very titles I had not heard of until then, I wrote to Faulkner on March 23 to let him know of my desire to be his translator, and I got in touch with his publisher, Harrison Smith. In October of the same year, Smith was kind enough to inform me that William Faulkner would be in New York at the very end of the month and would like to meet me over lunch. I would have forgotten the exact date of this meal if the dedication that Faulkner wrote that day on my copy of *As I Lay Dying* did not remind me of it: November 5, 1931. I returned to Princeton with the authorization to translate *As I Lay Dying* and any of the short stories I might like to choose from the volume which had come out two months earlier under the title *These Thirteen*. I knew that Raimbault and Delgove were working on a translation of *Sanctuary*. I had already prepared the ground by publishing, in the *Nouvelle revue française* for June, 1931, a short article designed to arouse the interest of French readers. Thus everything was ready for the offensive. Two stories, "Septembre ardent" and "Une Rose pour Emilie," appeared in early 1932, the former in the January *Nouvelle revue française*, the latter in the winter issue of *Commerce*. I had copies sent to Faulkner, and received the following letter from him, dated April 14, 1932:

> Please accept these belated thanks for sending me La Nouvelle Revue in which was Septembre Ardent. I thought the translation excellent there, but the one of A Rose for Emily, in Commerce lost nothing at all, even of that which a writer perhaps alone feels in his story but never quite gets into the actual words. But principally I wish to thank you for your critique among the Lettres Etrangeres in a recent number of La Nouvelle Revue, which I received from a friend in Paris. I see now that I have a quite decided strain of puritanism (in its proper

sense, of course; not our American one) regarding sex. I was not aware of it. But now, on casting back and rereading now and then or here and there of my own work, I can see it plainly. I have found it quite interesting.

Thank you again for your thoughtfulness in sending me the Revue.

The article in question was not as recent as he thought, since it dated from June, 1931. I had not mentioned it to him during our lunch in November, knowing that, even at that time, he had no interest in what people wrote about him.

Five years went by during which I do not recall having seen him again. In August, 1933, I published "Il Etait une reine" ("There Was a Queen") (*N.R.F.*, August) and finished *Tandis que j'agonise* (*As I Lay Dying*), for which, back in 1932, Valery Larbaud had written a preface, but which went on sale only at the beginning of 1934, after the appearance of *Sanctuaire* with André Malraux's preface. Nineteen thirty-five was a productive year. I gave a story, "Soleil couchant," to the magazine *Europe* for its January issue. This prepared me to attack *The Sound and the Fury* and predestined me to translate *Requiem for a Nun*, since Nancy already appears in it, not working for Temple Drake but for the Compson family. Nineteen thirty-five is also the date of *Lumière d'août* (*Light in August*). I do not remember when I decided to undertake the translation of *The Sound and the Fury*, but a letter from William Faulkner, postmarked "Hollywood" and dated February 26, 1937, proves undeniably that I must have written to him right at the end of 1936, for in it he says:

> This is mainly to ask your pardon for not answering your letter about 'Sound & Fury'. I probably stowed the letter away unopened, since I do not recall receiving one which I knew to be from you. I would not have been so discourteous otherwise.
>
> Write me in care of the address below and I will give you any information you wish and I can about the book. After reading 'As I Lay Dying' in your translation, I am happy that you are considering undertaking S&F. I want to see this translation, indeed, because I feel that it will probably be a damned poor book, but it may be a damned good one (in French, I mean, of course) but in either case, particularly in the latter, it will be Coindreau and not Faulkner, just as the Rubáiyát which English speaking people know is a little more Fitzgerald [sic] than Khayyám. Have you any such feeling about it? Anyway, I wish you luck with it and I will be glad to draw up a chronology and genealogy and explanation, etc. if you need it, or anything else.

I will probably be in the East some time in this autumn. If I am, I hope we can have a meeting.

We met sooner. No doubt, when I thanked him for his kindness I told him that I expected to spend the summer at Mills College, on San Francisco Bay, for on June 4, 1937, he wrote me:

> I have your letter. I will be here until August 15 and I will look forward to seeing you at any time you come to California at which time I will be glad to answer and try to explain any confusions in the book, though if you wish I will try to answer the enclosed questions by mail. I will await to hear from you again.

So I arrived at his house June 20. He lived in Beverly Hills, in a pretty little California-Spanish style house at 129 Ledoux Boulevard. He would go to the studio in the morning, leaving me alone with his majestic Negro maid who had come with him from Oxford to keep house for him and to make sure that he lacked for nothing. She worshipped him and never ran out of things to say about him. How I regret that I did not take notes on everything she told me as she went about cooking and sweeping, her pipe in her teeth! In the evening, after dinner, I would bombard Faulkner with questions. This was still the period when self-styled serious critics claimed that, if one did not understand his books, the author himself did not know the meaning of what he wrote. Actually, he seemed to know *The Sound and the Fury* by heart, referring me to such and such a paragraph, to such and such a page, to find the key to some highly enigmatic obscurity. Only once was he unable to give me an answer. Unfortunately, I don't recall what sentence was involved. He read it, reread it, then began to laugh. "I have absolutely no idea of what I meant," he admitted. "You see, I usually write at night. I always keep my whiskey within reach; so many ideas that I can't remember in the morning pop into my head. As for the sentence in question, I must have had something in mind, but I can't tell you what." Similarly, the day I asked him why he had entitled one of his stories "Carcassonne," he was unable to give me a clear-cut answer.

"It's a vision," he said, "a poetic vision . . . a young man who sees a horse. . . ."

He drank. That was no secret to anybody. He did not try to hide it, nor did he boast of it like certain other writers of the "lost generation." He would go

through tragic periods, but would emerge from his crises just as a strong
swimmer succeeds in escaping from the undertow that carries him away.
Personally, I never saw him give any embarrassing signs of drunkenness.
While I was staying at his home, he drank constantly, but without seeming
to be affected by it. On one occasion, however, he made me somewhat nervous. It was the day before I left; we had been to dinner at the home of a
friend of his, a rich Englishman named Davenport, whose lush gardens over-
looked Hollywood. There were a good many people present at this dinner,
which was actually more a cocktail-picnic, and the evening went on till quite
late. I had noticed Faulkner drinking constantly and felt rather uneasy thinking about the long ride in his high-powered convertible, over roads with hair-
pin curves. He got behind the steering wheel and set out at high speed. He
did not go through one red light or scrape one curb, and got me home safe
and sound without having said a word. I had not been in my room five minutes when he knocked at the door. He was holding in his hand a book and a
few sheets of paper between two blue pages. "I would like you to take this
volume as a souvenir of your visit," he said to me, "and take this story too.
You expressed a desire to reread it. This way you will have the complete
works of Ernest V. Trueblood." The book was a first edition of *Absalom,*
Absalom! (which had come out in October, 1936), on which he had written
his signature and the date, June 26, 1937. The pamphlet bound in blue paper
was the typed copy of "The Afternoon of a Cow," which he had read aloud
one evening, after a dinner at which he had assembled around his table two
old friends from Oxford, Mr. Davenport, and myself. In the review *Fontaine*
(June 1943), I have related the life and death of Ernest V. Trueblood, the
nonexistent secretary whom Faulkner had invented merely to have him write
that "in the manner of" which he later used in *The Hamlet.* Such is the only
testimony I can give as to William Faulkner's behavior in a highly intoxicated
state. That was twenty-five years ago. I saw him several times afterwards in
varied circumstances: at the dinner Robert Haas held in his honor in New
York, on the eve of his departure for Stockholm; in Princeton, at the home of
his friend Saxe Commins; and in meetings with university students. I never
saw him other than sober, or at least apparently so. As far as I am concerned,
no unpleasant recollection stains his memory.

After attaining fame, he raised ever higher the wall behind which he shel-
tered (in that silence whose existence Dominique Aury revealed in two won-
derfully true and penetrating pages) the dark secrets of Yoknapatawpha
County and the ghosts of Jefferson with whom he kept company. But his

deeper nature did not change, and if, on occasion, he rid himself of some pest with a devastatingly laconic remark, he was also capable of surrounding certain of his gestures with a surprising graciousness. For example, in the first week of June, 1953, having stopped at Princeton with Mrs. Faulkner while en route to Pine Manor, the school where their daughter Jill was finishing her studies (and where he had agreed to give a short speech for the graduation ceremony), he had his editor, Saxe Commins, at whose house he was spending the night, phone me. He wanted, his host told me, one of my translations of one of his books; any one would do. The next morning I took him a copy of *Lumière d'août*, and, intrigued by this odd request, I asked him for an explanation. "It's for a lady at Pine Manor," he answered, "who, my daughter wrote me, would like to have a signed copy of one of my novels. Since she is in charge of the French courses there, I thought that one of my books written in the language she teaches would give her twice as much pleasure." Whether the lady found out what was behind this gift which, no doubt, she would have preferred to read in the original language, I could not say; but, on the other hand, I am certain that, when he offered it to her, Faulkner said nothing to enlighten her, for he was extraordinarily reticent about his inner feelings. Taking someone into his confidence would have struck him as unseemly, and, judging others by himself, he would have feared to embarrass them.

Hence, when he signed his books—and he did so very rarely—he confined himself to the minimum. On my copy of *As I Lay Dying* he simply put: "With gratitude to M. Coindreau, the translator"; on *The Sound and the Fury* and on *Light in August*, my name, his signature, and the date. On *Absalom, Absalom!* he added the place, Beverly Hills. His dedications were equally concise. Once, however, he let his heart speak—the day he dedicated one of his most famous books, *Go Down, Moses,* to his family's Negro servant: "To Mammy, CAROLINE BARR, Mississippi (1840–1940), who was born in slavery and who gave to my family a fidelity without stint or calculation of recompense and to my childhood an immeasurable devotion and love." He had waited until the beloved centenarian had been dead for two years to pay her this touching tribute, for *Go Down, Moses* dates from 1942.

If he wanted to speak well of you, he preferred to do it when your back was turned. It has been reported to me several times that in the course of his talks with students at Princeton or at the University of Virginia, he mentioned my translations in terms which might have flattered my vanity. He never did it when he knew that I was in the room; and the two letters I have quoted above are the only written documents I could bring forward to attest his satisfaction. One evening, however, in the privacy of a dinner at Dorothy Commins' home—this was in 1959, and I never saw him again—he brought me around, by way of replying to a mildly eulogistic phrase, to expressing my ever present fear of not having done full justice to his works and of having betrayed him, involuntarily of course. He then became almost garrulous.

"You don't have to worry about that," he said to me. "As soon as my books are put on sale, they no longer belong to me. They belong to those who buy them. They can do as they please with them. I am no longer their owner."

"Still," I said, "Haven't you ever protested against Hollywood's infamous adaptations?"

"No. Why should I? First of all, I haven't been to see them, and, then, they too are free to use my books as they see fit. After a novelist has finished a book and given it to the public, there's only one thing left for him to do—start another one. The preceding one is no longer his."

This attitude, so rare among writers, can be easily explained (just as "the Faulkner mystery" can, assuming that there is a mystery) if one always keeps in mind the fact that Faulkner, beginning with the day he wrote *Sartoris*, no longer lived in our world. That is the meaning which must be given to the very true remark of Michel Mohrt: "He died with Bayard Sartoris, aboard a fighter plane, in the sky over France." Thereafter he only "appeared" among us. His true domain was the town of Jefferson and Yoknapatawpha County. For him, it was not Alceste's "desert"; rather it was Wonderland—a land of wonders often hideous and terrible—where the whiskey bottle played the role of Alice's mirror. For he drank far less to destroy himself than to create. With the odds and ends of reality offered by Oxford, Ripley, and the history of his family as a basis, he had begun to build his imaginary city and to people it with inhabitants. If he had been as stupid as certain people would have us believe, he would have made the Compsons and Sartorises paragons of all the virtues. But such is not the case. His "unvanquished ones" are just as vice-ridden as the Snopeses: "Faulkner [I borrow this quotation from Dominique Aury; I could not possibly improve on it] is no more merciful to his people than the Creator to the race of Cain and Abel. He holds them in his hand, turns them around, turns them back again without comment, puts them on display, and keeps silent."

It was in the silence of long nightly vigils that he cast the spells drunk from a liquid which, in Poe's time, would have been called "ignoble." This silence was not to be broken by anyone. Hence he avoided anyone who might have asked him troublesome questions or tried to sneak behind his back into that little kingdom of which he was the lord and master. I have often thought that he must have done violence to his own feelings to reveal to me, as he did in 1937, the origin of *The Sound and the Fury,* to explain to me its obscure points, and to confirm me in my idea that *Light in August* meant *Lumière d'août,* as I had translated the phrase in 1935, and not *légère en août,* as Isabel Paterson had suggested in 1933, long before Malcolm Cowley had set forth, in a different form, the same absurd opinion.

I repeat, Jefferson belonged to him and to him alone, and no monarch ever had such docile subjects. If he needed one of them, he would call him and restore him to life without worrying about whether what he was going to have him do was or was not compatible with the role that he had played in previous works. Sticklers for detail, armed with calendars and family trees, point out contradictions, chronological impossibilities, and odd reversals of the seasons in the chronicle of Yoknapatawpha. To these finicky people, Faulkner replied that his characters belonged to him, that he took them wherever and whenever he liked, heedless of other considerations. A creator is not bound to be a courthouse clerk as well.

But, however docile Jefferson might be, she found a way to take her revenge. She made her master her slave. She imposed attitudes, opinions, and ideas which transformed him into a citizen of Jefferson. The people, the animals, the buildings that he loved were part of the landscape of Yoknapatawpha. He was a great hunter, and his game was occasionally a bear, more often 'possum or raccoon, because that was what Major de Spain or Boon Hogganbeck might have hunted. Even if it had occurred to him to go off to the green hills of Africa in quest of more dangerous and more photogenic beasts, Jefferson would have forbidden him to go in for such safaris à la Tartarin. When he came into some money and bought what he called his "farm," what did he do but become the owner of an old house in Jefferson with its white columns and tree-lined walk, the kind of house where Colonel Sartoris, Miss Rosa Coldfield, Miss Jenny, and perhaps even the perverse Miss Emily might have lived? A citizen of Jefferson does not build a Le Corbusier-style house for his abstract paintings, with swimming pool and garage doors that open at the mere sight of lighted headlights. That would give evidence not only of real foolishness, but of an unforgivable lack of taste. For Faulkner's readers, Jefferson is the ghost of Oxford; for William Faulkner, Oxford had ended up by becoming the ghost of Jefferson. Thus he was seen strolling around town with an absent-minded expression, lost in his visions, just as, in *Light in August*, Reverend Hightower, sitting at his window, listened to the sound of military fanfares and cavalry charges in a past of which he was the prisoner.

While our relations were always most cordial, they grew no closer during the thirty years that they lasted. The last time we met, it was just as if we were seeing each other for the first time. He was not one of those people who slap you on the back and call you by your first name five minutes after being introduced. He had not forgotten our long conversations in 1937, and I knew that, though he was not seeking me out, he did feel some pleasure at seeing me again. But there was nothing of the citizen of Jefferson about me. As familiar as his work was to me, what I knew of it was the printed volumes which had become the fare of readers, critics, and moviemakers—prodigal sons who had left their father's house—in other words, stories in which he had lost interest, as animals lose interest in their young, who are guarded and protected at their birth as jealously as Faulkner guarded and protected the creations of his genius before allowing them to leave Yoknapatawpha and go out into the world.

The gods gave him the death he would have wished for. He had finished the Snopes trilogy. The chronicle of Jefferson was closed. The Compsons, the Sartorises, and the Sutpens had given way to the Varners and Snopeses, just as the Chickasaws of Ikkemotubbe, along with their queen Mohataha, had given way to the Sutpens, the Sartorises, and the Compsons. The cycle was complete. Only the final stroke was lacking, and this stroke was a burst of laughter, a piece of buffoonery—*The Reivers*. Then, the heart of the novelist, who for thirty-five years had suffered all the passions of his tortured characters, suddenly found itself out of work. It stopped beating. Faulkner could not die like Hemingway or Marilyn Monroe—the big, splashy leave-taking (an accident? suicide?). There are no question marks after Faulkner's death. The man who had never wanted people to talk about his life was granted an end which could not lend itself to any gossip. It was a beautiful, simple, clean death—exactly the kind he deserved.

Faulkner In Hollywood
Laurence Stallings / 1932

From New York *Sun*, September 3, 1932.

William Faulkner has been in Hollywood working with Howard Hawks on a story of war pilots. It is said that his running gags and his bits of business are the best seen around this town in MSS.

Faulkner is a little stocky man with a perfect civil war face. It is dark, flushed, framed in tightly crisped, grayish hair. His nose is eaglish, his chin curving. Ten years ago D. W. Griffith would unhesitatingly have cast him as a confederate brigadier. His favorite drink is Bourbon. Four fingers. No water.

Faulkner is of the opinion that the entire region known as Southern California is destined to crumble away at an early day. "A hundred yeahs from now," Faulkner says, "the archaeologists will go digging around here and find nothin'. It's all too perishable to wait for the archaeologists. The only thing they'll find will be these yeah iron stobs the folks from Iowa drive into the ground to pitch hoss shoes at. Funny thing, but these heah little iron pegs are all that will survive the test of time."

Faulkner was driving with me along Wilshire Boulevard. Ahead of us, out of the medley of electric signs, loomed a 300-foot tower. "That a filling station or the segregated district?" he asked politely.

Negroes on the Faulkner plantation in Mississippi, hearing that the young massa was in Hollywood on fabulous terms, have taken advantage of his absence. Four couples have been divorced there by Negro law. For each divorce he has received a bill for $25. Faulkner is going to put a stop to it. "I don't care if I am in Hollywood," he says, "they can't start living in sin."

The Faulkner reaction to Hollywood has been original. He has lived in a $30 per month cottage in Culver City and has done his own cooking and housekeeping. Unlike practically everyone else, he has remained cold sober. He bought one book to read over his lonely nights. It was a second-hand twelve-volume edition of the Cambridge edition of the Holy Bible.

Faulkner thinks his best book is *As I Lay Dying*. Actually it was written in six weeks while its author was engaged as a coal passer in a steam power station. "Long toward midnight," he says, "the peak load had passed and we could ease up on the boilers. I got a note book and a pencil, and I'd crawl

back to a comfortable spot in the coal burners and write another chapter by
about 4 A.M. I think the hum of the dynamo helped me. If ever I get rich I'm
going to have a little dynamo built to hum away in my room."

Faulkner, at 19, joined the Canadian air force. After two hours instruction
in France he went out with a squadron for combat. He was in a Camel.
Camels rarely banked to the right, and could be turned to the left only after
first making the motions for a right bank. The German who engaged him
evidently knew this. "No matter how many motions I'd make," he says, "that
German knew all along which way I'd have to turn. I'd kick her rudders and
do what was best, but he'd be hanging there waiting. I'd know it before I'd
looked on account of tracer bullets going through my wings. After a little of
this I couldn't turn at all. I noticed then I didn't have any ailerons. I ran along
the ground about a hundred miles an hour. Suddenly I turned the other way
and ran just as fast. Then it turned over."

"Did you get the engine in your lap?" I asked him.

"No," said Faulkner pleasantly. "I came to hanging from the belt. . . . I
never did figure out how I broke my legs."

Faulkner is a taciturn man. On a Saturday he showed up at our house
complaining of a sore throat. He claimed he was going out of town for Sunday. On Monday he returned, as taciturn as usual. By Thursday we learned
that on the Sunday he had been absent he had gone down town and found a
doctor who dissected his tonsils for $50. He had paid cash. He did not know
the doctor's name.

Faulkner's new book is *Light in August*. He awaits with great eagerness
the interpretations that the soothsayer critics will bring to an explanation of
the title. He has told me his own. After all the reports are in I will collate
them in this column and print his own.

Faulkner and I were watching a foreign officer manage a spirited brown
mare. After half an hour of this Faulkner removed his pipe to say: "He's got
her real good and fretted now. Let's go. It'll be twenty-four hours before he
can fret that mare that bad again."

Faulkner likes "All the Dead Pilots" best of his short stories. I like "A
Rose for Emily." . . . James Boyd of Southern Pines, who was out here
watching the Olympic horses, likes "Spotted Horses" in Faulkner's saga of
the Snopes family. (Incidentally, Faulkner is doing a grand book on the
Snopes family—whittling away at it—for about 1934.) . . . Faulkner thinks
Ernest Hemingway's "Fifty Grand" is just about the top in contemporary
short-story writing.

James Boyd was eager to see the Olympic lacrosse teams in action. Faulkner and I went along. From the moment play began Faulkner started laughing. He laughed fifteen minutes. "I was just thinking," he said apologetically to James Boyd, "of how the Injuns must have looked playing shinny, with their stony faces."

Afterwards I asked Faulkner if he knew James Boyd's *Drums*. He waited until Boyd was out of earshot. "I've read it a dozen times," he said. "I'm goin' to read it ten more."

Faulkner has gone home to Mississippi. He never ceased to complain, while here, of the lack of rains and cloudy weather. In his letter from home he wrote: "I am sitting on the back gallery eating watermelon and watching it rain. Beautiful cloudy weather here."

The Faulkners: Recollections of a Gifted Family

Robert Cantwell / 1938

From *New World Writing* (1952), pp. 300–15.

In the early winter of 1938 I was assigned the task of writing an article about William Faulkner for *Time* magazine. The article had originally been planned for the preceding year, at the time *The Unvanquished* was published, but at the last minute a different cover was scheduled, and the managing editor decided to wait until Faulkner's next book appeared. This was *The Wild Palms*, and while I felt uneasy about introducing the deepening involutions of Faulkner's style to the magazine's readers, the fact that his writing was growing steadily more obscure suggested that the difficulty might be greater in the future, and that unless the story were done quickly it might not be possible to do it at all. I arranged to meet Faulkner at the Hotel Peabody in Memphis, and took the Southern Railway from New York.

My preparations for the journey consisted only in re-reading Faulkner's novels and in going over the available biographical material on him. In this only one new item appeared, which I was turning over in my mind as the train swayed across Tennessee. *The Mississippi Guide of the Works Progress Administration* devoted some space, in its account of the town of Ripley, Mississippi, to the career of Colonel W.C. Falkner, identified as the grandfather of the famous Mississippi novelist, and referred to as Ripley's most colorful personality.

The Guide went on that as a barefoot child of ten Colonel Falkner walked the several hundred miles from Middleton, Tennessee, to Ripley, to make his home with an uncle, and that on arriving at dusk he found the uncle in jail, charged with murder; he sat down on the courthouse steps and swore that he would some day build a railroad over the route he had walked. *The Guide* further stated that Colonel Falkner was the author of a novel, *The White Rose of Memphis*, that after the Civil War he built the Ripley, Ship Island and Kentucky from Middleton to Ripley, and that in 1899, after his second election to the legislature, he was shot down and killed on the main street of Ripley by Colonel R.J. Thurmond. In another note, describing the Hindman house, which still stands near Ripley, *The Guide* said that it was built by Thomas Hindman, who was killed in a duel with W.C. Falkner and buried "20 yds. w. of the house."

It subsequently developed that most of this was wrong. Colonel Falkner was William Faulkner's great-grandfather, not his grandfather. Middleton is only thirty miles from Ripley, not several hundred miles. Colonel Falkner was killed on November 5, 1889 after his first election to the legislature, not in 1899. Colonel Faulkner never fought a duel with Thomas Hindman, nor any other duels at all. He was not a typical Southerner of his time, but had worked for years in Ripley jail, employed by the sheriff, while he went to school. Thomas Hindman was not killed by Colonel Falkner, but lived to become a celebrated Arkansas politician, a Congressman and a Confederate major-general. But despite its many errors, the Mississippi *Guide's* brief biography was valuable, for it directed attention to the factual background for his Sartoris novels, and for the character of Colonel Sartoris which he based on his great-grandfather.

When I entered the lobby of the Peabody, I was struck by a terrific tumult, shouts, laughter and the blowing of horns. I made my way to the desk and asked what was going on, and learned that was the day of the Tennessee-Mississippi football game. As soon as possible I retired to my room to wait for Faulkner. He arrived at exactly five o'clock. He was dressed in a gray suit coat, and trousers that did not match it, and wore brown leather gloves. My notes on the greet card read: "Walks with quick short steps, very erect, head slightly thrown back. Gives an impression of slightly military self-conscious bearing. Also, quite short. Extremely thin lips concealed by his mustache. Very sharp eyes, dark. Wavy hair, now graying, gray in back. Pleasant, but not easy in his manner." He sat down on the bed, apologized for the delay, and asked, "Are you all packed up?" It took me a moment to realize that he wanted to start for Oxford immediately. "I'm sorry about your waiting here," he said. "My wife sent the telegram and she didn't know that I was going to be busy today."

It was necessary for me to call the *Commercial Appeal* to arrange for a photographer to come to Oxford and take pictures of him—something I could not arrange until I had his permission. "I've got a Leica you can use," he said, a little impatiently. But he gave me the necessary permission.

Outside, the tumult in the halls increased. There were outcries from the other rooms, the shouts of the returning football crowd, and the shrill cheerful screams of drunken women. While waiting for the arrangements to be con-

cluded with the photographers, we spoke briefly of *The Wild Palms*. I said I
thought the convict in "The Old Man" section was wonderful. He smiled
briefly and replied: "I kind of liked him myself."

Conversation flagged again. There were more shouts from the hall. "This
would be a hell of a place to sleep tonight," Faulkner said.

The phone rang, the arrangements were completed, and we left the room.
There were a number of drunks waiting at the elevator, which was a long
time coming. Faulkner said, "They must have rented the elevator space too."

At last, we managed to get into a car, in which there were more drunks,
some aged couples, and two college girls talking about a psychology exami-
nation next Wednesday. "I didn't know it was next Wednesday!" said one.
"Yes honey," said the other. "Six weeks!" "Yes I did too hear something
about it!" said the first.

I thought they were singularly attractive, and their fresh Southern voices
and rattling inconsequential talk gave me the same feeling I had earlier in
the day, when I entered the lobby and it was filled with football revelers—
namely, the genius of the South for being always out of date, for turning on
a 1929-boom-year football atmosphere in the midst of the New Deal's grim
sociological determinisms, or for evoking the days of the village band concert
at a time when the mood of the rest of the country was that of a court-packing
plan and the end of the Spanish Civil War. I suppose it comes from the
Southern consciousness of always being before an audience, or from the
value placed on quickness of response, and the form of Southern politeness
that consists in pretending to be (with ingenious variations) what the rest of
the country believes Southerners are. The particular Southern revival of the
pattern of the twenties seemed a kind of conscious re-enactment, no less
deliberate than the rough breaks in chronological sequence in Faulkner's novels—a device that might seem artificial in fiction dealing with a different
story. The tricks that Faulkner plays with time, jumping from 1928 to 1910
or scrambling the intervening years, as in *The Sound and the Fury*, have a
parallel in a part of Southern life; and you can sometimes find in a Southern
gathering a layer of 1912 thought, then a layer of 1890 culture, a fragment of
reconstruction pottery, a broken piece of pre-Civil War belief, as archaeologists find the bronze above the Stone Age in their excavations.

We pushed through the dense crown in the lobby and went out to Faulkner's car. It was a Ford touring, tan, with one broken side curtain. Two boys
were sitting in the front seat. They climbed into the back. Faulkner introduced

them as Malcolm and Johnny, his stepson and his nephew. We got away into traffic.

"Sleeping in that hotel tonight," said Faulkner, "would be like sleeping in a fraternity house."

We drove cautiously through a traffic jam.

"This is Beale Street," Faulkner said.

The boys looked cautiously out through the side curtains. One of them said it was unsafe for a white man to be out there at night. Or even in the daylight, added the other.

"You sure can get some bargains in Beale Street pawn shops," Malcolm observed.

There was no further conversation for a long time. We drove grimly out of Memphis on the highway to Oxford, seventy-five miles away. I settled myself for a long and tiresome drive. Faulkner drove carefully, the car swaying and pulling to the right. One of the front tires was soft. It was discovered the next morning. Faulkner's hands seemed to bother him as he drove. He took off his gloves at intervals and clenched and unclenched his fists. The boys in the back seat said nothing at all. The road went through a series of low hills beside a railroad. The hills grew higher, the road going through a cut at the top of each hill, bright white under the new moon. There were few cars on the road. Now and then we passed a Negro couple walking along. The fields were desolate with stalks of corn or cotton and deep guillies washed out in the hills. There were a few scrubby, scattered pine trees. Now and then there was a Negro settlement, a few wan, tumbledown cabins, a patch of cleared ground, dim lights inside. They looked cold.

"Forty to nothing," said one of the boys in the back seat.

"Tennessee has a great team," said Faulkner, with something like a sigh. "When they'd come around the end I never saw so many yellow sweaters at one time."

"The first touchdown on the fourth play," said one of the boys.

We drove on.

"Well, Malcolm," said Faulkner at last. "You lost your bet."

"I sure did," said Malcolm, in a high, grieved, twanging voice. "I didn't think Ole Miss'd get beat like that. After the L.S.U. game . . . ."

"I reckon Tennessee must have just about the best team in the country."

"I reckon so."

"I reckon Tennessee must have just wanted to prove they should have been picked for the Rose Bowl."

"I reckon."

A fortunate reference to Colonel Falkner ended the long silence between Falkner and myself. Somewhat to my surprise, he was glad to talk about his great-grandfather. His principal interest seemed to be in Colonel Falkner and the Civil War, and he spoke about the independence of Civil War soldiers, their resistance to the regimentation of modern warfare—the war itself to him represented resistance to the regimentation of modern life. Outside Colonel Falkner's military career there seemed to be little in his life that interested him. He thought that the *White Rose of Memphis* was pure escapism—"The men all brave and the women all pure"—and that the Colonel had no humor and probably no sensibility.

I asked how it came about that a military man and a railroad builder turned to writing fiction.

Faulkner said he thought Colonel Falkner was probably an overbearing man. He had to be big dog. He built the railroad after the Civil War because he wanted to make a big pile of money. He made it. He built the railroad by will power, raising money during the week to pay the men on Saturday night, and raising the capital from among the neighbors. There were originally three partners, but one got scared and dropped out, and Falkner and Thurmond kept on. Building a railroad in those days was like starting an airline in 1928. A train would start out and they wouldn't hear of it again for a week. They'd be out chopping down trees, clearing obstructions, the engine would go off the track and be put back by hand and then the engine would blow up entirely. But as soon as Colonel Falkner had the railroad running and had made a lot of money he lost interest in it. He wanted to go into politics, so he did that, go himself elected to the legislature, but didn't like that, at least he didn't try to go on. He wrote the novel *The White Rose of Memphis* because he wanted to be the best in that. But then he never wanted to write another. Sir Walter Scott was apparently the only writer he ever liked or read, and he named the stations on his railway after the characters in Scott's novels. "The people could call the towns whatever they wanted," Faulkner said, "but, by God, he would name the depots."

Faulkner had grown animated as he spoke. He talked carefully, with characteristic pungent phrases, and grew eloquent, his words so composed and telling they could have gone down on paper without the change of a sentence. He described the Colonel's energy and arrogance, the attitude of the people toward him, the failure of his enterprises, the violent end of his life. He was overbearing, he said, hard to get along with, and he and Thurmond quarreled.

"I don't believe Thurmond was a coward," Faulkner said. "But the old man probably drove him to desperation—insulted him, spread stories about him, laughed at him."

"Besides," Faulkner said thoughtfully, "he had killed two or three men. And I suppose when you've killed men something happens inside you— something happens to your character. He said he was tired of killing people. And he wasn't armed the day Thurmond shot him, although he always carried a pistol."

I asked what happened to Thurmond. "He left the country, went out West," Faulkner said. It was obvious that he was not really interested in Thurmond. "The feeling in Ripley did not die out with Colonel Falkner's death and Thurmond's leaving. I can remember myself, when I was a boy in Ripley, there were some people who would pass on the other side of the street to avoid speaking—that sort of thing."

The road went straight through the winter night, past the same cold Negro cabins, along the railroad where Colonel Falkner had fought his cavalry battles, through country that seemed to me to be increasingly cold and depressing. "One of my kinsmen is buried on that hill," Faulkner said at one point, indicating a gloomy patch of deeper darkness.

He described that country around Ripley where Colonel Falkner had lived and worked, and where his legend persisted. "People at Ripley talk of him as if he were still alive, up in the hills some place, and might come in at any time. It's a strange thing; there are lots of people who knew him well, and yet no two of them remember him alike or describe him the same way. One will say he was like me and another will swear he was six feet tall. . . . There's nothing left in the old place, the house is gone and the plantation boundaries, nothing left of his work but a statue. But he rode through the country like a living force. I like it better that way."

Faulkner had been writing about Colonel Falkner, in the character of Colonel Sartoris, when the concept of his great cycle of novels took hold of his imagination. He was halfway through *Sartoris*, after writing his first two novels, when "suddenly I discovered that writing was a mighty fine thing—you could make people stand on their hind legs and cast a shadow. I felt I had all these people, and as soon as I discovered it I wanted to bring them all back."

We had come to Holly Springs. We drove past the big buildings of the Negro college and the new courthouse and into the crowded main street. "This was just a country lane when Van Dorn rode down and burned Grant's stores," Faulkner said.

The boys wanted to stop at a service station. We stopped. "There was a quality about these people you don't seem to find anywhere else," Faulkner said as we waited for them. "The war didn't seem to change their private lives. My great-grandfather raised his own regiment. It was attached to Long-street's corps in Lee's army. As you probably know, the men elected their officers once a year. They elected somebody else colonel. So he just packed up and came home. If he couldn't be colonel he wouldn't have anything to do with the war. But after awhile he raised a bunch of men, mostly from his own place and around, and fought when it suited him . . . ."

"Van Dorn burned Grant's store and kept Grant from getting into Vicks-burg from the rear," he said again after a moment. "That was a pretty gallant thing to do. But about a week later some fellow caught him in bed with his wife and killed him. He might have been good for a dozen more victories. But honor meant a lot to them."

I asked him about the sources of his history.

"I never read any history," he said. "I talked to people. If I got it straight it's because I didn't worry with other people's ideas about it. When I was a boy there were a lot of people around who had lived through it, and I would pick it up—I was just saturated with it, but never read about it." He said that he had grown up with a Negro boy like the boy in *The Unvanquished.* "There were no toys in this part of the country when I was a boy," he said. "We used to play Civil War games—we would fight over the battles and the old men would tell us what it was like."

Presently we came to Oxford. It was pleasant, tree-shaded and peaceful. There was a big Saturday night crown in town. At the base of a long hill leading into town there was the square and the tall courthouse, gray and lighted at night. Floodlights were playing on it. "There were no American flags here when I was a boy," Faulkner said. "You never saw one except on the Federal building. But they came in during the war and now every store has a socket for a flag."

Oxford is a town of no less interest than Jefferson in Faulkner's novels. It is not an old town by Southern standards, having been founded in 1836 by a physician, Thomas Isom, and it is a college town, dominated as it has always been by the University of Mississippi. The University was projected about the time the town was founded, and was established in 1848 on a level plot of oak-shaded ground a mile from the courthouse square.

Jacob Thompson, the organizer of the Confederate secret service in the

Middle West, was a pioneer Oxford resident and a trustee of the college from the start. There was a good deal of Unionist sentiment in the college before the Civil War, the flag of Mississippi flying over one dormitory and the Stars and Stripes over the other. One of the early presidents was a friend of Lincoln, and one of the professors a friend of Grant's family. But the college was closed during the war, and the students, organized as the University Grays, reached the highest point of the Confederacy, forty-seven yards beyond the farthest point reached by Pickett's men at Gettysburg. They never held a reunion.

The college buildings were converted into a Confederate hospital, the friend of the Grants remaining as caretaker. Of the 1,800 wounded cared for, beginning with those from Shiloh not far away, 700 died, and the records of their graves beside the campus were hopelessly scrambled. When Grant burned Oxford he spared the College buildings, supposedly after a plea by the friend of his family. In 1889, the year of Colonel Falkner's death, this venerable professor was abruptly discharged. He walked across the campus to his home and killed himself. The Negroes said that the building he lived in was haunted, and claimed they could tell because of the peculiar sweetish odor, like that of rattlesnakes, attributed to ghosts.

No trace of these grim events now remains over the grounds of the school. They have the shaded loveliness one often finds in these old Southern colleges, red brick buildings and white Jeffersonian pillars emerging through the foliage and beyond the expanse of grass like tangible portions of the past surviving independently of the more practical edifices around them.

Even if the college did not bulk so large in the community about which Faulkner writes, another factor would relate it closely to his fiction. The Faulkners moved to Oxford about 1900, at the beginning of the fight of the great demagogues, James Vardaman and Theodore Bilbo, against the old Bourbon aristocracy that had controlled Mississippi since Reconstruction days. The target of their attack was the traditional code and the standards of taste and intelligence that held the governing class together, and consequently they centered their fire on the institution that tried to sustain these standards, the University, of which Faulkner's father became treasurer.

For example, one of the planks of the Vardaman-Bilbo platform was the abolition of college fraternities. It was charged that non-fraternity men were ostracized by Oxford society (pop. 2,890). The student leader of the movement to abolish fraternities was an Oxford resident, who became Bilbo's right-hand man, eventually governor, and finally Bilbo's rival. During his second administration, Bilbo decided to put the university out of business altogether by combining it with the agricultural and mechanical college and moving both to his capital at Jackson. In the course of the dispute he discharged 169 faculty members and administrative officers. His Senate floor leader became dean of men.

The tactics of the Vardaman-Bilbo small fry, stalwart enemies of big business, radical-regionalists, whatever they were, were such as to make one believe that their primary target was human reason. Their anti-Negro, anti-aristocratic demagoguery was doubly provocative in a region where there were relatively few Negroes, and where the aristocracy consisted of a small professional class in moderate or straitened circumstances and a few farmers, often living in unpainted houses. Both the power and the unreality of their politics are reflected in Faulkner's novels. They are not a fictional documentation of the Vardaman-Bilbo movement, but their account of the monstrous Snopes family, gradually infiltrating the town of Jefferson, multiplying by the tens, and then apparently by the hundreds, certainly becomes more meaningful in the light of the careers of Vardaman, Bilbo and such lesser figures as Russell, of whom the country never heard.

When we drove past the square at Oxford Faulkner said that in the old days there were balconies out over the street, with doors from the second floor offices opening on them, and that in the evening the doctors and lawyers would sit in chairs on the balconies and talk. "For years the mayor was old man Stevens, with a beard that reached to here," he said. "Elections were just a formality because nobody ever thought of running against him. But now it's all changed and the people have learned political corruption all the way down."

In entering Faulkner's driveway we turned past the home of Jacob Thompson. His house was burned when Grant took Oxford and only the kitchen remained. This had recently been rebuilt into a low, modern cottage. Malcolm said that during the rebuilding a great stack of Jacob Thompson's papers were found in the attic and dumped in an unused cistern to help fill it.

The driveway of Faulkner's place was a wide curve, lined with cedars. The lights were lit on the front porch and in the big rooms, illuminating the cheerful exterior and the tall white columns. A little girl, blonde, pale and very pretty, came running from the house when Faulkner approached, but stopped suddenly to let him come up to her.

This was his daughter, Jill, who was then five. She was self-possessed and met me gravely, talked with the boys about the game—she won a nickel—and told me she had learned to ride a bicycle. I told her that my daughter had learned to ride a bicycle. A look of displeasure flashed across her features at learning that her accomplishment was not unique. I hastily asked when she was going to school. "That's for Mother and Daddy to settle," she said coolly.

She stretched out on the floor. "I certainly like to lie on the floor," she observed.

Mrs. Faulkner, a charming, hospitable, young-looking woman, had an air of having been surprised about something. We settled down and went into the Southern Conversation. This is a semi-formalized ritual that inaugurates a Southern visit, like the prologue of an Elizabethan play. It is almost identical in content from one household to another. Mrs. Faulkner was expert at it, and with great charm told us of Jill's mammy, who had been taken by the Faulkners to California, but she had gotten sick, and had to go to the hospital, which cost Billy $400, and in the hospital she and her husband were addressed as Mr. and Mrs. with the result that they remained in California and no power on earth could ever get them back to Mississippi. Sometimes these pleasant inconsequential Southern conversations are edged. That is, someone may have died, or some terrible catastrophe may have taken place, but the conversation goes on just the same. I think it began during the Civil War, when the hostesses of Vicksburg pretended that nothing was happening when a shell came through the window.

For some reason the conversation turned to fishing. "Billy buys all sorts of tackle but never uses it," Mrs. Faulkner said. "So Jill and I do the fishing."

"Billy fishes," said Johnny, "but he throws them all back. He says they're too small."

"You fish like a nigger," Malcolm said to his mother. "You keep everything, no matter how little."

"Would you have gone to that game, Mac," Faulkner interrupted him, "if you had known how it was going to turn out?"

"Yes," said Malcolm thoughtfully. "I wouldn't have believed it."

The next day Faulkner took me to interview his Negro mammy, Aunt Caroline Barr, then 77, who lived in the old slave quarters behind the house. She was a bright-eyed, small, high-voiced old lady, and I got an impression of her as shrewd and humorous, but we did not have much to say to each other. Aunt Caroline is said to be the original of the magnificent portrait of Dilsey in *The Sound and the Fury*. She was physically unlike Dilsey, for Dilsey is pictured as having been "a big woman once" and the massive kindly slowness of her ministry of the dying Compsons was not summoned up by the trim figure of the old colored woman in the flesh. Until three years before, Aunt Caroline had called Faulkner by a childish mispronunciation of William, calling it something like Meme, and Aunt Caroline called him that. About 1935, to his bewilderment, she started calling him Mr. Faulkner.

Standing in the thin sunlight outside the old slave quarters, Faulkner began talking about horses. His earliest recollection was of getting a pony at the age of three and waiting for the saddle to be made. He could not remember the name of the man who had made the saddle, and after thinking about it for some time decided to drive out to his farm to find out. An old Negro there, Uncle Ned, had been Colonel Falkner's servant, and had cared for three generations of Faulkners. "His is a cantankerous old man," said Faulkner, "who approves of nothing I do."

We drove twenty or thirty miles into the pine woods and came to a cluster of cabins under the trees in a converging fold of the hills. They formed a little settlement. John Faulkner, the novelist's younger brother, appeared from a frame house some distance apart from the Negro cabins, dressed in riding breeches and boots. Two years later John Faulkner published *Men Working*, the first of a series of wildly comic books of his own, followed by *Cabin Road* and *Uncle Good's Girls*, satirizing bureaucracy and the exaggerated political passions of Mississippi as these subject have never been satirized in American literature. But he then expressed no literary or political interests, and the two brothers talked about the farm.

Presently John Falkner went on and William Faulkner and I walked up a slope to Uncle Ned's cabin. It had grown quite cold. The cabin was sealed tight. There was a dish of some savory stew cooking in the fireplace. "In the wintertime they just go to bed and stay there," William Faulkner said. "They keep something cooking and when they get hungry they get up and eat, even if it's the middle of the night."

Uncle Ned greeted Faulkner almost ceremoniously. He seemed incredibly aged. Faulkner explained that I was interested in Colonel Falkner. The thought seemed to make Ned older. We did not get very far with our conversation about him, and presently Faulkner asked, "What was the name of that man who made a saddle for me? Had a shop down by the depot?"

Ned thought a long time. He could not remember. Then he exclaimed, "Cheek!"

The recollection pleased them both enormously. It was Mr. Cheek, that's right, a very fancy saddle, made with a special thread and a tree whittled out in the shop.

Presently we returned to the subject of Colonel Falkner. Faulkner tried to draw Uncle Ned out on some personal characteristics, but the recollections seemed troubling. A silence settled on the room. We sat there for awhile. It was nearly dark. I know now that the tragedy of Colonel Falkner's life brooded almost oppressively over that cabin in the woods, but then I felt that I had intruded enough; I sensed its reality, not so much to Faulkner as to the old man, and after some further polite conversation we went on our way.

My Friend, William Faulkner

Stephen Longstreet / 1944

From *Cavalier*, 15 (April 1965), pp. 58–61; 15 (May 1965), pp. 50–52, 85–86. Reprinted by permission.

Coming across a batch of drawings I had done of William Faulkner when I lured him out to the West Coast to write, looking at the black lines on the already yellowing paper, it all came back to me. The two of us sitting in my studio office, the late afternoon sun held partly back by the flapping window shades, the bottle of bourbon, the ice, and what he called "branch wattah" within reach, our feet on a low table, he looking at the drink to see if it was "above sea level." And saying in that low easy burr of his:

"We admire people who have small talents and are modest about it, sure. But artists with any quality of the heart don't need to have brains, unless they have no talent at all. Writing is a kind of nostalgic solace, a spontaneous affection yo' have for the folk who are the story. Just follow them along; they'll work out a book for yo'."

He held up his glass for a refill, and while I did so he lit up his little black briar pipe and puffed it alive, his hawk eyes half-hooded (it was prime 90 proof bourbon). "Yes sir, the undulation of all breathing things, yes sir."

Even the pencil notes I made on the backs of some of the drawings bring him back as he was—in need of money, most of his books out of print and favor. And scenes, whole scenes that were the color and taste of him, come back, too; scenes which have not yet become part of any definitive life of William Faulkner and perhaps never will. The cohesiveness and complexity of him is there in those scenes; maybe even the enigma, too, if one had the key.

My friend William Faulkner (not yet the Nobel Prize winner) and I were standing in front of the unbalustrated wings of Warner Brothers Studio in Burbank, California, waiting for our car pool. The year was 1944 and it was one of those fine lime-white sunny days, with motionless clouds at rest in the crayon-blue sky, the hills all umber and dry in the golden weather; the rain had failed to come.

Bill looked up and said in his soft slurred voice, "Look at it, Steve, one day *one* leaf falls in a damn canyon up there, and they tell yo' it's winter."

What led to my hearing this slur on the native seasons began in 1937, when Bennett Cerf first introduced me to William Faulkner in an editor's office—Saxe Commins, at Random House. I was producing black-and-white drawings for *The New Yorker* at the time, with no idea of becoming an author. I was paid nine dollars for a black and white drawing, but fifteen when I did the text for such stars as Peter Arno and Charles Addams. I was beginning to wonder at the higher value of my prose. Bennett, sagacious and tactful, had liked my texts and invited me over to talk of my writing a novel.

It was during that visit that I met a little man in unpressed English tweeds, who was hard at work tapping away on a typewriter. He had, I noticed, a proud hawk nose, his black hair already turning pepper and salt. He had the look of a shy wary man, yet with a patrician elegance, as we shook hands. I knew that his books were not selling well, and that some critics, Clifton Fadiman among them, had read him out of American literature as a failure. But the smoker had an unassertive confidence I liked.

He didn't look like a man who wanted to talk of his books—he was at the moment, Bennett had told me, engaged in rewriting part of a novel in his editor's office—so I asked Mr. Faulkner if they still ran hounds after foxes by torchlight at night in Mississippi and on foot. He smiled and took his little Dunhill pipe from his mouth and said, sure, a few did. By some instinct I had picked the right subject. And did they still drink "moon," an illegal, still-mashed, corn whiskey, around wood campfires after the hunt out of wide-mouthed quart Mason jars? They did. I could sense the conversation to the man was like a letter from home.

A half-hour later, having listened to Bennett's idea of turning me into a novelist, I came down to street level—Random House in those days was not yet in residence in the great Madison Avenue mansion it now shares with the Vatican's Papal organization, but was housed in a tall old slice of a building on East 59th Street, with a brass-laced elevator.

I was standing at the curb in introspective wonder at publishers, also trying to decide between going home or to the Modern Museum, when a slurred Southern voice behind me said, "Could I buy yo' a drink?"

It was William Faulkner, wearing a battered dark hat at an angle, pipe still in his mouth. I said sure, and he asked where. I recommended an Irish bar on Third Avenue where no newspapermen or advertising writers went. He said that would do fine, with that mundane disposition I got to know so well.

In the malty dark bar, half in gloom, with only a couple of horseplayers marking up a daily racing form, we talked about dogs, horses, touched on women. And both decided New York City was dirty, dank, too crowded, and the people had green-white faces and "pore" manners. He spoke in a low easy voice of intimate sensibility.

I nursed a couple of Beefeater Gibsons, but Bill drank steadily Old Forester with "branch wattah." He was a remarkable drinker in that he paid no attention to his drink except to absorb it casually, holding up the glass from time to time (with no word said) for a refill. I didn't count, but in the two hours we were in the bar he consumed a lot of prime bourbon whiskey and never showed any sign of it. He said something about adaptability not being essential to life, and held up his glass.

I never talk about writing or that square subject "literature" to writers. The closest Bill came to it was to remark that he'd be in town a week or more; his editor wanted certain changes in the new work in progress, and he was doing a lot of rewriting. Bill, always a fast worker, was not temperamental about changes, I found out over the years. He could rewrite a novel under pressure in a couple of weeks and, once started, he was like a greyhound after a rabbit. "I like to find that moment of time," he once said to me, "when the direction of things is about to change."

We parted that first day with a wave of hands. A week later I went to see Bennett Cerf again, at which time he offered me the fabulous advance of $2,000 to write a novel. I figured how many $15 captions it would take to reach that sum and I said I'd try. I'd never had $2,000 before in my life.

Faulkner was again at the typewriter in his editor's outer office. (Saxe was also to be my editor.) I put my head in the door; "Bill, how about my buying the first one today?"

He scratched a match alight, held it to his pipe and said, "Why sure, it's twelve o'clock." Later he told me he held noon to be the most dangerous of all hours.

We went back to the Irish bar and I told him I wasn't a writer, but Bennett thought I was and I had signed to do a novel. He swallowed some bourbon and looked at me with those gray-gold or hazel-colored falcon eyes (sometimes they seemed green-blue).

He said there was nothing much to writing a novel. "Yo' just keep the words coming. No trick to it at all if the writing is in yo'. Nothing will come if yo' haven't got the stuff. It's like one dog that can trail a scent and another dog that's not worth cuttin' up for catfish bait. It comes natural, yo' know, or it doesn't come at all. Everything comes: the people, the place, the story, and yo' just act like the fella feeding the cornshucker. Keep moving about and filling." He paused to refresh. "The rest is up to what kind of stuff yo' are made of, what kind of memory there is, and what there is in it for yo' to say. That's all there is to writing."

It was nearly the longest speech I ever heard him make. I didn't know if he was encouraging me, or kidding me, or being playful in that sadistic humorous way I was to observe in him at other times. There was a truculent cruelty in him occasionally, in spite of himself. It seemed a simple way to me to get over first-writer shakes. We parted, me a little woozy from the publisher's offer and the Gibsons.

With most great writers, as people, I feel an ultimate disenchantment—but not with Bill. We met about three times after that before he finished his own revisions and went back to Oxford, Mississippi. We remained on casual friendly terms, but Bill never relaxed his reserve, his too obvious Southern manners. He seemed in the grip of an adaptive necessity with people. While he smiled at times, I don't remember him ever laughing. And I don't remember him in anything but those oatmeal-colored tweeds. Perhaps he had several suits of them. He was a little sad, shabby, and I think he felt he had missed the boat. He had moments of silent lassitude.

It must be remembered that in 1937 Faulkner, while known to the avant-garde critics, was not at all a famous man. His books were not selling well. I was told his sales of a novel often averaged 1,300 to 1,500 copies a book. I formed no opinion of what the man was like inside, or why a dark shadow of brooding pain came through to me in his eyes, or how it entered his system. From what he said, I knew he lived in a big run-down place in Oxford and had trouble supporting his Negroes. He referred to them often as "his." He was very loyal to them and felt he was obligated to see to their welfare, as if some monstrous consequence would occur if he didn't.

Bill was a bit of a professional Southerner. His contempt for the North was rather amusing to me for I knew the self-imposed myth of the South well, but I did sense he was a good man underneath—plagued, tormented by something cutting inside him. And that he needed all that bourbon to keep his balance. As yet, I knew very little of his background, his education, the things that made him a writer. He was an enigma, and all that bobbed in view to me then was the little ramrod-backed man in gray tweeds, smoking that smelly pipe. He seemed all of a piece with no arbitrary inconsistencies once you grasped his pattern.

We wrote each other a few letters. He never said anything about my novel. (I had sent him a copy when it was published.) He was not much of a letter-writer to a drinking friend. Later, I found out he felt there was only one great writer in America—William Faulkner; and two excellent ones worthy to be ranked just below him: Thomas Wolfe (whom I despised and told him so) and Ernest Hemingway, whose muscles and travels and famous friends he envied very much.

Bill was mad about what he called "the quality" and the horseback riding set. He never showed any sparkle of interest about painters, poets, or musi-cians who made up the intellectuals, as I saw later when he had a chance to meet them in Hollywood: Huxley, Stravinsky, Frank Lloyd Wright, and others.

This isn't my story, but I have to say, to set the correct angle of my life with Bill Faulkner (he preferred Bill to William close up, so it's no pose on my part), that my first novel for some reason was a best seller and the second one was sold to Hollywood for a film. In 1941, loving the landscape, I went to live in California. And in 1944—I was at Warners, who had bought several of my books and were interested in *Stallion Road*—I heard from Saxe at Random House that Faulkner was desperately in need of ready cash to run his place and could use some help. I wrote Bill that if he wanted to chance the Hollywood mines again I would try to arrange a writing assignment for him. (He had had an earlier session in Hollywood which resulted in the often-repeated myth that he asked if he could work at home, and the studio said yes, so he went home to Oxford, Mississippi. He himself told me, "The story is a pure lie by some press agent fella.")

Through an agent and James Geller, the story editor at Warners, I got Bill hired to come to California again. When he came out, he was a little grayer, the suit looked the same (perhaps it was), he was still smoking a little black Dunhill pipe. He didn't say much the first day at the studio—just shook my hand and smiled.

He was not a man to discuss his personal problems. He held to silence with an extraordinary tenacity. For a week or so I could sense he in some way resented the fact that I had bailed him out when I had heard he was in diffi-culties. He had told me he refused to be the sport of forces outside himself. He had a lot of old-fashioned corny pride, and the people he often turned a cold hauteur on were sometimes people who did him favors.

Milt Gross, the cartoon satirist, after meeting him said to me, "Faulkner is still back there dreaming the plantations were never burned, the war lost, and the black folks enjoy tipping their hats and yakking it up for the Ole Massa. Then it all kind of falls away and he knows it's not true and he gets scared."

There were a lot of fine writers at Warners at the time: Christopher Isherwood; W.R. Burnett; John Collier of the fey mad stores; Heinrich Mann, a brother of Thomas Mann, a charity case who wrote in German (his work was translated into English and then thrown into the wastebasket). John Huston, Sammy Fuller, Richard Brooks, none of them yet a director, were also writing. But William Faulkner, his reputation rising with the years, was the uncrowned king of the Writer's Building. The only people who resented him were the old tired hacks, gagmen, writers of dismal commercial plays, popular writers of bad novels. His major enemy at the studio became an aggressive woman who was desperately trying for a long-term contract.

I knew there was war when Bill said, in the studio's Green Room, "Can't stand *that* woman. Ever see how she always puts out her cigarette butts in her butter patty?"

Which was true. She also reported to the front office that Mr. Faulkner kept a bottle of whiskey in his desk, and that he was often drunk by the late afternoon. What the woman didn't know was that the writers' secretaries had an underground FBI reporting back everything that went on in the front offices. Soon everyone knew the woman had turned in Faulkner. James Geller, the story editor, killed the report before it got as far up as the top brass. Geller, a fine intellect and well read, covered for Bill during several three-day bats. He was a great admirer of his work and he fought to keep Bill on the payroll.

When Bill heard of the woman's action he made no comment at all. He accepted it as a medieval prelate received treachery as part of life. But the woman panicked as the studio writers turned against her. She captured Bill one day outside the men's room; she was about six feet tall and looked nearly as wide. She began with no reticence, no shame, a shrill denial of her guilt. As she talked on, faster and faster, spilling words and sputtering, Bill's face never changed expression.

I was passing by, having been to a tea and cake party (cooking was forbidden in the Writers' Building but the secretaries all owned hot plates). I stopped to watch the match. Bill's only reaction was to puff a little slower on his pipe and stare with cold passivity and those gray-gold hawk's eyes at the bulk of protesting woman. She tried to circle him, but he kept the men's room wall at his back. She never stopped talking. Bill just speared into her with his eyes. She began to wilt, stammer, drool. At last, words failing, she died away, like a recording running down. Turning, she fled and was not seen any more that day.

Bill merely knocked the dottle out of his pipe into the palm of his hand and placed it into the pot of sand kept there for smokers. Ramrod stiff, he walked to his office after inviting me in for a drink. It had been a cool hypnotic performance and I told him so. He looked at me with a perverse introspective stare as he lifted his glass for his secretary to drop in the ice from the secretaries' icebox (also against rules).

"Don't know what yo' are talkin' about, Steve. I didn't hear a word she said."

He continued to be evasive at the studio, but not self-effacing. He seemed to exist on an internal validity above the lapses in taste and manners, the gaucheries of Hollywood. He was infinitely contemptuous of screen writers who didn't produce books. The Coast remained for him a predatory wilderness. He quoted D.H. Lawrence: "Culture in Southern California is the jade arse of the world."

Bill seemed to suffer in California an incurable ennui. He told me he found no equivalent of reality in the place. "It's too large for life or man, existence evaporates, slips from yo' grasp in all this sunlight. Experiences become fashions and styles, everything is a pattern for some facetious evasion."

He would talk like this, his face expressionless, smoking, his eyes looking directly into mine, and I'd wonder if he really saw me.

I advised him to buy a horse for company, and he did.

Everyone at the studio continued to stand in awe of Bill. After several weeks of riding in our car pool, as we were unloading one morning at the studio, the driver turned to me with a whisper.

"Mr. Faulkner must really like you."

"What makes you say that?"

"You're the only one he said 'Good morning' to."

I suddenly realized Bill had forgiven me for helping him out.

He was even ready to talk about women during our afternoon sipping. He had some dark obsession about the female, and I had read his books with an eye to seeing just how he treated them. His young women were not exciting, for all their longing and disquiet. They were sexual and had lusts and hates, and yet no man seemed to be fully happy with them. Knowing Bill, I began by talking about Madame Bovary and Mollie Bloom and *not* his characters. . . . He bit.

"Now yo' take them; interesting enough sure, for when a man needs a woman. But once a man gets caught up with them, he has to hold on to his sanity like to his hat on a windy day. I can do old ladies and middle-aged women—white or black—good as any writer. And I don't say my young girls aren't right. No." He stopped to puff on his pipe. "No, but with all their incomprehensible intensities, yo' know, in some things they do have a deficiency of understanding of a man's world."

I said I hadn't been too much impressed with the girl in *Sanctuary*, Temple Drake, who got raped with a corncob. It was, I admitted, the kind of scene and situation that can make a book, but Temple seemed to me more a symbol of an atrophied society, with a mean drive when turned on, rather than a true-to-life person.

I had said the wrong thing. He didn't care much for critics. "Women are all logically inaccessible; women are like elephants—they're fine to have around at times, but *who* wants to own one?"

I soon sensed that his attitude was a mixture. Part of him was steeped in the South's tradition towards children, women, horses, and dogs. He could get taciturn and stubborn about these. But a part of him ached with pain at the terrible inadequacies of the poor whites and the Negroes. "Damn the sadness of defeats and remembrances. Nowhere to nowhere is no goal."

If Faulkner was a prisoner of his own uniqueness, he was also isolated from his critics. Frankly, many of them puzzled him. Early he had been mocked for his dilatory form, his strange wandering sentences, those overloaded pages where phrases went on and on in long swirling loops.

"I can write prose as simple as anybody, but when you're trying to say, well, that desires and dreams are in the final scoring incompatible, yo' have to have between yo' and the reader a kind of veil that forms the mood and the color, that sets the fact that life is studded with pain, and to seek it is to expand one's own agony in a way, I suppose. To put it all in words is a hell of a hard thing, very hard." He stopped and with a finger brushed the ends of his well-defined mustache, first the right side then the left. "Too much damn talk about writing anyway."

I would quote to him what some critics were writing of him from time to time. That was when he had mellowed enough in the California sunshine to talk a bit of his work.

He couldn't go along with them much. "There is this group in England, run a very avant-garde magazine. Write about me a lot. Oh, with an immense reverence, I suppose. . . . Yo' know I don't know what they're talking about lots of times. They see symbols and significant intuitions in some of the craziest disjointed trivialities that have no more meaning than a hunter's dog taking a piss."

I said the critics felt he really hunted the dark insides of lives and had found something there other American writers didn't.

This pleased him I could see, but it also embarrassed him. He shrugged his shoulders, "For the right moment, I guess, yo' just have to wait."

When, in 1944, I persuaded Warner Brothers' studios to hire my friend William Faulkner as a screenwriter, my only desire was to help him earn some needed money. For his first assignment, the studio, to my dismay, gave him my novel, *Stallion Road*, to turn into a screenplay. Coming to my office in the Writers' Building, Bill gave me a very sad but belligerent eye. "I don't read much of yo' young writers, but they are paying me for this, so I'll go through it."

I said I hoped he had a good time with his screen version because, if he didn't like the original text, he *did* like horses.

He began the job with no beguiling protests. . . . Bill was going off on periodical drunks; during his entire writing term in Hollywood this was a constant problem. Geller, the story editor, would plead with me to have him at least turn in pages for the front office to see, even if he wasn't on the lot. When Bill did come back he had a humbled look.

Bill never made any comment on the novel, but I knew he was making progress on the screenplay because actors were being announced and directors talked of. One day I was called into the office of the jumpy little producer who had been assigned to the picture. He threw a bound bundle of yellow onionskin sheets at me. He told me my friend Bill had written an impossible script on *Stallion Road*. Would I forget his version and write my own screenplay? Those were orders.

I read the screenplay that afternoon, an original Faulkner manuscript (and as yet unpublished). I think I own the only surviving copy. I thought it was a magnificent thing; wild, wonderful, mad. Utterly impossible to be made into the trite movie of the period. Bill had kept little but the names and some of the situations of my novel and had gone off on a Faulknerian tour of his own despairs, passions, and story-telling. Today it could be made as a New Wave film. It had an enduring, authentic, fluid flow, a disquieting persistence.

I told Bill they were rejecting his script, but that I liked it for its quivering alertness. The next morning when I got to my office my secretary said Mr. Faulkner had been in and signed all my copies of his books. I owned almost all of his works, and six were then in my studio office. I had known better than to ask him to autograph his books. He had a dislike of people pushing a book and pen in front of his nose for a Faulkner signature. Of the many books mailed to him to sign I saw lots of them piled in a corner of his office; he never had any intention of signing or returning them. He calmly kept them, many of them valuable and rare items. As he phrased it: "My response to a pressure is to freeze still as a setting hen."

Of the six books he signed for me I have only retained the copy of *The Wild Palms*, in which he wrote with the smallest handwriting in the thinnest pen line:

For Stephen Longstreet
William Faulkner
Los Angeles
3 October
1944

Four of the other books were stolen the next day by some ardent but dishonest Faulkner collector, and one copy I gave to a Southern writer who used it to establish, in part, his social status among the town's intellectuals.

Bill went to work with collaborators on two screenplays, *The Big Sleep* by Raymond Chandler and *To Have and Have Not* by Ernest Hemingway. He wrote certain key scenes and situations and part of the dialogue in both pictures. But the director, Howard Hawks, pretty much kept his own style and signature on the films. There are hardly any true Faulkner touches in the pictures, and certainly the Hemingway was debased into a sleek love story. Several other writers contributed, but Bill turned out the most pages, even if they were not all used. This made Bill a problem child.

The unofficial Writers' Guild strawboss on the lot came to me.

"Faulkner is turning out too many pages. He sits up all night sometimes writing and turns in fifty to sixty pages in the morning. Try and speak to him."

I said no, I wouldn't do that. But Bill talked to me about it when we went to visit his horse. Bill patted the animal's neck. "Yo' think I'm turning in too many pages?"

"I don't think about the subject at all."

"I ain't one to give in to no calculated absurdity."

When Bill used *ain't* and his dialect got thick as corn mush, I knew he was playing country boy and trying to appear innocent. Someone among the writ-

ers must have spoken to him of his power of work. I said as long as he gave
the director what he wanted, at least he could afford to keep a horse in California. Bill mounted and rode off, looking very small on a very large mare.

I never rode with him, but people who did said Bill was a pretty poor
horseman. For all his love of horses and dogs he was not a sportsman, and in
fox hunts in Virginia—one of my former secretaries wrote me—he fell off
horses very often.

Bill's social life in California seemed to be kept down to as close to zero
as he could get it. He lived in a Faustian loneliness of his own making. The
college intellectuals (he called them "endowed loafers") tried to capture him.
His fame was spreading, but he avoided contact with what passed for culture
on the Coast.

I attended two dinners he could not refuse at the home of James Geller.
Bill spent the evening drinking, in a sort of pious complacency. He would sit
silently, the talk of art, literature, income tax, and film-making going on all
around him. He clutched a tall highball glass and held it up from time to time
to be refilled with bourbon, ice, and a little water. The gorgeous inanities of
the table conversation he ignored.

His was an easy prolonged drinking; no effort, and seemingly no reaction.
At dinner he kept a filled glass by his plate. He ate little.

Bill didn't care to meet many Californians. His private emotional life I
knew little of, and this is no place to write of it. The minimal core, the self-
sentence to loneliness, I didn't probe.

I did see Bill once with a Faulknerian woman, a character out of one of his
novels, an image hovering between realities. One night, I entered the Gotham
Delicatessen, a wartime eating place on Hollywood Boulevard. Seated at a
table was Bill, at ease, smiling at a woman who was sadly reciting some event
to him, her dark-ringed eyes shiny with melancholy. Even seated she looked
too tall, her dark lank hair had never been curled, and not combed too often.
Her dress didn't fit. She had bony shoulders. It was too much like one of his
novels. It seemed a planned joke. But it wasn't. She appeared to be in her
late 30s and met Bill drink for drink. I nodded to Bill and went to my own
table. The next day at the studio Bill said to me, "Very unfortunate woman."
Nothing else; I never did have any idea if she suggested any of his books or
came out of one.

The creation of one of his later books I did see through its early stages—*A
Fable*. Professors and critics have written long texts on its sources and its
theme; most are wrong. I had, carelessly, introduced Bill to a film producer

who was also a great salesman. He latched onto Bill with a hypnotic stare
and I saw Bill melt. His dualities and alienations calmed. It was the first time
in the nearly twenty years I had known William Faulkner that he let someone's personality engulf him.

The producer spoke of an idea he and a director had been working on. Bill,
he said, with a Promethean stare, was just the man to write the screenplay.
Bill politely asked what it was. The producer closed his eyes, seemed to go
into a trance, then announced the idea was the story of Christ and his Twelve
Disciples returning to earth as a corporal and his squad during World War I
to die again. I thought the idea was banal and vulgar. But looking over at Bill
I saw him nod. "Could be a pretty interesting thing."

Later I tried to talk Bill out of the idea. Then I heard he had actually
written the screenplay for the producer. It was rejected by the studios.

Those who doubt any of this about *A Fable* should turn to the footnote
near the title page of the novel and read Bill's thanks to the producer and
director "who had the basic idea from which this book grew into its present
form. . . ."

Many things were amazing about William Faulkner, most amazing was his
willingness—a curious impotence in his main purpose—to accept any kind
of hackwork in Hollywood, yet still keep his integrity and his image of himself as a great literary figure.

"The way I see it, Steve, this studio work, it's like chopping cotton or
picking potato bugs off plants; yo' know damn well it's not painting the
Sistine Chapel or winning the Kentucky Derby. But a man likes the feel of
some money in his pocket."

Bill was, I had long sensed, a kind of actor, and he would present several
facets of his country-boy character when trapped for an interview. His favorite answer as to why he wrote or what literature was became: "The drama of
the conflict in the human heart." I heard so many versions of this I wondered
he dared repeat it so often. The other favorite answer was when asked what
made a writer: "A little whiskey, a little tobacco, and paper."

As he grew older and fame came to him he became, some said, a snob; I
thought an amusing, harmless one. An act. The mustache grew longer in a
British guardsman's model, a bowler hat appeared, and he wandered around
with a tightly furled umbrella. The only people to whom he freely offered
signed copies of his work were dull hunt-club horsemen and fox hunters. I
sensed the self-examination and purification was over; these were Bill's last
self-indulgent years.

It was near the end of his Hollywood stay that I finally penetrated some of his defenses and disguises. I saw a man of great talent (and time may prove, a genius), an encumbered heart, a provincial with a certain naïveté, not given to any surface exuberances. Magnificently sensitive to the true stuff of life, he could make simple things nearly epic: the sound of grease in a hot skillet, the shade of a certain plant at a certain hour, the feel and smell of a hot day, the direct sexual reaction of a woman, the pattern of the perverse daemons that haunt us all. William Faulkner was the historian of the consequence of errors, of climate, and hereditary pride.

He himself was irrational and bizarre on the outside, a silent man who saw the world as a sad spectacle, an audible countryside sick with heat, lust, greed, for he had a fine ear. Correlation of words and eye he drew down into his own unadulterated self and ejected as his strange prose. ("I am a strangulated poet.")

We would sit in the late afternoon at the studio—not talking, yet aware. His sadness came naturally to him; he saw, he told me, the world needed the minimum of integrity to function. Ecstasy and disgust, he went on, are often two spellings of the word. "Most writers perpetuate the juridical lie."

His world was one of a disintegrating social fabric. He remained of the South and said if troops of a Federal government came to Mississippi to enforce some law they'd meet him at the crossroads with a rifle in his hands. Alcohol was his salve against a modern world he saw as a conspiracy of mediocrity on its ruling levels. Life was most bearable, he repeated, at its simplest; fishing, hunting, talking biggity in a cane chair on a board sidewalk, or horse-trading, gossiping.

Bill spoke rarely about writing, but when he did he said he had no method, no formula. He started with some local event, a well-known face, a sudden reaction to a joke or an incident. "And just let the story carry itself. I walk along behind and write down what happens."

He was bristly as a mastiff when one talked of his prose style. He wanted it shadowy and insubstantial, he once told me, "full of the dimensionless color of despair," a simplicity of spirit. He was trying to make of indefinable sensations a formal structure called the novel. He felt his world, his South, held too strongly to the desire for an irrevocable past; yet he, too, regretted its passing. He claimed he did not plan a book, it just grew; the people took over and made the story.

"We writers are dreadful liars, couldn't tell the truth on oath; don't know where fact begins, fancy starts up." At this point he'd usually start talking of

the conflict in the human heart. It was like a rest period for him, that phrase.
He though the best writing is usually recollection in tranquility, but said he
couldn't practice it himself. "I can write a streak when I've got a case of the
hots."

Bill, in all the years I knew him, never talked like his Nobel Prize speech.
Life was a mess of irrelevant detail, he often said, and the writer presented it
in a little order with a bit of poetry. "Poetry now, that's the highest form of
art. I wrote some in my youth. It wasn't much. When a man finds poetry isn't
for him, and the short story isn't everything, then all that's left is the novel."

But I suspected that, too, was one of his set interview pieces. He really
admired the great novels he had read as a young man. "Latent unconscious
ideas need giants to make their revelations valid." He did not read much
contemporary writing in later life. But for Hemingway and Wolfe, I never
heard him mention a modern writer with any degree of pleasure. He did dip
into Dickens and Balzac and the great Russians.

He was ashamed, at that time, of his lack of education and the fact that he
had never really flown as a fighter pilot with the Royal Canadian Air Force
in France. For years he gave the impression he had. ("It seemed to me then
the thing to do.") He felt he was a man harassed by inordinate instincts,
destined to express himself best in words. His premonitions and gropings
made him the artist he was. Inner conflicts and memory transmuted and artic-
ulated became texts as book followed book.

Like most readers, I wondered if he had from the first planned his strange
world of Yoknapatawpha County, its hillbilly Greek shadows, its sly red-neck
Romans, his symbols, into which the critics read so much that is universal.
In the little Bill said of it when I hinted about the subject, it would appear he
had planned nothing, had written of himself and his background, and had let
his people make their own themes.

"To feel happy without feeling guilty, now, yo' can say that's what I hoped
to find in my writing. The critics—I used to read them, I don't no more—they
found all that metamorphosis and labyrinth of purpose. Maybe they were
right. Oh, I tried later to make some of it fit together. I wasn't Zola or Balzac,
who had it all blueprinted for a series of books. I didn't have their brilliant
impromptus, either. I just wrote. Ideas are necessities not luxuries. It's people
I write about. Good and bad, I don't make them good or bad. Can't explain
some of them why they are as they are. People are an indestructible element.

Yet they're going to sicken, going to die, going to be forgotten, but leaving a sign of themselves sometimes saying, 'Kilroy was here.' The flesh has its own spirit I feel, free of the mind."

He didn't care to discuss the distortions or involutions of his sentences or his symbols. I think he sensed he didn't really fully understand them himself. Writing was a grand audacity, full of discrepancies, but the only thing he wanted to do.

I once quoted Hebbel to William Faulkner: "The heroes fall because they are overwhelmed; all tragedy is destruction." He seemed pleased to hear that, but just sat silently puffing on his pipe.

Hollywood, the studios, most of "the reprehensible, malicious hacks" did not care if William Faulkner stayed or left their world. I remember well the day I was called to a meeting of writer members of the Academy of Motion Picture Arts and Sciences. The problem, I was told by the group of highly paid screenwriters, was how to raise the low prestige of the studio writer before the next awarding of the Oscars?

I thought I had a good solution. "By picking out an outstanding great writer among us and giving him a special award. It would make world news if we gave William Faulkner an award for bringing his talents to our studios."

A shocked sea of over-cared-for faces turned on me as if I were demented. I sensed that to them William Faulkner was just a poor slob who wrote long-hair corn and had to come begging for a job in the studios; he wasn't acceptable. One of the writers, ignoring my suggestion, made one of his own. It was to cut down the writing awards by the Academy from six to four. Open-mouthed at this sterile *Alice in Wonderland* logic, I left and next day I re-signed from the Academy.

Soon after this took place William Faulkner left California. My last scene with him, like his last novel, was a kind of minor comic masterpiece. I was standing in front of the studio waiting to be picked up for the ride home. A battered car appeared with Bill at the wheel. A two-wheeled horse trailer was attached behind. It was his horse, the most pregnant mare I had ever seen.

"That's a mighty pregnant mare, Bill."

"Gotta get her to Mississippi. No mare of mine is going to throw a foal in California."

With a grind of gears he moved on towards the hills where extremities of details were fading into fragmentations of browns and golds.

I saw Bill only once more before his death. Years had passed; he had won the Nobel Prize, had been sent to Japan by the State Department, was a novelist-in-residence, had been a guest at West Point [that was his bowler hat and furled umbrella period, and they are on display there along with much military memorabilia]. He hunted with the Virginia fox hunters. He was much photographed.

I had been puzzled by his Nobel Prize speech; it did not express his true dark philosophy, nor was it the introspective, subtle language of the man I had known. It neither sounded like him nor conformed to the antagonistic brooding of his own personality.

The last time we met—in a dark mellow eating place—I told him my doubts about the speech. He sat a long time smoking, then looked at me and placed a hand on my knee. "We really live in the work of our mind, we only move about in the visible one. What I said I would have liked to be true." We left it at that.

I asked how the foal had turned out. He shrugged his shoulders and held up his glass to the waiter. He had, I saw, though better tailored and groomed, still retained the peculiar nobility and infusing grace of our first meetings.

The William Faulkner I knew for so many years is in part a series of drawings I made of him, a few sheets of notes in which I tried to retain some of the things he said that appeared worth remembering. I respect the great writer I think he was. The Nobel Prize winner—that man belongs to the public, the professors, the literary jackals who will fight over every morsel of him. And what they will recreate will be a very fine picture, a facade that will be impressive: A Harsh Lyric Voice of the South, The Creator of a Universal Social Scene. And lots more. We've all read them.

He was actually indifferent, in his middle years, to all this, only very dimly aware of it. He was a lonely solitary; "Life," as he once said to me as we walked between the palm trees, "Life is sort of leaning over a bannister to see who's knocking on the front door."

He lived so long and with such dignity on the flawed terraces of his personal purgatory that I prefer that sentiment of a writer's purpose than those of the too-easy prophet of the Nobel Prize speech.

William Faulkner

Fred Woodress / 1944 and 1949

From *Birmingham News*, June 9, 1957, Magazine Section, p. 8. Copyright by *The Birmingham News*, 1998. All rights reserved: reprinted with permission.

My most memorable wartime experience wasn't the Battle of the Bulge, the capture of Coblenz or the celebration of VE Day in East Germany. It was two glorious all-expense-paid months as a private at the University of Mississippi waiting for the Army to make up its mind at what college it wanted me to study engineering.

The fact the Army took two whole months to decide our future didn't bother us a bit. We had traded the all-male, dateless-Saturday-nights barracks life for a friendly man-starved campus populated by beautiful co-eds. To keep us busy they gave us refresher courses, originally intended to last several weeks until we were assigned to a college for Army Specialized Training.

It really taxed the ingenuity of the Ole Miss professors to keep refreshing us without actually teaching us a regular course. So you can imagine how our sociology professor wandered over to the subject of Oxford's most distinguished citizen—William Faulkner.

His humorous accounts of Oxford Faulknerlore intrigued us because most of us had never heard of William Faulkner. When the professor casually mentioned that Faulkner's sexy book, *Sanctuary*, had the university thinly disguised as its locale, much to the consternation of university authorities, we rushed to the library, checked out a copy and passed it around the dorm, reading aloud certain passages as guys will do.

One Saturday afternoon I walked to town and went into the Green Fern Restaurant to kill some time and drink coffee. I had heard Faulkner occasionally went to this restaurant, so I asked a waitress about him and if it were possible to meet him.

She said Mrs. Faulkner was in the restaurant right then and suggested I go over and talk with her. Mrs. Faulkner answered my question with: "Sure, you can go out and see him. He'll be glad to talk to you."

The shy writer who shuns publicity couldn't have been nicer. It was warm for January (1944), so we sat on the front porch, smoked his cigarettes, talked

58

and petted his dog who kept trying to nuzzle me. He told me about his son in service and advised me the way my Army career could help my writing ambitions was by "traveling as much as you can and by getting as much out of life as you can."

Nearly five years later with the Army and college behind me, I bought a Jeep, packed everything I owned into it, drew all my money from the bank and left St. Louis with two objectives: to see the United States and to free lance.

One of my first stops was Oxford, for an interview with William Faulkner. It embarrasses me now when I think back to the cocksure young man who was certain Faulkner had no better use for his time than to sit down and advise a guy who hadn't done much writing about how to write.

I have since learned how extremely inaccessible he is for newspaper and magazine interviews, preferring to use his time for writing. I blithely drove up his rutted drive that is lined with cedars, got out and shook hands with him. He was shyly cordial but very busy supervising his regular Negro handyman and a helper who were cleaning and dressing two hogs. It was a brisk December day, perfect for hog killing.

Faulkner excused himself to go to the doctor, so I hung around and watched the hog dressing. Then I asked the maid if I could say "hello" to Mrs. Faulkner. She couldn't have been more gracious to such a brash young man. She invited me into the living room and proved herself to be as much a conversationalist as her husband is not, asking me a lot of questions about myself and my family. I apologized when I found I was keeping her from ironing curtains, so she went back to work, leaving me with some magazines to read.

Faulkner returned, suggested I put on my coat because it was getting chilly, and took me outside to finish supervising the hog dressing and curing. He paid off the Negro helper and started to take him home when Mrs. Faulkner leaned out the window and said she needed the station wagon.

Faulkner muttered something about the other car not working and looked lost, so I volunteered. He started to climb in with me, but then there wouldn't have been room for the Negro and his dishpan full of chitlings, so he got back out.

When I returned and handed him the empty smelly dishpan, he thanked me and suggested we go inside the white porticoed house. He laughed when I reminded him of his earlier advice about travel and told him what had happened. It was nearly dusk and the living room was almost dark, but he didn't turn on a light. We smoked from a pack of Mrs. Faulkner's cigarettes as he answered my questions, thinking them over deliberately and moving about the room as he talked. I remembered Mrs. Faulkner's words: "Billy believes in taking his time in writing so as to do a job well."

Here are the highlights of our conversation:

About Writing—"Don't write by associating with other writers. . . I don't believe in it. . . Get to know people but not particularly writers."

About Style—"The writer with his novel, the composer with his music and the artist with his paintings are all doing the same thing—expressing themselves. It doesn't matter what your medium is—the main point is to express yourself. If you worry about style or about what medium to use, well . . . you're not a sincere writer."

About reading—"A writer must read. In the short space of his life he should become familiar with the printed word . . . of course this is impossible but he should keep up with new books and the classics."

About Education—Faulkner believes the best way to get an education is to "go to a library and browse around. Get to know the librarian so that she will let you in back of the shelves." About his own education he said: "Now I'm not an educated man. I ain't had much schoolin' "—coming from one of the world's greatest men.

About his writing—"These little Mississippi towns are all I know and that's what I write about . . . I have no particular favorite book. If I had time to reread them, I would want to rewrite them."

His lapses of silence grew longer, so I decided it was time to leave. I got up. About that time Mrs. Faulkner came in with their daughter Jill, whom Faulkner introduced; then she disappeared. He followed me to the door and we shook hands as I thanked him. "I'm heading for New Orleans," I said.

"You will enjoy it," he said, smiling. The large white door closed behind me and I got into my Jeep and drove down the cedar lined drive on my way to Water Valley, Jackson and New Orleans.

William Faulkner at Home
Sidney Landfield / 1946

From Chicago *Sun*, June 23, 1946, Book Week, p. 6. Reprinted by permission.

A few weeks ago Sid Landfield, a *Sun* reporter, and his wife were driving through Mississippi en route home from their vacation. Realizing he was in Author William Faulkner's home country, Landfield sought him out.

"Mr. Faulkner will be back shortly—he's making funeral arrangements." his wife explained pleasantly as we took advantage of the 10 minutes until his arrival to examine great piles of empty beer and ale bottles all over his back porch.

A docile brown cow relaxed on the front lawn and mooed. My wife and I had followed the avenue of huge cedars leading to William Faulkner's large, ante-bellum home, all white but for the green shutters and now 115 years old. Just as two of his several dogs began lapping at our dusty heels, Faulkner drove up in his '39 model Ford, a touring job with a few fancy gadgets. He was wearing a two-tone sport jacket and off color slacks, a matching tie and handkerchief and even a bachelor's button in his jacket lapel.

"Hope you haven't been waiting long," he apologized, "but I've just been to town (Oxford, Miss.) arranging about one of our family who passed away." (We learned after questioning that the "relative" was a trusted and loved servant who had been with the family for years.)

Hair and mustache a steel gray, with sharp features and jet black eyes, Faulkner seemed at 49 to blend with the house and its surroundings: sturdy, gloomy, exciting.

We asked him about work and if he had anything "going."

"Yes," he answered, "I'm at a novel now, but it's just a mess of notes and ideas. But let's talk about my farm. It's some 17 miles from here—it's large and it takes most all of my time." He explained that farming was charming and that novel-writing was "oh so terribly slow and hard when you get my age."

We had a camera and Faulkner insisted on pictures, all the while trying to remember when and where he had written *As I Lay Dying*, *Sanctuary* and

other of his earlier novels. "I guess they were written most everywhere," he
said finally. "In this house a lot, in New Orleans—in half a dozen places."

He told us over and over again that he loves Oxford. As for his house, the
older it gets the better it is and the more he likes it. As we started for our car
he said, "Come on back soon, and let's talk some more about farming. . .
and Chicago." Then he led us down the narrow path from his house to the
road, all the while explaining about this old tree or how good an animal the
cow was; we drove half a mile or so across peaceful countryside lined deep
with trees until once again we came to the main road—a gravel stretch that
led a mile or two until suddenly the highway appeared.

Back again in Oxford, we had an overwhelming desire to appease a curiosity. So, even though on our way to his house we had purposely inquired of a
dozen people to find Faulkner, we once again stopped men and women,
young and old, on the streets of the town, to ask "Where does Faulkner
live?" Once again everyone knew, "Back yonder a piece and near the woods,
I reckon." Everyone knew William Faulkner, even the 12-year-old Negro
boy who shined my shoes, as he put it, "extrah real good if you know Mistah
Faulknah."

Stopping for gas some 15 miles past Oxford we asked the gas station
attendant, "Ever hear of William Faulkner in these parts?"

"Sure," he answered immediately and happily, "he lives back to Oxford
and then down yonder a piece—but just ask anyone in town."

We knew then why Faulkner loves Oxford and the surrounding country.

Faulkner on Writers and Writing

Gene Roper, Jr. / 1947

From *The Faulkner Newsletter and Yoknapatawpha Review,* 3 (April–June 1993), pp. 1, 3. Reprinted by permission.

(Editor's Note: Faulkner's biographers and others have reported at length on Faulkner having met six classes at the University of Mississippi in April 1947 and the furor over publicity being given to his sessions with the students. The matter is documented by A. Wigfall Green in "First Lectures at a University," from notes made by one student, Richard M. Allen, in *William Faulkner of Oxford,* edited by James B. Webb and Green (Louisiana State University Press, 1965), and by Joseph Blotner in *Faulkner: a Biography* (Random House, 1974, 1984). One person on the scene at Ole Miss that April who has not been heard from until now is Gene Roper, Jr., who was in Ole Miss public relations and serving as a correspondent for *The Commercial Appeal,* the Memphis morning newspaper. Published here for the first time is his report, written the week following the April 14–17 class sessions, and sent to *The Commercial Appeal,* which honored a request by Ole Miss not to publish it after Faulkner had objected to publicity. Roper's article, on yellow copy paper, was kept by Paul Flowers, book editor and Greenhouse columnist for the Memphis newspaper, and is now in the William Boozer Collection.)

William Faulkner, who ordinarily shuns public assemblies like a young colt shies at snakes, established a precedent last week by not only appearing at the University of Mississippi, but by giving forth with utterances on literature—his own and others—for the open-mouthed consumption of literature students at the university.

This was a William Faulkner who could talk with authority on the field of contemporary literature, and many of the anecdotes which are told of the oft-read but seldom-seen author who lives within a couple of miles of the school went by the board as he answered questions candidly and freely, answered them to the satisfaction of his listeners and gaining stature with every statement.

This was the first opportunity that his student neighbors—who are well acquainted with Mr. Faulkner's reputation through his books and the stories that circulate around him, increasing the legendary atmosphere that surrounds him—have had to meet the noted writer, since public appearances on his part are in the nature of a literary event. No advance publicity was given to his visit to the campus because of his passion for avoiding such spotlighting. However, from the students who fired questions at him are available many of the answers he gave to their interrogation, and many are of a literary yardstick caliber.

He named Thomas Wolfe, author of *Look Homeward, Angel* as one of the greatest contemporary authors, then listed second William Faulkner; John Dos Passos was third in his estimation, followed by Ernest Hemingway and John Steinbeck.

Questioned on that stroke of light which inspired him to start writing, he announced that it was strictly a utilitarian mood, prompted by an association with Sherwood Anderson back in the days of Prohibition when Faulkner asserted he was running whiskey for a bootlegger in New Orleans. Inferring from Anderson's vacation existence that all writers had it easy, he decided to try his own hand at turning out copy. Thus was begun one of the South's greatest writing careers.

His first effort was *Soldiers'Pay,* which he induced Anderson to ship to his publisher. Anderson made the one stipulation that he would not be required to read the production. Then, in typical Faulkner tradition, William took off for Europe as a deck hand on a freighter. While abroad, he received a check from the publisher for $200—which he was unfortunately unable to cash.

Some of the questions posed were in something of this fashion: "What is your favorite character in your books, or do you have one?," to which he replied "the one I think I would enjoy talking to would be my detective lawyer. I think that one of the characters I would choose is the Negro woman in *The Sound and the Fury.* Dilsey's a fine woman. I'm proud of her."

Asked if he ever felt influenced by the reading public, Mr. Faulkner answered in the negative, inasmuch as he never thinks of writing in terms of money. The subject of criticism was brought up, and Mr. Faulkner explained that he is not only intolerant of criticism, but even goes to the trouble to insult those people who think well of him.

He paid tribute to the greats of literature when he explained "primarily I'm not a prose writer, I'm a poet. I write that way because I can't write like Shakespeare or Shelley." Then he asserted that a writer can't be both an artist and a reformer, he must be objective.

He passed off as a symptom of the times the fact that women are writing detective stories, but professed to liking women poets "when they are good," naming Sara Teasdale and Emily Dickinson as two examples.

Asked various questions about authors and works, he referred to *Forever Amber* as trash, classified *Native Son* as a very good book while putting *Black Boy* in the propaganda category. He defined James Street, his Southern contemporary, as a "newspaper man," whose people are round. But he was of the opinion that Mr. Street is lacking in imagination, that his intention is not to uplift but to tell the reader something. It was Mr. Faulkner's belief that the "artist has the intention of uplifting the heart."

He discarded the idea that style is everything by stating that this basis of writing is nothing, that technique is nothing, supplanting in their place the theory that they invent themselves as you go along and need them. And he laid down the rule of hard work for those ambitious to become authors, insisting that they would never get anywhere without the sweat of toil.

In the process of preparing a novel, he expressed the theory that a character does his own talking once he becomes alive, asserting that "you can have no more control over him than you would an incorrigible child."

He claimed that Hemingway's style is synthetic, but added later that there is a great deal of Hemingway in his own novels.

He classified Shakespeare's works as the "case book of mankind," adding that if a man has a great deal of talent, he can use Shakespeare as a yardstick. He thought that perhaps Shakespeare might have wanted to become a prince, to have taken part in a tragic romance, but inasmuch as the Bard never got around to his desires, he wrote about it instead. The author added somewhat skeptically, "he also probably wanted to make money."

He paid the highest off tributes to Sherwood Anderson, reminiscing that "he was a sweet man. He was really a fine, unassuming, kind, generous—well really more kind that generous—he had known poverty too well to be really generous."

These and other statements Mr. Faulkner interlaced with hints to prospective authors, admitting that he was ashamed of *Sanctuary* because "I think it isn't honest." He stated that "the conception of that book is shameful, " insisting that it was simply to "portray yourself to make a little money," humbly asserting that "my whole intention was base."

An Interview with William Faulkner

Lavon Rascoe / 1947

From *The Western Review*, 15 (Summer 1951) , pp. 300–04.

In April 1947, the English Department of the University of Mississippi invited William Faulkner to meet one English class a day for a week. He consented, and at his request the classes were conducted by his answering questions; also, the teacher of each class was asked not to attend. The following questions were asked by the Creative Writing class on April 16.

Q: In *Sanctuary*, did "Popeye" have any human prototype?

A: No. He was symbolical of evil. I just gave him two eyes, a nose, a mouth, and a black suit. It was all allegory. Not a very good book. I was probably wrong in a good many places in my characterization of Popeye because I was equipped with no approach of a scientific nature.

Q: Did you read into "Popeye" characterizations similar to those found in Milton's Satan?

A: That's assuming that a trait is good or evil in its own right. You must study the result. Anything that brings misery is bad. Consistency is good only in its result. You have to stretch a character through the length of the book.

Q: What about Temple?

A: Women can stand anything. They are even tougher than evil itself. A man cannot stand what a woman can. A man would have cracked under a strain comparable to Temple's.

Q: Which of your books do you consider best?

A: *As I Lay Dying* was easier and more interesting. *The Sound and The Fury* still continues to move me. *Go Down, Moses*—I started it as a collection of short stories. After I reworked it, it became seven different facets of one field. It is simply a collection of short stories.

Q: In what form does the initial idea of a story come to you?

A: It depends. *The Sound and the Fury* began with the impression of a

66

little girl playing in a branch and getting her panties wet. This idea was attractive to me, and from it grew the novel.

Q: How do you go about choosing your words?

A: In the heat of putting it down you might put down some extra words. If you rework it, and the words still ring true, leave them in.

Q: What reason did you have for arranging the chapters of *The Wild Palms* as you did?

A: It was merely a mechanical device to bring out the story I was telling, which was one of two types of love. I did send both stories to the publisher separately, and they were rejected because they were too short. So I alternated the chapters of them.

Q: How much do you know about how a book will turn out before you start writing it?

A: Very little. The character develops with the book, and the book with the writing of it.

Q: Why do you present the picture you do of our area?

A: I have seen no other. I try to tell the truth of man. I use imagination when I have to and cruelty as a last resort. The area is incidental. That's just all I know.

Q: Since you do represent this picture, don't you think it gives a wrong impression?

A: Yes, and I'm sorry. I feel I'm written out. I don't think I'll write much more. You have only so much steam and if you don't use it up in writing it'll get off by itself.

Q: Did you write *Sanctuary* at the boilers just to draw attention to yourself?

A: The basic reason was that I needed money. Two or three books that had already been published were not selling and I was broke. I wrote *Sanctuary* to sell. After I sent it to the publisher, he informed me, "Good God, we can't print this. We'd both be put in jail." The blood and guts period hadn't arrived yet. My other books began selling, so I got the galleys of *Sanctuary* back from the publisher for correction. I knew that I would have to either rewrite the whole thing or throw it away. I was obligated to the publisher financially and morally and upon continued insistence I agreed to have it

published. I reworked the whole thing and had to pay for having the new
galleys made. For these reasons, I didn't like it then and I don't like it now.

Q: Should one re-write?
A: No. If you are going to write, write something new.

Q: How do you find time to write?
A: You can *always* find time to write. Anybody who says he can't is living
under false pretenses. To that extent depend on inspiration. Don't wait. When
you have an inspiration put it down. Don't wait until later and when you have
more time and then try to recapture the mood and add flourishes. You can
never recapture the mood with the vividness of its first impression.

Q: How long does it take you to write a book?
A: A hack writer can tell. *As I lay Dying* took six weeks. *The Sound and
the Fury* took three years.

Q: I understand you can keep two stories going at one time. If that is true,
is it advisable?
A: It's all right to keep two stories going at the same time. But don't write
for deadlines. Write just as long as you have something to say.

Q: What is the best training for writing? Courses in writing? Or what?
A: Read, read, read! Read everything — trash, classics, good and bad; see
how they do it. When a carpenter learns his trade, he does so by observing.
Read! You'll absorb it. Write. If it is good you'll find out. If it's not, throw it
out the window.

Q: Is it good to copy a style?
A: If you have something to say, use your own style: it will choose its
own type of telling, its own style. What you have liked will show through in
your style.

Q: Do you realize your standing in England?
A: I know that I am better thought of abroad than here. I don't read any
reviews. The only people with time to read are women and rich people. More
Europeans read than do Americans

Q: Why do so many people prefer *Sanctuary* to *As I Lay Dying*?
A: That's another phase of our American nature. The former just has more
commercial color.

Q: Are we degenerating?

A: No. Reading is something that is in a way necessary like Heaven or a clean collar, but not important. We want culture but don't want to go to any trouble to get it. We prefer reading condensations.

Q: That sounds like a slam on our way of living.

A: Our way of living needs slamming. Everybody's aim is to help people, turn them to Heaven. You write to help people. The existence of this class in Creative Writing is good in that you take time off to learn to write and you are in a period where time is your most valuable possession.

Q: What is the best age for writing?

A: For fiction the best age is from thirty-five to forty-five. Your fire is not all used up and you know more. Fiction is slower. For poetry the best age is from seventeen to twenty-six. Poetry writing is more like a skyrocket with all your fire condensed into one rocket.

Q: How about Shakespeare?

A: Their *are* exceptions.

Q: Why did you quit writing poetry?

A: When I found poetry not suited to what I had to say, I changed my medium. At twenty-one I thought my poetry very good. At twenty-two I began to change my mind. At twenty-three I quit. I use a poetic quality in my writing. After all, prose is poetry.

Q: Do you read a good bit?

A: Up to fifteen years ago I read everything I could get hold of. I don't even know fiction writers' names much now. I have a few favorites I read over and over again. (Note: Dickens is one of Mr. Faulkner's favorites.)

Q: Has "The Great American Novel" been written yet?

A: People will read *Huck Finn* for a long time. However, Twain has never written a novel. His work is too loose. We'll assume that a novel has set rules. His is a mass of stuff—just a series of events.

Q: I understand you use a minimum of restrictions.

A: I let the novel write itself—no length or style compunctions.

Q: What do you think of movie script writing?

A: A person is rehired the next year on the basis of how many times his name appeared on the screen the previous year. Much bribery ensues. In the old days they could give a producer three hundred pounds of sugar and be reasonably sure of getting their names on the screen. They really fight about it and for it.

Q: To what extent did you write the script for *Slave Ship*?

A: I'm a motion picture doctor. When they find a section of a script they don't like I rewrite it and continue to rewrite it until thy are satisfied. I reworked sections in this picture. I don't write scripts. I don't know enough about it. (Note: Besides the filming of *Sanctuary* and *Intruder in the Dust*, Mr. Faulkner's name has appeared on such films as *To Have and Have Not* and *The Big Sleep*.)

Q: It is rumored that once you asked your boss in Hollywood if it would be permissible for you to go home to work. He gave his approval. Thinking you meant Beverly Hills, he called you at that address and found that by home you had meant Oxford, Mississippi. Is there anything to this story?

A: (laughingly) That story's better than mine. I had been doing some patching for Howard Hawks on my first job. When the job was over, Howard suggested that I stay and pick up some of that easy money. I had got $6,000 for my work. That was more money than I had ever seen, and I thought it was more than was in Mississippi. I told him I would telegraph him when I was ready to go to work again. I stayed in Oxford a year, and sure enough the money was gone. I wired him and within a week I got a letter from William B. Hawks, his brother and my agent. Enclosed was a check for a week's work less agent's commission. These continued for a year with them thinking I was in Hollywood.

Once a friend of mine came back from England after two years stay and found 104 checks inclosed in letters that had been pushed under his door.

They are showing a little more efficiency now, so those things don't happen much anymore.

Q: How do you like Hollywood?

A: I don't like the climate, the people, their way of life. Nothing ever happens and then one morning you wake up and find that you are sixty-five. I prefer Florida.

Q: On your walking trip through Europe how did you find everything?

A: At that time the French were impoverished, the Germans naturally servile, I didn't find too much.

Q: Did your perspective change after travel to Europe and to other places?

A: No. When you are young, you are sensitive but don't know it. Later you seem to know it. A wider view is not caused by what you have seen but by War itself. Some can survive anything and get something good out of it, but the masses get no good from war. War is a dreadful price to pay for experience. About the only good coming from war is that it does allow men to be freer with womenfolks without being blacklisted for it.

Q: What effect did the R.C.A.F. have on you?

A: I still like to believe I was tough enough that it didn't hurt me too much. It didn't help much. I hope I have lived down the harm it did me.

Q: Which World War do you think was tougher?

A: Last war we lived in constant fear of the thing catching on fire. We didn't have to watch all those instruments and dials. All we did was pray the plane didn't burn up. We didn't have parachutes. Not much choice. World War II must have been tougher. (Note: Mr. Faulkner had both legs broken in a plane crash in World War I.)

Q: Is association (such as a boarding house) good or bad as a background for writing?

A: Neither good nor bad. You might store the facts in mind for future reference in case you ever want to write about a boarding house.

Q: How much should one notice printed criticism?

A: It is best not to pay too much attention to a printed criticism. It is a trade tool for making money. A few critics are sound and worth reading, but not many.

Q: Whom do you consider the five most important contemporary writers?

A: 1. Thomas Wolfe. 2. Dos Passos. 3. Ernest Hemingway. 4. Willa Cather. 5. John Steinbeck.

Q: If you don't think it too personal, how do you rank yourself with contemporary writers?

A: 1. Thomas Wolfe: he had much courage and wrote as if he didn't have long to live; 2. William Faulkner; 3. Dos Passos; 4. Ernest Hemingway: he has no courage, has never crawled out on a limb. He has never been known to use a word that might cause the reader to check with a dictionary to see if it is properly used; 5. John Steinbeck: at one time I had great hopes for him—now I don't know.

Q: What one obstacle do you consider greatest in writing?

A: I'm not sure I understand what you mean. What do you want to do? Write something that will sell?

Q: I mean whether the obstacle is internal conflict or external conflict.

A: Internal conflict is the first obstacle to pass. Satisfy yourself with what you are writing. First be sure you have something to say. Then say it and say it right.

Q: Mr. Faulkner, do you mind our repeating anything we have heard today outside of class?

A: No. It was true yesterday, is true today, and will be true tomorrow.

First Lectures at a University

A. Wigfall Green and Richard M. Allen / 1947

From *William Faulkner of Oxford*, ed. James W. Webb and A. Wigfall Green (Baton Rouge: Louisiana State University Press, 1965), pp. 127–39. Reprinted By permission.

Professor A. Wigfall Green, for thirty-five years a member of the University of Mississippi faculty and for the same period a friend of the Faulkner family, in 1947 made preliminary arrangements with Mr. Faulkner to appear before students at the University in a series of informal "lectures." This was the forerunner of later appearances by the writer, most notably as writer-in-residence at the University of Virginia.

"First Lectures at a University" is an account of negotiations with Mr. Faulkner and of what he said to the students, the latter based upon notes taken by Richard M. Allen, then an undergraduate, now an Indianola, Mississippi, attorney.

By the early 1940's Faulkner's earlier popularity had declined. But after the appearance of Malcolm Cowley's *The Portable Faulkner* in 1946, critical interest was revived. When Faulkner lectured at Ole Miss, he had not published a book in five years.

With the Second World War over and the happy return of many of our faculty from soldierly to scholarly pursuits, our neighbor William Faulkner, poet, fly-boy, and novelist, seemed closer than ever to us—so close that we hoped we could transform him temporarily into a fellow zombie and get him to talk to our advanced students in English at the University of Mississippi. Two members of the English staff individually and courageously urged him to help us. But they attempted to seduce by remote control: by letter and telephone. The result made it seem that both U.S. mail and Southern Bell had broken down; an imperious "Nay!" would have been preferable to the impenetrable silence.

It was my turn. Because I, too, was chicken-hearted, I resorted to proselyting by remote control, the telephone. Mrs. Estelle Faulkner, ever gracious, played intercessor with her husband. But he reacted typically: "I have never lectured; I can't lecture"; and the novelist shrilled further, "and I won't lecture!" To myself I said, "I must stall for time; I must use force." Mr. Faulkner agreed to talk with me and he was gracious, though surprised, at my instanta-

73

neous appearance at his house. "Mr. Faulkner," the plea began, "our students
need to hear you. Talk about anything: your flying during the Great War; your
South; the evolution of your characters; why you are a novelist; or anything
else that you wish to talk about. No faculty people will be in the room; and,
if you wish, no notes will be taken." He brightened, but he was still timid.
With bravado he rationalized, "I shouldn't think of doing such a thing except
for—MONEY!" Knowing that he was bluffing because he was then almost
rich, it seemed that his bluff should be called with a grin. "All right, Mr.
Faulkner," and I grinned, "we'll pay you a hundred dollars for meeting a
couple of advanced English classes," a daring offer because the department,
as always, was broke. He laughed, shook my hand heartily, and agreed.
Somewhat later arrangements were made by the chairman of the department,
Professor W. Alton Bryant, for him to give six lectures beginning on Monday,
April 21, 1947, for $250.

Mr. Faulkner's original wish was that no verbatim record be made of his
answers to questions, but later he said that he had no objection to anyone's
discussing or repeating anything that he had said, for "it was true yesterday,
is true today, and will be true tomorrow." The following answers to questions
are the purport of what Mr. Faulkner said.

Asked how he happened to become a novelist, Faulkner replied that it was in
New Orleans that he became really interested in writing prose. During the
prohibition era he worked for a bootlegger there. After the seamen on schoo-
ners from the Bahamas had transported whiskey bottles with Scotch labels
and had buried the bottles in sandbars, it was his job to dig them out of the
sand and transport them to New Orleans. He had previously met in New York
through Stark Young a Miss Prall, who later married Sherwood Anderson,
and through her he met her husband, then living in New Orleans. He envied
Anderson his easy life: writing at home during the morning and walking
around, talking, and drinking in the afternoon. Not satisfied with his poetry,
Faulkner decided that he would attempt a novel. Mrs. Anderson relayed this
information to her husband. "You're writing a book?" Anderson said to
Faulkner, "Well, if I don't have to read it, I'll send it to Liveright."* Liveright
accepted the novel for publication. In the meantime, Faulkner had sailed for
Europe on a freighter. He received the $200 publisher's advance for *Soldiers'
Pay* while in Paris, but no one would cash it.

---

*Horace Liveright, of Boni & Liveright, was Anderson's publisher. The firm published
Faulkner's first two novels, then rejected his third, *Sartoris*.

The question, "What is your purpose in writing?" was a good one, Faulkner said, but one that he really couldn't answer. It was probably because of the hope that someone somewhere might say, "Yes, that's true!"

He said that for him writing was hard work and that he followed no rigid schedule, but that he found he had less trouble writing in the morning than at other times. The writer, he added, must set aside a part of his time to be an introvert. But he must not await a certain environment or a mood that would be conducive to writing; he must find time to write. Anyone who says that he hasn't the time is lying to himself. To this extent depend on inspiration: when inspiration comes, jot it down. Don't wait. The sooner you put it down, the stronger the picture will be. Don't wait until later to try to recapture the mood and color.

As for subjects, he said, there are only three: love, money, death. Titles of novels, he added, sometimes generate themselves. The title can be important; it can establish the whole tone of the book. Sometimes an author finds such a good title that he writes a book around it.

A novel begins in various ways. There is no rule. Sometimes the basic idea is an anecdote or an incident; sometimes a character is created first and then the story. *The Sound and the Fury*, Faulkner said, began with a mental picture of four children: first, Caddy, the girl; and then, almost immediately, her brother Benjy, the idiot boy. Another character being necessary for the story, Quentin, another brother, was created. Then a devil was needed and Jason, the youngest brother, was put in to represent the devil, even in the earliest scene when the four children are playing in the stream. *Absalom, Absalom!* began with the character of Colonel Sutpen, and the story worked itself out around him. A vision of a pregnant woman walking down a road from Alabama to Mississippi in search of the father of her child was the initial idea for *Light in August*. The woman wasn't tired and probably didn't feel that she was undergoing any great hardship as a woman of a different class would have felt. Hers was the natural strength of the earth—a strength different from that of Dilsey in *The Sound and the Fury* because Dilsey's derived from oppression.

Asked whether the character Popeye in *Sanctuary* was modeled upon an actual person, Faulkner said that he was simply the protagonist of evil: he had given Popeye two eyes, a nose, a mouth, arms and legs, and a black suit so that he would be recognizable. "Popeye is a contemporary Satan manufactured in carload lots for, let us say, Sears Roebuck." The whole thing was allegorical, but the portrayal was probably bad because it was impossible to use anything like a scientific approach. Anything, like Popeye, that brings misery is bad, but there was no attempt to ascribe to Popeye qualities of evil like that in Milton's Satan because, to do so, is to assume that a trait is good or evil in its own right. Temple Drake, of Sanctuary, he said, proves that women are tougher than evil and can stand almost anything. Sanctuary was written to make money, two or three earlier books not having sold. The publisher said, "Good God! We can't print this. We'd both be put into jail!" Then the blood-and-guts period came in and the earlier books began to sell and the publisher wanted *Sanctuary* back; but Faulkner rewrote the entire book and had to pay for new galleys: for these reasons, the author never liked the book. Darl, of *As I Lay Dying*, he said, really did go insane; he was schizophrenic. The structure of *The Wild Palms* was deliberately made mechanical to bring out the contrast between two types of love: one man gave up his freedom for a woman; another to escape from a woman.

Sometimes, Faulkner said, he revised a good deal; sometimes not. *As I Lay Dying*, a successful tour de force, was written without changing a word. He said that he always felt a letdown when he completed a book and that he could do a better job if he could begin it all over the next morning.

It was difficult for him to answer in straightforward fashion the question, "What is your favorite character in your own books?" Dilsey, the Negro woman, he said, was the stabilizing influence in *The Sound and the Fury*; she was also one of his proudest creations. "Dilsey's a fine woman. I'm proud of her."

"How long does it take you to write a book?" Only a hack, Faulkner replied, can answer that question. The time varies. He wrote *As I Lay Dying* in six weeks because he knew exactly the direction in which he was going; *The Sound and the Fury* took six months; *Absalom, Absalom!* three years.

To ask an author of many novels to name his favorite, he said, is like asking the father of many sons to name his favorite. *Go Down, Moses* was a favorite because it started as a collection of short stories, but as he revised it he derived pleasure in creating of it seven different facets of one idea. In a different way, *As I Lay Dying* was a favorite in that it was the easiest and most pleasant for him to write and in that it continued to move him.

The South, Faulkner said, was what he knew best, and he wrote about it because it was what he knew best. But his point of view would have been essentially the same had he lived in any other section. He had to use the material he had without considering the reaction of people of other sections to his pictures of the South; but even had he foreseen their reaction he would have written as he had done and let the chips fall where they might. His purpose was to tell a story as best he could, to tell the truth about man, the truth inside the heart. The setting was incidental. He used exaggeration only when he had to, and cruelty only as a last resort. A poet, he said, has to overemphasize. He admitted that his pictures of the South were misleading, distorted, and he regretted that they were; but he tried to show not fact but truth.

The South, Faulkner said, is too closely tied to the other states for it to have a fate of its own; the fate of the South is the fate of the nation. He would not predict what was going to happen in the United States but he was certain about what was going to happen in his make-believe county, Yoknapatawpha: the Snopeses would drive out the aristocracy.

Faulkner said that he did not use living people as characters even though one may today see a lot of Shakespeare and Balzac characters on the street. Every writer, he said, is vain enough to believe that he can invent characters a little better than Nature can, though he probably cannot. A good creation is a real, three-dimensional character who stands up of his own accord and can "cast a shadow."

His characters, Faulkner said, do not express his opinions but speak only according to their own natures. When he began to write about his characters, he did not know how they were going to develop, but he knew that if they came alive he might have no more control over them than one would have over an incorrigible child.

There is, he said, only one way in which to learn to write dialogue: listen when other people talk. In the heat of writing, words must be put down rapidly. Later some of them may seem a little off and may need alteration. If, however, when the writer goes back over his work to redo it, the words still ring true, they must be left in. Sometimes the meaning of a word in its context transcends the dictionary definition.

It is not good to copy the style of another writer, Faulkner said. If an author has something to say, the story will evolve its own type of telling, its own style. An author wastes time in trying to invent a style. Style changes, so much, indeed, that sometimes even the author, much later, will not recognize it. Faulkner then cited an example. A magazine once rejected one of his stories, but kept the manuscript. Ten years later the editor sent him a check and a copy of the story. Faulkner did not recognize the story, the characters, the style, or anything about it; but it turned out later that it was his own work.

The author will never get anywhere writing style for the sake of style; he must still have something to tell.

Faulkner added that he wrote as he did because he had to; he wished to God sometimes that he had a different style.

In reply to questions about the relationship between poetry and prose and the poetic element in prose writing, Faulkner said that primarily he was a poet and not a prose writer; that he began writing verse when he was seventeen; and that he quit writing poetry at twenty-three because he could not write so well as Shakespeare and Shelley had written and because he found his best medium to be fiction; but because he still thought of his stories as a poet would, his characters often do things that don't happen in Oxford but which are true to man. Poetry is like a skyrocket: all the fire is condensed in one rocket. Outstanding poetry is written by young men, he said; but he was interrupted by the question, "How about Shakespeare?" Conceding that there are exceptions, he noted that Shakespeare wrote much in both youth and later years.

Asked about Allen Tate, Faulkner said that Tate is an able poet. He replied to another question concerning women poets: he liked them when they were good, and he named as good Emily Dickinson, Sara Teasdale, Elinor Wylie, and Edna St. Vincent Millay; but he concluded that nobody was writing good poetry any more and that, as a symptom of the times, women had started writing detective stories.

A student, picking up earlier mention of Shakespeare, asked Mr. Faulkner to name his favorite plays by Shakespeare. *Hamlet,* he thought, is probably technically the best play, but his favorites were the Henry plays and *A Midsummer Night's Dream.* His favorite characters were Prince Hal and Falstaff. Shakespeare, it seemed to Faulkner, probably would have liked to be a prince and take part in tragic love, but, since he never got to, he wrote about it. Shakespeare also probably wanted to make money. The value in Shakespeare is that his work is a case book on mankind: if a man has a great deal of talent he can use Shakespeare as a yardstick.

Faulkner did not hesitate in replying to the question, "What makes the stories of other writers good?" Because, he answered frankly, of the truth that comes out of them—not fact, but truth. Fact and truth have very little to do with each other. Truth is the sum of things that make man bid for immortality, that make him generous in spite of himself, or brave when it is to his advantage to be cowardly—the something that makes him better than his environment and his instincts.

Huckleberry Finn, Faulkner said, approaches the "great American novel" and Twain the "great American novelist," but Twain never really wrote a novel, assuming that a novel has set rules. His work is too loose, a series of events, "a mass of stuff."*

The father of modern literature, Faulkner thought, is probably James Joyce, but the father of modern American literature is Sherwood Anderson. Anderson, he said, was an unassuming man, a fine, kind, sweet man who talked much better than he wrote. Before Sherwood Anderson, writers had written in the European tradition, used European phraseology and diction, looked at their work through the eyes of Europeans; they had looked east, but then they looked back west. He was the forerunner not only of Faulkner but also of Hemingway (whose style was strongly influenced by Anderson and Gertrude Stein), Dos Passos, Tom Wolfe, Caldwell, Steinbeck—of this entire group. Anderson's style was not derived from Europeans but was completely his own; it made it seem that Anderson had never read anything because it consists of short, jerky sentences: "I see a dog. The dog can run."

Faulkner answered candidly another question on his evaluation of his American contemporaries. In his opinion, he and all the others whose names had been coupled since they had begun to write had failed: Hemingway, Wolfe, Cather, Dos Passos, and Steinbeck. Wolfe made the grandest failure because he had a vast courage—courage in that he attempted what he knew he probably couldn't do; he banged around "like an elephant in a swimming pool"; he wrote as though he didn't have long to live—and Faulkner showed humility at the mention of Wolfe's name. Hemingway had always been careful and had never attempted anything he could not do; he had been like a poker player who plays close to his vest; he had never made mistakes of diction, style, taste, or fact; he had never used a word the meaning of which couldn't be checked in the dictionary. Faulkner once had great hopes for Caldwell, but now he didn't know. He would rank the group: Wolfe first; then Dos Passos, Hemingway, Cather, and Steinbeck. When a student called the writer's attention to his failure to rate himself, a faculty infiltrator said, "I'm afraid you're taxing Mr. Faulkner's modesty." But he rearranged his list: Wolfe, Faulkner, Dos Passos, Hemingway, and Steinbeck. (With modesty

---

*Twenty-five years earlier, in an essay in the Ole Miss student newspaper, Faulkner called Twain "a hack writer who would not have been considered fourth rate in Europe, who tricked out a few of the old proven 'sure fire' literary skeletons with sufficient local color to intrigue the superficial and the lazy."

and only upon the insistence of the class Faulkner ranked—and perhaps underrated—himself.)

Native Son, he said in answer to a question about Richard Wright, is a very good book, but *Black Boy* is propaganda; a writer cannot be both an artist and a propagandist. He praised the work of Frank Norris, Theodore Dreiser, and Elinor Wylie; and he paid tribute a number of times to the stories of Willa Cather. Faulkner lost his usual reserve and smiled as he volunteered information about Eudora Welty, whose *The Robber Bridegroom* he had recently read and had found to be a "charming and fantastic story."

Some people can survive anything and some get good out of it, he said in responding to a question on the value of war experience to the potential writer. But war, he continued, is a dreadful price to pay for experience, and experience alone is not enough to make a story. He still liked to believe that he was sufficiently tough that the RFC/RAF did not hurt him much; it did not help much either; he hoped to live down the harm. The only good that can come from any war, he said, is that it allows men to be free of their womenfolk without being blacklisted for it.

With pretended ingenuousness he answered another question: the experience of having lived in a boardinghouse is neither good nor bad except in that the writer might want to some time to write about a boardinghouse.

One's perspective doesn't change after travel in Europe, and travel is not necessary preparation for writing. "Homer did okay without it." Just talk to people!

The best training for writing—and Faulkner ignored "courses in writing" and "experience" included in the question—is reading. "Read, read, read! Read everything—trash, the classics, good and bad, and see how they do it, just as an apprentice studies the master. Read! You'll absorb it! Then write. If it's good, you'll find out. If it's not, throw it out of the window." Observation also furnishes material. He did not, Faulkner said, have much confidence in the present system of education. Preparation for writing must be in the library. Just as one studies law from books and not from life, likewise the young author can learn more about human life from books than from life. Read everything! Talent and hard work are both important, but one never gets anywhere without hard work. Don't merely talk about writing. "If you want to write, do it now," whether it is poetry or prose; and remember that the poet burns out much sooner than the prose writer. Don't put off writing either poetry or prose. If it doesn't sound right to you, put it away and write something else; come back later to what you have written.

The best period for writing verse, Faulkner said, is from seventeen to twenty-five. The writing of prose is slower and the fire within the writer lasts longer; the best age for writing novels is from thirty-five to forty-five, when the author knows more than at any other age.

Returning to the subject of books, a student asked the speaker about his own reading. Faulkner replied that for many years he read anything and everything but that—deliberately understating—he had not read any new fiction for fifteen years. Nowadays he read only a few favorites, but he did read again, probably once every twelve months, the Old Testament, *Don Quixote*, the Henry plays of Shakespeare, some of Balzac, *Madame Bovary*, *Moby Dick*, *Pickwick Papers*, *Vanity Fair*, *Henry Esmond*, and *The Nigger of the Narcissus*. The Russian novels were the greatest novels of the nineteenth century, and they influenced his writing, as did the Old Testament, Melville, and the verse of Swinburne. Both Balzac and Conrad had a strong influence on his writing, but it was one of which he was more or less unconscious.

"Is humanity decaying?" seriously asked the youth who, like many others, believes that the creative artist is part prophet. Faulkner said that it is going through a phase of change; he had faith in human beings as individuals but not as a race. Americans hear the radio program of Fred Allen which ridicules American life but they are too blind to see that what he has to say is true; they laugh at characters like Senator Claghorn but haven't sense enough to realize that life is in a pathetic mess.

People prefer *Sanctuary* to *As I Lay Dying*, he said in answering another question, because the former has more commercial color. "That's another phase of our American nature."

After a discussion of current writing, detective stories, and cheap stuff full of blood and thunder without soul, Faulkner, said that the condition of the human spirit is now poor and that what one writes must uplift the heart, or otherwise it is not great writing. Reading is, "like a clean collar and heaven, necessary but not important." We want culture, but we don't want to go to any trouble to get it. When someone in the class remarked that his statement seemed to be a slam on "our way of life," Faulkner replied that it needed slamming. Everyone aims to help people, to turn them to heaven, he said. The author also writes to help people.

At ten each morning Mr. Faulkner was free. His was not much of a hand for clutching coffee and sharing professional conviviality, but, sportsman that he was, he tagged along with several members of the English staff and gave to the chatter what originality it had. At ten fifteen each morning he rose formally from the table and said, "I wish you gentlemen would excuse me. I must go home and let the cow out." At ten fifty-five each day he got back, after having let the cow out, and met his class. Free again at noon, he offered to remain to answer any other questions. In the classroom Mr. Faulkner was always gracious but retiring to the point of shyness.

On the last day after his last meeting, he looked a little sheepish but more victorious. Had he known in advance how pleasant it would be, he would have given five hundred—a thousand—dollars to talk with interested, even adoring, students. He seemed a little tired but also quite refreshed.

All had gone well. Each had come to have respect for the others: Mr. Faulkner for the faculty and the cow, and the faculty for the cow and Mr. Faulkner. But a Big Bertha was fired when Mr. Faulkner learned that the Ole Miss public relations office was planning an article for the *Saturday Review of Literature* based on his answers. "I just hate like hell to be jumbled head over heels into the high-pressure ballyhoo which even universities now believe they must employ," he wrote in reply to a letter of explanation and apology which the chairman of the department of English had written to him. "The damned eternal American BUY! BUY! BUY!

'Try us first, our campus COVERS ONE WHOLE SQUARE MILE, you can see our water tank from twelve miles away, our football team almost beat A.&M., we have WM FAULKNER at 6 (count them: 6) English classes!' That sort of thing I will resist with my last breath." Then he resumed his mild manner and said, "But if the English department, not the publicity dept., uses the material, I shall have no qualms and fears." In the next to last paragraph he said, "If you decide on a 'repeat,' let me know." The last paragraph contains five words: "Thank you for the check."

The Private World of William Faulkner

Roark Bradford / 1948

From '48 *The Magazine of the Year,* 2 (May 1948), pp. 83–94.

William Faulkner is a Southern Democrat, a literary figure, and a legend. It is as difficult to dissociate him from his home town of Oxford, Mississippi, as it is to fix him and his work in time. There is Faulkner and there is Oxford. It is yesterday and tomorrow; it is before the Civil War and a hundred years hence; it is always now, with the Sartoris family and their friends struggling with the ramifications of genealogy and land titles and what to do when the fox gets a man down wind.

Some of the more serious appraisers of literary figures have called William Faulkner the second milestone in the development of American letters — Mark Twain being the first to emerge from the cross currents that became American culture. They point out that while Twain caught the bumptious humor of America's energetic growth, Faulkner is catching the unsubstantial threads of its tragic disintegration. The Faulkner legend is the inevitable outcome of Faulkner's aversion to personal exploitation. "Because I write," he says, "doesn't make what I eat for breakfast or think of the international situation a matter of news or public concern." He thinks present methods of advertising—"selling something you haven't got to someone who doesn't want it"—are obscene. "I don't hold with bad manners, under any circumstances," he says. Faulkner never discusses for publication either himself or his work, and he never reads criticism of his books. And so, the boys in the newsrooms have set to work unhampered by facts.

He is a Southern Democrat, which merely means that he is an individualist. He is not what is called a rugged individualist, although Bill Faulkner can be rugged enough when the occasion arises. His individuality, both in his life and in his writing, requires no adjective. It is part of his breeding, background, and nature.

The spirit of individuality asserted itself publicly early in Faulkner's career. Like so many other Southern boys who wanted to do things, it was necessary for Bill to support himself while he struggled through his apprenticeship. He got the job of postmaster at the University of Mississippi post office, but his duties began to interfere with his writing. His letter of resignation to the Postmaster General is one of the brighter items on file in Washington.

"As long as I live under the capitalistic system." he wrote. "I expect to have my life influenced by the demands of moneyed people. But I will be damned if I propose to be at the beck and call of every itinerant scoundrel who has two cents to invest in a postage stamp. This, sir, is my resignation."

Being averse to publicity does not make Faulkner a freak or an eccentric. You have to understand Oxford and Faulkner together and that each is a part of the other to appreciate why Faulkner refuses to be publicized.

He lives in a big white house on the edge of Oxford with his wife and his teen-age daughter. The house is set in thirty-five acres of ground. There are dogs, horses, cows, hogs, and cats. There are Negroes, ranging in age and importance from Uncle Ned, who was personal attendant to Bill's grandfather and father, to Pom, who functions as houseboy when not in school. Uncle Ned rules the whole complex life of the farm. Every living creature on the place, human and brute, falls into the spirit of whatever project he plans.

There are lots of dogs around—blooded pointers, a fine Dalmatian, a dachshund, and a few feists which once wandered up, made friends with Uncle Ned, and become a permanent part of the establishment. There is a fine Persian cat and a short-haired cat that dropped in one day and took up residence. There is also daughter Jill's pet saddle horse.

Recently, Uncle Ned decided to school a couple of half-breed hound dogs in trailing possums. The old man had managed a trade for a possum. He penned him up in the barn. When the air got right, the possum would be set free and the half-hounds taught to trail it.

"One morning, just before daylight," Bill related, "the household was awakened by the damnedest ruckus you ever heard. I slipped on my robe and ran out to see what the trouble was. The possum had broken out of the cage and tried to escape. But he didn't get more than a couple of hundred yards before he had to take to a tree.

"When I got there, every dog on the place, the two cats, and Jill's horse had formed a circle around that possum, holding him up the tree. The dogs were yipping fit to wake the dead. The two cats were yowling as loud as they could, and the horse was glaring defiantly at the possum. Pretty soon, Uncle Ned came, fussed at the dogs and cats, and put the possum back in his cage."

I liked the picture of all the animals entering into the spirit of Uncle Ned's

scheme, although I knew that only dogs with hound blood would, instinctively, trail a possum. Possibly the other dogs would follow for the mere
excitement of a chase. The cats, I figured, were added by Bill just to round
out the picture, and the horse—"Do you mean," I said, with what I considered sly sarcasm, "that the horse wasn't whinnying?"

"Of course not," Bill answered. "It just isn't in the nature of a horse to
whinny when he trees a possum."

Oxford is different from many other small Southern towns. Like some of
them, it is situated in the heart of poor, hillside farming country and is surrounded by poor people, black and white, whose lives are made bleak by the
constant struggle for a livelihood. Yet, Oxford is the site of the University of
Mississippi, an institution that has built a fine tradition of culture. The State
of Mississippi has allocated to its other colleges the duties of teaching the
technical trades that have swamped most centers of learning, and has kept
"Ole Miss" remarkably free from the trade-school brand of education. In
turn, the University has created a kind of erudite dignity which rises above
the blatant, scheming, angle-figuring self-aggrandizement by which aggressive people are seeking life's fulfillment. This influence has been felt in the
town and surrounding country, and the effect of it on the unlettered poor
whites often produces strange phenomena.

Discussing politics with me, a farmer once told me proudly: "Old Bilbo
lived long enough to fix that fellow Taft's clock, when he said Taft was like
a baby mawkin' bird, all mouth and no bird! 'Y God. Pericles might'a said
hit purtier, but he couldn't 'a said hit no truer!"

Only a character from a Faulkner tale or a Faulkner world could, believably
and logically, speak of Pericles and Bilbo in the same sentence. Perhaps it is
the impact of these two extremes of culture, unsoftened by any appreciable
middle ground, that gives Faulkner his feeling for the tragic, and for the grisly
humor with which he relieves it. It is not, however, that time stands still either
for Faulkner or for the University; both exist in the timelessness of the arts.
Each has something to give in the way of beauty, and neither will be dis-
tracted by current fads.

But press agents must work. A man who writes novels that astound and
startle, and frequently confuse, ought to be Grade-A copy. Yet, Faulkner puts
out no copy. The result is that a rumor grows into a story, a fact quickly
expands into a legend.

Among the legends that have grown up about Faulkner is the one that he
is a prodigious drunk. Like most Southerners, Bill likes an occasional drink

of good whisky. Probably during his fifty-odd years he has lost a couple of week ends, now and then. Now, in a morality of calomel, cornwhisky, and the Old Time Religion, Bill is not considered a heavy drinker. Yet, most of the yarns that have grown up about him have to do with Herculean binges.

One tale that is fairly indicative of the crop concerns Faulkner's first experience as a Hollywood writer. He was one of the first big names to be employed in the movie capital, and the moguls wanted to do the thing up right. They selected Nunnally Johnson, who is both a writer and a Southerner, to be the link between moviedom and this strange wild man who wrote about idiots, folks getting raped with corncobs, and people having their coffins built as they lay dying.

Johnson decided that the way to handle Faulkner was to overwhelm him with Hollywood grandeur and with the czarlike importance of an Executive. To this end, he took the biggest and most elaborate office in the studio. The room was a hundred feet long, with three levels of floor. On entering, one had to walk the full length of the room, through long-napped green carpet, then descend two flights of marble steps, to arrive eventually before the broadest and shiniest desk in Southern California. It was calculated to be both impressive and disconcerting.

Promptly on schedule, Faulkner entered, and Johnson immediately began handling telephones, papers, and push buttons. Faulkner walked through the carpet nap and down the steps, slowly, casually, like a man who had a heap of walking to do and was in no particular hurry to get it done. At the desk he removed his hat and held it in his left hand.

"Are you Mr. Johnson?" he asked.

"I am. Are you Mr. Faulkner?"

"I am."

There was an awkward silence. During this silence Faulkner fished into his hip pocket, took out a pint of whisky and began uncorking it. This act was complicated by the fact that the bottle had been sealed with heavy tinfoil. Bill dropped his hat on the floor and went to work with both hands. In the process, he cut his finger on the tinfoil. He attempted to staunch the flow of blood by wetting the wound with his tongue, but it was too deep a cut for that. Next, he looked around for a suitable drip pan. The only thing in view was the hat at his feet. Holding the bleeding finger over the hat, he continued to work, methodically and silently, until the bottle was finally uncorked. He then tilted it, drank half its contents, and passed it to Johnson.

"Have a drink of whisky?" he offered.

"I don't mind if I do," said Johnson, finishing off the pint.

This, according to the legend, was the beginning of a drunk which ended three weeks later, when studio sleuths found both Faulkner and Johnson in an Okie camp, sobered them up, and got them to work.

I for one have made no effort to verify this story; I am not a man to spoil a good tale with statistics. One Faulkner story, however, I did spoil. It was not a very good story, but it had had wide circulation. It is also about Faulkner's first Hollywood writing experience:

After a couple of weeks, according to this story, Faulkner felt ill at ease in his work. He suggested to his boss that he be allowed to do his writing at home. The boss, having visions of Faulkner in a hotel room banging away at his typewriter, said that would be all right. When they next heard from Faulkner he was in Oxford, Mississippi, two thousand miles from Hollywood. He had gone home to complete the assignment.

"I have heard that one," Bill said. "And since they told it, themselves, I don't suppose the truth will do anybody any damage. Here are the facts:

"I was working with the brother-in-law of the head of the studio, and we were pretty friendly. But as soon as I had as much money as I wanted, I decided to quit. My friend urged me to remain until I had a lot of money.

" 'I've got more money than anybody in Mississippi, now,' I told him. 'I won't ever need any more, I reckon.'

" ' If you ever do,' said my friend, 'just let me know, and I'll get you back on the payroll.'

"I came home and went to work on my novel. But I had a few debts to settle, and what with one thing and another, my money began to run short. So I wrote to my friend to get me another job in Hollywood. This was late in November. The first week in December, I got a check from this man's brother—my regular salary, less 10 per cent. This brother had just finished at Yale, and wasn't able to swing onto anything out there, so I suppose the family had set him up as an agent. Anyway, the checks came in every week, and I cashed them. This went on until about June, when they assigned me to work with Tod Browning. When I finished that assignment, I went off the payroll. And that," grinned Bill, "Is the true story of how I worked in Oxford, Mississippi, for Hollywood."

Bill's younger brother, John, author of *Men Working* and *Dollar Cotton*, has probably contributed to the Faulkner legend.

"Old Bill," said John, "just naturally hates to see anybody make a fool of himself. After Bill had been writing a long time and nobody was paying much attention to him, he wrote *Sanctuary* and suddenly got famous all over the country. The editor of a big magazine decided maybe some of the stories he had refused might be a little better than he had thought, now that Bill was famous. So he came down to take another look.

"Bill was hospitable, but he wasn't interested in selling him the stories that had already been turned down. But word got around that a big magazine editor was in town, and everybody else had something they wanted to sell. Among these was a lady from the University who had a thesis. She got her thesis and a bottle of whisky and lured the editor out to the back porch. She'd give him a drink with one hand and try to sell him the thesis with the other.

"Well, sir, when old Bill walked out and saw what was going on, it made him so disgusted he just naturally took off his shoes and went to El Paso, Texas."

There is a sureness, an unswerving certainty, in Faulkner. He sees the play and he calls it exactly as he sees it. There is no false modesty, nor is there the slightest taint of egotism. What people think of him isn't important; what he thinks of other people is important. "It will be another fifty or a hundred years before my novels are enjoyed and appreciated," he said. "Right now, it is considered sissified and unmanly for folks to love the arts. That is because, at first, the men had to work all the time, and only the women had any time to take up artistic appreciation. That isn't necessary now, but the men had rather pretend they think art is unmanly than take the trouble to acquire an appreciation for it."

From the course which his most widely read novel, *Sanctuary*, followed, this view seems justified. *Sanctuary* catapulted him from obscurity into fame and notoriety, although it followed *The Sound and the Fury* and *As I Lay Dying*, both of which are rated as greater novels. Most American readers instantly associate the name of William Faulkner with the corncob episode in *Sanctuary*, and remember him for that alone. Yet some of Faulkner's most beautiful, most soul-searching passages, as well as some of his most ribald drollery, are contained in this novel. Feminine taste in the arts, it would seem, prefers a violently unusual form of vicarious rape to penetrating insight into tortured souls.

The younger psychologists are beginning to take up Faulkner's characters for study; but almost invariably they put them down again. Their Messiahs, it seems, did not attempt a system which included the complicated mental make-up of the worn-out generations from Faulknerland. In another fifty or hundred years, perhaps, the psychologists will drop their Freud, Jung, or

Adler systems and try to get at an understanding of how Pa Bundren, of *As I Lay Dying*, and a stinker to the ground, could be so shiftless in all things and at the same time so logically tenacious in getting his wife's body back to Jefferson.

In the meantime, Faulkner has novels to write, and he must keep at it. At the time of my visit, he had been working three years on his latest novel, and had completed five hundred pages of it. It will be a fable based on the interval between the Crucifixion and the Resurrection. A hundred years ago, or a hundred years hence, Pericles or Bilbo, a Sartoris or an Armstid, a Harvard graduate or a babbling Benjy, will all dovetail logically and beautifully into the Faulkner pattern.

Recollections on Two Artists at Work in Courthouse Square

Stuart Purser / 1949

From *The Faulkner Newsletter and Yoknapatawpha Review,* (January–March 1983) pp. 1, 3. Reprinted by permission.

A month or so after I arrived in Oxford, Mississippi, in June 1949 to assume the position of chairman of the newly-established Department of Art at the University of Mississippi, I took a Saturday off to sketch the colorful groups of town and country folks gathered at the Courthouse Square.

Absorbed in the subjects I was sketching, it took me a few moments to realize the presence of someone looking over my shoulder.

"Do you always draw this type of subject?" the stranger asked. I nodded affirmatively without looking around, not wanting to become involved in conversation while trying to sketch the moving crowd. But the man persisted, wanting to know if I always drew blacks in preference to white people.

It was a question that I had been asked before. I had been told by a gallery director at the closing of an exhibition in New York that my paintings had not sold because of the limited subject matter, mainly black people. The director had asked about this and I replied that I liked the contrast of black people against light backgrounds. "If it is contrast that you want, why not paint white people against dark backgrounds," he said. Recalling that incident, I explained to the man standing behind me on the Square in Oxford that I found the blacks more interesting as subjects.

"I hear that you judged the local art exhibit at the Mary Buie Museum several weeks ago," my onlooker continued. "Yes," I said. I was anxious to get back to my work. "Did you give my brother John Faulkner the graphic award because you thought the drawing had merit?" was the next question. It was then that I realized that the man behind me was William Faulkner.

It wasn't clear to me at the time whether he wanted to know if I considered his brother John talented or whether he wondered if the name of Faulkner had influenced me. I realized later that he really wanted to know if it was a good drawing. But conscious of the fact that everyone wanted to meet him and that the Faulkner name was prominent, I thought he might be a little suspicious of my motive. I explained that the drawing wasn't signed and that I had no idea who had made it. The drawing in question was of a 'possum hunt done rather expressively in black ink and wash. I pointed out that my interest in the subject and the unique way in which the artist had handled the media in relation to his idea had influenced my decision.

Several Saturdays after that I saw Faulkner moving among the country folks, talking to both black and white, not groups but to individuals. It was near the end of the summer before he again engaged me in conversation. This time he ventured a remark rather that a question: "You get your ideas and inspiration from observing these people, while I get mine through talking with them." We got into a discussion about the words and expressions of blacks. I remarked that I too found that interesting but that their dialect was of little use to me as a painter.

I told him about a mural that I had painted for the post office in Leland, Mississippi, and having spent several weeks in Leland while installing it. I had had trouble getting what I called a good cup of coffee. After trying all the restaurants I finally found coffee to my liking at the main hotel in Leland. An elderly black man with a white chef's cap and uniform stood by the coffee urn. I complimented him and asked if he had a special secret for making such good coffee. "Well, boss," he said, "I guess it's because I'se jus' peculiar." While I was trying to figure that out, a native helped translate by asking if he didn't mean "particular" instead of "peculiar." He agreed. "That's it, boss, particular . . . particular."

As Faulkner and I continued our conversation I showed him some sketches in my book that I had made of blacks fishing at Sardis Dam. He mentioned that he had a houseboat on Sardis Lake and that there was much boating and fishing activity on his side of the lake.

That fall I made several sketching trips to that area and sketched from his houseboat. From these I made a series of paintings which I labeled "Ecru Lake Fishermen." One of these was purchased by the Atlanta Museum and is now in their collection. Another, entitled "Ecru Lake #2," is owned by the Alexandria, Louisiana Museum. The water in Sardis Lake at certain times during the year appeared to be yellow, or ecru, in color. I had also borrowed the name "Ecru" from a town in Mississippi which I discovered during the summer.

Ecru brings to mind another conversation that I had with William Faulkner. Perhaps I should say another response to a Faulkner question, because most of our verbal exchanges were prompted by questions that he asked.

Shortly after our move to Oxford, I was driving through the one-store community of Ecru when I noticed cement sculptures of Joe Louis and George Washington Carver in front of a two-room cabin which was surrounded by several acres of cotton. My curiosity aroused, I knocked on the door. An elderly black woman came to the door and, I explained my reason for stopping, invited me in. On the walls of the two rooms were paintings done by her son, M.B. Mayfield. I became interested in M.B. and persuaded him to move to Ole Miss as the custodian of the department's art gallery. There the faculty helped him with his creative and academic work and he exhibited in several local shows. He even gave talks and workshops at black schools.

Faulkner had heard about M.B.'s work. One day when I was sketching on the Square, he asked, "Does Mayfield have real talent, or is his work getting attention because he is black?" I answered that you could safely say for both reasons. I pointed out that M.B. Mayfield, having only gone through the seventh grade, had never had an art lesson, or known as artist, but had made his paints from plants and flowers and painted on shirt cardboards. I added that many of my art students didn't do as well although they had adequate materials and some instruction.

"He is also a Renaissance man," I told Faulkner. "He writes poetry." I had been looking through M.B.'s sketch book when I had noticed some poems. After complimenting him he told me hesitantly that some of his poems had been published in *The Commercial Appeal* in Memphis, in Paul Flowers' "Greenhouse" column. When I read these poems I noticed that he had attached a *nom de plume* to his contributions. He explained that he was afraid the editor wouldn't publish them if he knew that he was black. Faulkner indicated that he knew Paul Flowers and that it wouldn't make any difference to him. He also said that he would be interested in reading the poems.

I carried the Greenhouse clippings around in my pocket book until I finally ran into Faulkner again on the Court Square and showed them to him. He didn't respond. I felt it was my time to ask a question. "Would you say that he is talented or that they are just pretty good for a black boy?" He smiled and said, "I think that he had better stick to art." He asked if M.B. needed art materials, indicating that he would like to provide some. I explained that John Phay, a professor at Ole Miss, had agreed to furnish his materials.

In the fall of 1950, students at Ole Miss raised money to pay for M.B. to go to Chicago to see the Van Gogh show at the Art Institute. Faulkner was one of the contributors.

There were a few times when Faulkner told me of sayings and remarks of some Negroes and farmers he knew. I don't remember them. I do remember that our conversations were usually prompted by a question and were about an area in which Faulkner was unfamiliar but interested. Paul Flowers once referred to Faulkner as a friend of mine. I hurriedly corrected him because Faulkner never made what would be called friendly conversation, always moving on after he had been given an answer to a particular question. If he didn't have a question, he always greeted me but never bothered to stop and talk.

I'll never forget a remark made by an Ole Miss librarian when I rejected a suggestion that William Faulkner was unfriendly. "Oh yes, he loves to talk to Negroes and poor white trash," the man countered.

Several years ago I read an article in *The Christian Science Monitor* by the Pulitzer Prize winner, Dr. Robert Coles, whose books on "Children in Crises" are a landmark in the wider and deeper understanding of our society. "Here in the United States William Faulkner made it his business to spend hours with his townsmen in Mississippi—he made brilliant use of his dreams and fantasies—but he also knew that his understanding of others made him a rich man. He was willing to be taught by his neighbors."

Although my conversations with William Faulkner were usually brief and to the point, I feel that I, learned from him.

Novelist's Advice Put New Spring in Youth's Step

Pinckney Keel / 1952

From Nashville *Banner,* July 6, 1962, pp. 1–2. Reprinted by permission.

Ever since my childhood I'd heard of William Faulkner, the novelist who belonged to the South and who in turn gave the South to the World.

Fresh out of college, I decided, while job-hunting, to go to Oxford, Miss., to see the fabled author and let him tell me newspaper work was my goal. I knew it was, anyway, but I wanted be sure. I wanted him to tell me.

Oxford was my family home. My family and Faulkner's grew up within a stone's throw of each other. That alone, I thought, would earn me an interview with Faulkner.

Arriving at Oxford by bus from Jackson, Miss., I went to my uncle's house and told him why I'd come.

"Sure, go talk to ol' Will," he told me. "He'll be glad to see you," he added, with a smile that said I'd never get a foot inside the front door.

I found his home, a gracious ante-bellum-type structure, with a driveway lined with sentries of tall, slender poplars.

I listened hard for the click-click of typewriter keys. I knew he would be at work. I heard nothing, so I knocked on the door, expecting a butler, housekeeper or maid.

Faulkner answered my knock. He was in walking shorts, white T-shirt and pipe.

"Whom did you wish to see, sir?" Faulkner asked.

Taken aback by being confronted by the man himself, I stammered a little, then blurted: "I want to see you. I want to write."

"Well, you come on in and we'll see what we can do to help," he said, turning into his living room with a motion for me to follow.

Sipping delicately at the stem of his pipe poked between his white moustache and tiny chin, the little man of enormous dignity asked: "Exactly just what do you want?"

I told him I wanted to write like he did.

94

"Then go plow a while until a thought comes. Then sit under a tree and write it down."

Feeling a premonition of a newspaper editor's displeasure at my plowing and tree-sitting to write, I told him I wanted to be a reporter.

"Always wanted to work for a paper," he said, looking into a far corner of the amply-furnished living room, "but found out I'd rather write books."

Faulkner kept talking in a quiet voice, at times almost inaudible, as he explained that the characters he wrote about were people right in Oxford. "You don't have to look for people to write about," he said, staring into the glowing bowl of his pipe. "They're everywhere."

I found enough courage to tell him: "People around here think you are different."

Smiling faintly, Faulkner crossed and uncrossed his legs and said, "In Mississippi the people work for their money and you can understand how they feel about writing, why it puzzles them. In Mississippi, a man goes out in the sun and sweats for his dollars."

I asked to see his typewriter from which had poured volumes, including a 1949 Nobel Prize-winner. He ushered me into an adjoining room, cluttered with magazines, written notes and, commanding the spotlight, a battered machine he proclaimed to be "the oldest in the country." It was, he said, about 30 years old then, and that was 10 years ago.

"I don't need anything fancy for these two fingers," he said. "It will last as long as I need it, I guess."

I asked for advice.

"Just keep writing," he murmured, and I pictured his keen mind already at work on another novel.

Only once during the visit did he raise his voice. It was as I walked down the shaded walk. "Good luck," he shouted, and a new spring came into my walk.

Faulkner Without Fanfare

Robert N. Linscott / 1953

From *Esquire*, 60 (July 1963) , pp. 36, 38. Reprinted by permission of *Esquire* magazine. © Hearst Communications, Inc. *Esquire* is a trademark of Hearst Magazine Property, Inc. All rights reserved.

During the early Nineteen Fifties, when I was an editor at Random House, I saw Faulkner almost every day whenever he was in New York. Some of the notes that follow were made at the time; some years later when news of his death quickened old memories.

Took Bill to the annual show at the Whitney Museum. The paintings were mostly abstract. I could see that he wasn't happy, so we skated through in jig time. When we got out on the street, he said: "It made me nervous. It's like being in a crowd of people all shouting in a foreign language"

We walked over to my apartment, where I read while Bill dozed with a copy of *Life* on his lap. He was feeling low as a result of pre-travel shots (he was flying to Europe to write a movie script on location) and because he hated the idea of going abroad at that time. On the way over I had asked him why he was going, since the money meant nothing to him. He replied characteristically and as if surprised at the question: "Why, I've got to go. Hawkes asked me. He's done me favors in the past, and I can't let him down now."

At five o'clock, Bill revived over a bourbon and water, and became (for him) quite loquacious. The paintings we'd seen reminded him of modern poetry which, he said, had got out of step with life. "I used to read the young poets, and sometimes the feeling came across even when I wasn't sure what they were talking about. Lately, though, I just haven't bothered. Don't seem to get enough out of it."

He sat swishing the bourbon and listening to the tinkling ice, and that set him off on the subject of liquor. His grandfather used to give him heeltaps (the last drops left in the glass), he said. Then later he drank a lot to ease the pain when he was in an airplane crack-up. But mostly, he thought, his drinking was a matter of chemistry. He'd go along for weeks or months at a normal gait—two bourbons at luncheon, two more after five, a martini before dinner, and half a bottle of wine with it, and maybe another bourbon or two to nurse along during the evening. And then the craving would come. Most often he'd fight it off. But once in a while something would happen that would "get me all of a turmoil inside," and liquor seemed the only escape. It was only when he was caught in a situation he couldn't easily cope with that he'd give in to what he called the chemistry of craving and go overboard. You would be aware of the symptoms of increasing tension—drumming fingers, evasive looks, monosyllabic replies to questions—then he'd disappear, and, when you next heard of him, he'd be out cold.

Bill wandered around helplessly in *A Fable* for years. Finally he decided he couldn't write in Oxford, Mississippi, anymore, and came up to New York to finish it. (He said then: "A man writes for glory and I guess I'd had all I needed. Then someone came along I wanted to impress so I made the extra effort.") Random House gave him a room and a typewriter at their office. He'd come in around ten o'clock, type steadily for maybe half an hour, get up and pace the floor for ten or fifteen minutes, then sit down and type some more. When I asked him why he did it that way, he said: "It's just my cussed laziness. I hate to retype, so I figure out exactly what I want to say as far ahead as I can remember it, then sit down and type it out." Sometimes, instead of pacing, he'd read a magazine or come into my office for a talk, though talk is hardly the right word, since he generally sat silent for a while, then looked at his watch, said, "Well, fifty minutes more" (meaning until time for a drink and luncheon), and went back to his typewriter.

I asked him if these special interludes meant he was wound up too tight and had to unwind. He grinned and agreed, as he agreed to any theory about his writing you happened to advance, not caring in the least what ideas were attributed to him. Here's another example: He and I had luncheon one day with an eminent critic, and the next day with another, equally eminent. Both quizzed him on the subject of *The Wild Palms*. One critic asked if he hadn't put together those two unrelated themes as a stunt. Bill replied that yes, he had written two stories and when he found that neither was long enough to make a book, he'd just mixed them up together. The other critic congratulated him for what he called a superb piece of counterpoint, each them giving contrast and meaning to the other. And Bill agreed just as courteously as he had with the first critic. His attitude to critics was one of complete indifference. If they wanted to read into his books meanings that weren't there, it didn't bother him. What did it matter? The books spoke for themselves. I recall once telling him about a critic who read deep and subtle Freudian meanings into *The Sound and the Fury.* He laughed and said: "Well, maybe it's all there, but I sure didn't know it."

In all the time I knew Bill, I only once heard him speak a word of self-commendation. One day at my farm in The Berkshires he astonished me by running his finger along a shelf full of his books and saying: "Not a bad monument for a man to leave behind him." He had many quirks, but the quirkiest of all was his complete disinterest in what he had written. He didn't care how his books sold; he didn't want royalty statements, preferring just to draw money as he needed it; above all, he didn't want even to glance at reviews of his books. This resolute shutting his eyes to what the world thought of him was so rare—for most authors devour their reviews like hungry dogs—that I thought it might be an act; the conscious building up of a legend. So I laid a little trap. One day when he was staying at my apartment, I said: "Bill, here's a new collection of articles about you written by fifteen famous critics. There's a piece in it by Jean-Paul Sartre that develops quite a fascinating theory about your writing. I wish you'd read it and tell me if you agree." Bill grunted noncommittally, and I left the volume exactly aligned with a crack on the table so I would know if he picked it up. (It was *William Faulkner: Two Decades of Criticism*, and I knew he hadn't seen it as I had just received an advance copy from the publisher.) When I got back that night, the book had not been touched. "Did you read that piece?" I said. "No," he replied, "I didn't bother."

Bill was window-shopping with me on Fifth Avenue when a woman rushed up to him and cried: "Oh, I know who you are. You're William Faulkner. You look just like your pictures." Bill said coolly but courteously, "Madame, you're mistaken. I am not William Faulkner. But I have been told before that I look like him."

This was typical of the man; he had a deep aversion to public recognition. When he was presented with the annual booksellers' award, the crowd closed in to shake his hand, and he beckoned to me to escape with him. At the hatcheck counter, he laid down the award," the hatcheck girl cried. "You must be Mr. Faulkner." "No, ma'am," said Bill. "I ain't Mr. Faulkner. I just saw this thing lying on the table and walked off with it." "That's awful," she exclaimed. "I'll have to call the house detective." So Bill and I slid out the side door and into a taxi. Another time at a banquet he was placed between two earnest women who bombarded him with questions about his literary and political beliefs. I could see his eyes rolling like marbles as he looked more and more wildly for an avenue of escape. Finally, with a bow and excuse, he came to me and whispered: "For God's sake, get me out of here. I'm getting nervous."

Time once decided to do a cover story on Bill, an accolade with which most writers, or most anyone for that matter, would be very pleased. But not Bill. He refused to answer their phone calls, telegrams or letters; nor would he give an interview. *Time* was persistent, and finally Bill called up from Oxford with a plaintive request: "I wish you'd tell Mr. Luce to stop bothering me."

Bill had another run-in with the Luce organization. One morning he came into the office chuckling over a letter he'd just had from his mother. "She says *Life* has a piece about me that's full of lies so she wired them to cancel her subscription. It's the first telegram she ever sent in all her life." I replied that Bob Coughlan, the author of the piece, was a good guy and I was sure he'd want to correct any errors, especially since it was to be part of a book. So the three of us had luncheon at the Ambassador. When Bob asked for a list of the errors, Bill said, "I can't give them to you. I haven't read the piece." "But how can I correct the errors," Bob asked, "if you won't tell me what they are? Will you read it and mark what's wrong?" "Thanks," said Bill, "and no offense to you, but I'd rather not. Just let it go along as written."

But while Bill would retreat when demands were made, he would sometimes advance when they were not. There was a young meat cutter in a provision store in Northampton, where I shopped on the way to the farm, who was a great admirer of the Faulkner novels, and had read every one. The next time we were passing through this town, I told this to Bill. "Maybe he'd like it if I went in to see him," said Bill. So we stopped at the store, Bill shook hands with the butcher, and chatted with him a while. The butcher told me afterward it was the greatest thing that ever happened to him, and he'd never forget it. Kindness and consideration of this sort were typical. In the absolute sense of the word, Bill was a gentleman.

Soon after I met Bill, he and his wife and I drove to Boston. I thought he'd enjoy an overnight stop at the ancient Wayside Inn at Sudbury, which Henry Ford had bought and restored. So I phoned ahead that we were coming and asked that Bill be given the Longfellow Room, the most elegant of their bedchambers, which was preserved just as it was when Longfellow stayed there to collect material for his *Tales of a Wayside Inn.* This turned out to be a disaster. Bill was miserable at the fuss made over him, and flatly refused to sleep in the Longfellow Room. Instead of sitting before the open fire in the old barroom and drinking cider as I had planned, he escaped from the inn and walked down the road until bedtime. And to compound his troubles, he lost himself in the winding corridors when he got up in the night to look for the bathroom. But all he ever said was: "I can't seem to like antiquity when it's self-conscious."

To say that Bill was taciturn and unresponsive doesn't begin to do him justice. He was wholly without the loose change of small talk. He'd sit with you for an hour without speaking. If you asked him a direct question, he'd answer in a word or two, and again be silent. Strong men would leave a tête-à-tête with Bill, shaking and mopping their brows, for silence is a hard thing to take. In time you learned that this was no reflection on you. It was just his natural way. He didn't believe in chitchat, or in talking unless he had something to say. When he did talk, he talked slowly, softly and well; mostly about people or about the South, rarely about public affairs or intangibles. If he liked a woman, his natural courtesy led him to make an effort; hence one sometimes heard women say: "Oh, I get along fine with Bill. He talks to *me*." I remember an evening with James Thurber, whom he admired, when he talked about Hollywood: good talk and very funny. Mostly Bill liked to listen, now and then making an observation, watching the faces, relaxed and at ease.

Bill seldom wrote letters, and the few he did write were as laconic as his conversation; just a sentence or two to make a date or ask a question. His aversion to writing letters led to an equal aversion to reading them on the ingenious theory that if you hadn't read a letter you didn't have to answer it. He'd hold a letter up to the light to see if there was a check inside; if not, he'd toss it into the wastebasket. "This is a free country," he'd say. "Folks have a right to send me letters, and I have a right not to read them." Admirers begging for an autograph, eminent critics or would-be biographers asking for an interview; all scanned the post in vain. For Bill, like Thoreau, believed in stripping life to its essentials. His job was to write novels, not letters. Though in public, he wouldn't even admit this, maintaining that he was just a farmer who only wrote when he needed money.

Bill and I usually lunched at one of the handy midtown hotels—the Drake, Berkshire or Ambassador—because the dining rooms were spacious and quiet and I could sign for the meals. ("We'll never starve as long as the pencils hold out," he used to say.) Dinners were *his* treat, and his preference was for Michael's Pub, the Oak Room at the Plaza, or downstairs at the Pierre for Indian curry. The selection of the proper wine was a ritual, arrived at after a prolonged study of the wine list and consultation with the sommelier. He seldom went to a play or movie, preferring a long, leisurely dinner, after which he would stroll back to his hotel where he would read himself to sleep with a murder mystery. By the time I knew him he didn't read much else except an occasional magazine, and I don't recall ever seeing him settle down to serious reading. Come to think of it, I never saw him read a newspaper. But he must have read widely in his youth, and I remember one occasion when he dipped into his literary reservoir most aptly. It was at a party where a guest was indicting modern poetry on the ground that all good poetry must be clear and simple. When he paused for breath, Bill quietly recited Shakespeare's *The Phoenix and the Turtle*.

Let me describe the kind of time Bill most enjoyed. I'm thinking of a midwinter day he spent with my wife and me at our farm. He got up at six, got his own breakfast, and did his own dishes, doing as always more than his share of the work. That morning he and I crossed the ice of our big beaver pond and climbed a rocky hill to watch a neighboring farmer gathering timber. He would hitch his old horse to a big hemlock log and the horse would snake it down the hill to where the farmer's helpers were waiting to load it on the wood pung. Then the horse, unguided and unaccompanied, would plod up the hill for another log. Bill was fascinated, and talked for a long time with the farmer about the technique of logging in the North. Then we went home to a midday dinner of New England clam chowder and pumpkin pie, for Bill preferred simple cooking, native to the region. Afterward we introduced Bill to the pleasure and labor of a walk through the woods on snowshoes.

That evening Bill sat at ease before the open fire, tinkling the ice in his bourbon and talking, with long pauses, about the South. He said in effect: "The South's the place for a novelist to grow up because the folks there talk so much about the past. Why, when I was a little boy, there'd be sometimes twenty or thirty people in the house, mostly relatives, aunts, uncles, cousins and second cousins, some maybe coming for overnight and staying on for months, swapping stories about the family and about the past, while I sat in a corner and listened. That's where I got my books."

He went on to say that for years people in Oxford thought he was trash, doing no work to speak of, just writing books that nobody read. "Why some folks wouldn't even speak when they passed me on the street. Then MGM came to town to film *Intruder in the Dust*, and that made some difference because it meant I'd brought money into Oxford. But it wasn't until the Nobel Prize that they really thawed out. They couldn't understand my books, but they could understand thirty thousand dollars."

He talked a little about the problem of race relations, which he thought was more economic than racial. "What you folks want is coming, but it's going to take a long time because you can't reason with prejudice and emotion. And the more you push, the harder we'll resist." And, finally, he talked about the books he was going to write. "I want to tell what happened to Quentin after she climbed out the window [*The Sound and the Fury*]. And there are a couple of Snopeses I've got to deal with."

This was the kind of day that gave Bill deep pleasure; a day of simple natural things that required no effort and made no demands. In later days he often spoke of it. And there was a postscript I liked. The next time I saw him he said: "Well, I made quite a stir on Park Avenue. I was practicing snow-shoeing so I'd get onto the hang of it next time I visit you. Folks saw me going along all bent over with my feet wide apart and they thought I was crazy."

Faulkner Speaking
Time / 1954

From *Time,* 64 (August 23, 1954), p. 76. Reprinted by permission.

Novelist William Faulkner, notably tight-lipped on home soil last week found tongue for some reflections on life, letters and Faulkner, while attending the International Congress of writers in Brazil.

"I confess honestly that *A Fable* [his latest novel] does not please me. It took nine years to write that book and I once tore up its first version.

"Generally I don't read my countrymen's books. In fact I read little. At my age (56), I prefer to read Flaubert, Balzac, Cervantes' *Don Quixote* and the Bible . . . The few times I tried to read Truman Capote, I had to give up . . . His literature makes me nervous.

"I do not necessarily have a system to work. Normally I write at any time, but for me expression comes easier when it is hot, or precisely during summertime when the blood boils in my veins, or during sleepless nights when I work until early morning. I always carry pencil and paper with me, since at certain moments on the saddle of a horse or leaning on a fence, I proceed with work under way.

"Failure brings me stimulation to try to do better in each new book. I have something to say, but I know I will not have time to write all the books I want. I hope to write three or four more . . . I am happy to be a novelist, but I would like to be a poet. In fact, I am a frustrated poet.

"American literature and poetry are being killed by our mechanical civilization. We Americans once had the beautiful dream of every man's being free. What happened to that dream? . . . We failed in that we forgot the needs of the rest of mankind, perhaps because we are too self contented and too rich."

My First Day at Random House with William Faulkner

Hiram Haydn / 1955

From *Words and Faces* (New York: Harcourt Brace Jovanovich, 1974), pp. 80–93. Copyright © 1974 by the estate of Hiram Haydn, reprinted by permission of Harcourt Brace & Company.

On that first morning, I arrived early. At the receptionist's desk I asked, as instructed, for Donald Klopfer, and was told to go up to his office. The vast spiral staircase between the first and second floors of Random House must have persuaded as many courted authors to join the firm's list as the partners or any editor. It was majestic, as was the whole house, from its stately court-yard and front door onward. Built for the Villard family of railroad fame, it was bought by Joseph Kennedy while he was ambassador to Great Britain. Bennett and Donald acquired it by winning the favor of Cardinal Spellman for their publication of Étienne Gilson's work on Thomas Aquinas. The Cardinal "instructed" the Ambassador to sell it to them! Or so Bennett told me.

For this old stone mansion at the corner of Madison Avenue and Fifty-first Street shares a large cobbled courtyard with the Archdiocese of New York. Now that Random House has moved to a new building on Third Avenue, the north wing of the mansion has been reclaimed by the Church.

At any rate, that first morning the stairs awed me, as they had on earlier visits. I proceeded to Donald's office and paused in the doorway. He was in the midst of what sounded like an emotional telephone conversation.

"No, no, Dorothy," he said. "You tell Saxe that nothing has changed, that we love him just as much as we always have. I'm terribly sorry about the ulcers kicking up again. We'll have his new office ready in a couple of weeks and we want him all well by then. Now, Dorothy, make him see sense. You know we really love him." He was manifestly upset, even pleading.

When he hung up, he turned and saw me. For a moment of eloquent si-lence, his dark, mobile face expressed surprise, embarrassment, sadness and chagrin. Then it lighted up into a smile, and he spread his hands wide in that immemorial gesture that confounds both the tragic and the comic.

"So you heard." Then, more briskly, "Life must go on. I'll call Bob."

It was not clear why both Haas and Klopfer were needed to escort me to my office halfway down the hall, but I decided that they felt I needed support after our conversation of the previous week. It had been only then that I had learned I was to have Saxe Commins's office, and he was to be moved up to the fifth floor, into a new one. I had protested; Bennett and Donald had charged me with undue sentimentality. I had replied that I was not being noble, but practical. My taking over Saxe's office would prejudice his friends and colleagues here against me: it wasn't fair to force me into such a position.

They insisted. They were being practical, too. If I was to be their head editor, they must have easy access to me; my office must be on their floor. Moreover, no one would blame me; everyone would know it was their decision. I capitulated because there was nothing else I could do.

Bob and Donald escorted me those thirty or forty steps, as firmly as policemen, to the office I had not wanted to occupy.

We entered. A small, neat, silver-haired man was seated at a table.

Bob Hass spoke his piece.

"Bill, this is Hiram Haydn, our new editor. Hiram, this is William Faulkner. You'll share the office just for two weeks; then we'll move you upstairs, Bill, to Saxe's new office."

Mr. Faulkner gravely acknowledged the introduction. The two partners tumbled out, perfidious dissemblers, and left me alone with William Faulkner.

Now I understood why Haas had been summoned: to break the news to Faulkner. It was he who had been Faulkner's publisher before they both came to Random. And I was particularly angry that they had not told me that when Faulkner worked in New York he shared this office with Saxe.

After a few polite remarks, Mr. Faulkner turned back to his work, and I was left to simmer in silence. My files had not yet arrived from Bobbs-Merrill; I had no desk work to do. There were many useful telephone calls to be made, but how could I talk naturally to anyone when the greatest novelist in America was sitting a few feet away, working on a new book?

Bennett had no such scruples. A half hour later, he came in, moving in three-quarter time, and saying, "Hi, Bill! Welcome to Random House, Hi!"

Then his manner abruptly changed. Ten days before, I had deposited a manuscript with him, saying that I was not recommending it to him but that it seemed to me an interesting one over which to get acquainted with each other's publishing judgement. I thought it a quite salable but trivial and vulgar story.

Now Bennett plunked it down on my desk and said sharply. "Here's that miserable piece of trash you gave me to read. I'm surprised at you, Hiram." and left the room. His staccato heels beat a forced march away. I listened to their diminishing echoes while a slow but devastating heat mounted to my head.

For another three-quarters of an hour I sat either in alternate rage and despair. I doodled fiercely; I wrote my resignation twice. I felt humiliated, furious and desolate.

Then at last William Faulkner slowly turned around in his swivel chair—a progress so slow and deliberate that it seemed to me I watched for minutes.

He looked at me; his eyes were clear and kind.

"Why, Mr. Haydn," he said, "I don't reckon you're doin' hardly anything."

I acknowledged the truth of this with a strangled gurgle.

He smiled, and asked me if I was concerned about disturbing him at his work. He assured me that, whether he was at home in Mississippi or here in Saxe's office, no amount of talk or noise affected his concentration.

I made some feeble response, and he looked at me thoughtfully.

"Are you troubled," he finally asked, "about being here in Saxe's office? You don't suppose that I think you wanted to take it away from him, do you? Why, Mr. Haydn, no man in his right mind would want to come in and do that. I never have considered such a thing. It's those great monopolists down the hall—" he pointed—" they arranged it this way because they're sensible men. Now you forget all that—especially about my work—and do the things you're here for."

All this in the gentlest of Southern voices. I felt healed. And for two weeks I did what I was "there for," what he had suggested, except that I did still lower my voice—I hoped effectively but no conspicuously.

I was, of course, intensely curious about Faulkner at work. (The new novel was *The Town*.) Several times that week he left for lunch before I did. Each such time, without shame—as I report it without shame—I went over to study the sheet left on the table at which he worked or in the typewriter on the nearby stand. For he wrote in longhand at the table, then (it had seemed to me) rose when he finished a single page, and carried it to the typewriter, where (apparently) he rewrote it. Surely his *furor poeticus* was not submissive to such quantitative measurement!

Yet it was—if that's what it should be called. Twice the evidence was unmistakable. In each case the page in longhand had ended in the midst of a sentence: once with the word "and," once in the middle of a prepositional phrase. I pondered these breaks and became aware of the possibility that I was being preternaturally naïve: that it was not a question of Faulkner's being the slave of a quantitative slide rule, but rather being so open to the dictates of what Montaigne called *"le patron dedans"* that he could leave off anywhere and regain the flow simply by waiting and listening for that master voice to resume.

It was early in the second week that I finally managed the temerity to ask him about this process. Every morning, punctually at eleven, he would lay down his pencil or still the typewriter and swing around to face me. He would light a cigarette and begin to talk. It was our social hour, and, in anticipation of it, I would carefully clear away in advance whatever interruptive debris might interfere with it. I even arranged with the switchboard operator to take all calls between 10:45 and 11:15. Had Faulkner known this, I think it would have amused and pleased him. A hint or two suggested to me that he enjoyed veneration if it was not explicit or vulgar.

He would talk for no more than ten minutes, and although he made polite attempts to draw me out about myself and my work I preferred listening to him. As a result, neither of us said much that would gracefully survive repetition.

But on this Monday or Tuesday morning I blurted out my confession about peeking, and asked my question. He laughed.

"Why, Mr. Haydn," he said, "haven't you ever heard that I wouldn't know a sentence if I saw one? I don't read those reviews, but I hear about them. And I just suppose that it's more interesting this way. If you stop at 'and,' why, you can go anywhere. And that's what we all want, isn't it—to feel that we can go anywhere?"

It sufficed, and we continued our polite and casual acquaintance. Only on the very last day he shared the office did I really secure another insight.

I had an appointment for lunch that day with a young woman named Charlotte Payne. I had published her good first novel, called *Milo*, at Bobbs-Merrill the previous year. Charlotte had come north from Mississippi to write novels. She had discovered that there was more to the process than writing if one desired also to eat. Being naturally gifted, she became a Powers model.

She was announced, and I asked the receptionist to send her up to my office. As her heels clattered through the small coat room that led to the office proper I witnessed a transformation in Mr. Faulkner. I swear that the small hairs on the back of his neck bristled, and in instant reflex he began the slow movement of the swivel chair that would bring him around to face me.

I rose to greet Charlotte, who burst into a stream of rapid chatter. I interrupted her.

"Charlotte," I said, "I want you to meet William Faulkner. Mr. Faulkner, Miss Payne."

She acknowledged his bow briefly, turned back to me.

"But Hiram," she said, "I want to tell you—"

Then she froze, and in obedience to the classic double take, swung back to face that small elegant man. She gasped.

"Why, Mr. Faulkner," she said. "Mistuh Faulk-nuh. Why, I guess this is the proudest moment of my life."

He bowed again, courteously, and smiled.

She rattled on, reciting a list of all his novels, interjecting sighs and "why" and "oh my goodness" from time to eloquent time. Then she finally stilled herself and looked at him with unmistakable reverence.

"I know I'm making a fool of myself," she whispered, "but you can't know what this means to me. Mr. Faulkner, I'm from Mississippi!"

That debonaire man inclined his head again.

"So am I," he said. . . .

That afternoon he returned from lunch, smiled at me and showed me a copy of the paper-bound edition of *Milo*.

I missed him badly when he moved upstairs.

Conversations with William Faulkner

John Cook Wyllie / 1955

From Richmond *News Leader*, January 31, 1955, p. 11. Reprinted by permission.

The annual pouring out of the spirits occurred last Tuesday in New York at the National Book Awards. In the awards proper, Faulkner came in first, and the rest (Wallace Stevens, poetry; e.e. cummings, ditto; Krutch, miscellaneous) were nowhere. In the speeches, Senator Fulbright had the audience standing up in applause. In his clarion, tobacco-juiced, Arkansas accents, he was for freedom of speech. To Fulbright, it is wrong to enter an indictment of illegal assembly against a man who is merely collecting his thoughts.

Among the guests, Richmond was represented at least by Miss Peggy O'Neill and Mr. Willam Ellyson, Jr., both of them scouting for Richmond's Book and Author Dinner; and by your humble servant. There were 750 other guests, 250 of them authors, including the gentle Carl Sandburg, who stood on the edge of the crowd looking tired and seedy.

Your correspondent, also looking tired and seedy, didn't feel in the mood for interviewing Sandburg, having already interviewed Faulkner, so he plunged bravely into the crowd, found that close to the likker, the authors got thicker. Came on home, brooding darkly over Yoknapatawhpa County and the indignity of man.

Here is this interviewer's off-the-cuff impression of 57-year old novelist William Faulkner.

He is a small man, shy, sincere, nothing of the smart-aleck. He gets clothes-dummy frozen before banked cameras or a press-gang, thaws readily in a group of two or three people if one of them has a kind or an understanding word. The two Oxfords (Mississippi and England) are strong in him: rough edges of the country-store philosopher and the sophisticated reserve of the housebroken British; a Mississippi accent in Swinburnian rhythms, but too faint to hear unless you listen intently.

His eyes are black, his hair white. The sharp, forward, ferret taper of his face and the fixed public stare give him a zoo-like appearance, something between a chicken and a fox, but he is handsome even in his mask. He carries a red bandanna handkerchief that he tucks up his left sleeve. His public voice

109

is an inaudible, inexpressive monotone. As a public speaker, he is a total loss, but what he writes to speak is golden.

Before a panel of interviewers, the caged impression is re-emphasized. The newspaper questioner becomes the man with the long pole, poking. Faulkner, surprisingly, never snarls, but he has no love for the poke. He plays no game. There is no enjoyment.

Interviewers from New York and Chicago to Texas and California asked these questions, got these answers:

Q: Does Mr. Faulkner intend to return to Yoknapatawpha County in future novels?
A: He never left there.

Q: Does Mr. Faulkner think his writing has ever been obscure?
A: Has never intentionally written obscurely, would consider obscurity a defect, knows of no obscurity in what he has written.

Q: Has any author a right to express himself obscurely?
A: No.

Q: Did Mr. Faulkner see combat in World War I?
A: No, was still in training at war's end.

Q: Does Mr. Faulkner still think well of his original proposal to print *The Sound and the Fury* in different colored inks?
A: His original fear that the reader might need such a device seems not to have been valid, now has no desire to see the novel so printed.

Q: What does Mr. Faulkner think of the critical notices of his recent work?
A: He never reads them.

Later, in brief conversation, your correspondent reopened the right-to-obscurity questions in a somewhat less turgid atmosphere. Is the required clarity due the author or the reader? Makes no difference: the author is expressing deep emotion; for whomever he expresses, he must be as clear as he can be. But isn't the deepest of emotions from the most obscure of causes? The effort to express is the effort to clarify.

This interviewer came away puzzled, but with an undiminished respect for Faulkner; and for his own part, still thinks Faulkner obscure, still believes Faulkner has a right to be obscure, believes now that Faulkner moves under intense artistic compulsions, hovering between sophisticated coma and sav-age convulsion of which your interviewer has only a dim and unsatisfactory comprehension.

Here, at all events, is a fleeting impression of the most influential, the most original, and the most vilified novelist living, each of whose works has en-riched all his others. Hemingway (Faulkner's closed rival in contemporary literary fame) has been too personal to support followers, too attractive not to produce imitators, but Faulkner has been sinking deep roots, while Hem-ingway has only been blooming and fading.

Editor Twice Met Faulkner at National Book Awards

Mary Stahlman Douglas / 1955

From Nashville *Banner*, July 13, 1962, p. 22. Reprinted by permission.

When a great man dies, little men always rush to get into the act—to boast, if they can, that they "once saw Shelley plain," that he did stop and speak to them and they to him. Thus it is now with William Faulkner. There will be a rash of recollections of the shy individualist of Oxford, Mississippi who, after receiving word he had been awarded the Nobel Prize for Literature, took his daughter to high school, went to the back yard and chopped wood, strolled to the post office, chatted with friends and never once mentioned winning the world's highest literary award. It was all his family could do to get him to go to Stockholm in December, 1950 to accept his award, made for the previous year when it had been witheld, along with Britain's Bertrand Russell who received the 1950 award—the first time two full Nobel literary prizes had been awarded simultaneously.

The following March, 1951, the five-man jury for the National Book Awards selected Faulkner's *Collected Stories* for the Gold Medal in fiction, to the disappointment of many of the visiting critics from throughout the country who had hoped the newly established awards of the entire publishing industry would honor younger and fairly unknown writers to whom it might prove a "leg up." It was a decided anti-climax to the Nobel Prize for Faulkner, who failed to come and get it and had his editor, Random House's Saxe Commins, accept for him. The judges passed out a lagniappe to youngish Brendan Gill (35) in the form of a special citation for his novel, *The Trouble of One House.* Mr. Gill was there to get his "diploma" and to make a few forthright remarks. He was the only recipient of honors under fifty.

The visiting critics, authors and the hundreds of representatives of the publishing industry who had been disappointed in not seeing Faulkner in the flesh in 1951 were to receive a surprise at the festivities in 1953 when he turned up apparently "just for the heck of it." He hadn't won a thing but he stood shyly over in a corner with Editor Commins and completely stole the show from the winners as the most distinguished writer present. All the re-

112

viewers and book editors tried to meet him and when going through my files
to be sure I had my facts straight, I found a photograph sent me later by Pike
Johnson, then of Doubleday, proving I did see and talk with Faulkner. Doubleday's man-of-the-hour, Justice William O. Douglas, the speaker for the
occasion and the guest of honor at a swank buffet supper at the St. Regis
Penthouse, was also in the picture.

Two years later the faithful NBA attendants had another chance to talk
with Faulkner when he and the poet, Wallace Stevens, became the only authors twice honored with the National Book Awards, Faulkner receiving the
gold medal for *A Fable* which also won a Pulitzer, and Stevens for *Collected
Poems.* (He won in 1951 for *The Auroras of Autumn.*) This reminds me that
Faulkner's first published work was poetry, *The Marble Faun* (1924); his first
novel, *Soldiers' Pay* (1926).

At the informal forum preceding the awards, Faulkner answered questions
by critics with precision and droll humor. We were all flabbergasted, however, to hear him declare: "I never, no never, read any reviews of my books."
To which Clifton Fadiman, emceeing the events quipped: "I know a great
many reviewers who don't read the books." Which reminds me of my favorite story told by Irvin S. Cobb about the Irish wit and critic, Oliver Hereford,
who when asked what he thought of Arnold Bennett, replied "Something I
once wrote about him in a critical way so prejudiced me against the man, I
could never bear to read any of his works."

Meeting him after the ceremonies, I asked Mr. Faulkner if the report that
he was then living in New York were true, to which he averred: "No, I came
up here just before Christmas and I am going home to Mississippi tomorrow."
It was in his beloved Oxford that he died of a heart attack last week.

Faulkner read his brief acceptance speech too rapidly without inflection,
in too low a voice to be heard even by first rowers, but from the mimeo-
graphed address furnished us we learned that the writer's mission is "to create something that was not here before him," knowing that he is doomed to
failure but that if what he is doing is "valid," then "even failure is worthwhile
and admirable, provided only that the failure is splendid enough, the dream
splendid enough, unattainable enough yet forever valuable enough, since it
was of perfection."

He closed by pointing out that one of the things wrong with our country is
success. "There is too much success in it. Success is too easy. A young man
can gain it with only a little industry. He can gain it so quickly and easily

that he has not had time to learn the humility to handle it with, or even to discover, realize, that he will need humility."

We should like to take this occasion to salute the alert editors of the New York *Herald Tribune Books*, which appeared on Sunday, July 8 (Faulkner died on July 6) with a full-page portrait of Faulkner on the cover and two following pages of pictues, life chronology, list of 27 published volumes, an excerpt from his memorable Nobel acceptance speech and a delightful article by Hodding Carter, editor and publisher of the Greenville (Miss.) *Delta Democrat-Times.*

In case you're thinking that Faulkner is only for the literati, the cognoscenti, a wire this week from Jay Tower of New American Library, also "on the ball" as usual, gives the staggering information that since April, 1947 when *Sanctuary* was introduced for the first time in paperbounds through Signet Editions, ten of Faulkner's books have climbed to a printing of about 8,000,000 to date.

Faulkner, Lured to Preview, Bares Long Link with Films

Commercial Appeal / 1955

From Memphis *Commercial Appeal,* June 14, 1955, p. 17. Reprinted by permission.

The quiet genius that is William Faulkner, although obviously preferring the sanctuary of his home in Oxford, Miss., or the contemplative activity of the hunt, nevertheless sparkled brightly at a cocktail party held in his honor at the Gayoso yesterday.

Mr. Faulkner was in Memphis, with his family, to see a special private preview screening last night of *The Land of the Pharaohs,* CinemaScope, WarnerColor spectacle-drama of ancient Egypt for which the Nobel and Pulitzer Prize winner wrote the screenplay. His hosts yesterday were Joe S. Young, manager of Warner Bros. Pictures Distributing Corporation here, and Eli H. 'Slim' Arkin, manager of the Warner, where the film will open June 29.

It is perhaps not too widely known that screenplay writing is no recent activity for the famed Missisippian. He has been doing them for some 25 years, he said. But it takes some doing on the part of a producer to get Mr. Faulkner to work on a script—and particularly if it means he must be pried away from Oxford.

Once, his aunt, Mrs. Walter B. McLean of 944 Peabody, recalled yesterday, Howard Hawks called him from Hollywood to Oxford seven times—and got seven refusals. "If he calls me the eighth time, I'll have to do it," groused Mr. Faulkner. Hawks did, and Mr. Faulkner did.

Hawks, a longtime close personal friend of the author's, is producer and director of *The Land of the Pharaohs.* An additional reason for his wanting Mr. Faulkner to do this story of the building of the great pyramid was that Mr. Faulkner had visited Egypt, and Hawks knew it.

On the topic of movies, Mr. Faulkner expressed himself as feeling that a story has to pass through too many hands for maximum effect and impact. By the time it has gone through several studio processes and dozens of hands, the author's original story has been altered or even lost, he feels.

115

Television, radio, the screen and the novel present separate problems and challenges to the writer, Mr. Faulkner said, but indicated he felt that a competent craftsman should be able to handle them all. One of his own books, *Intruder in the Dust*, has been filmed.

A gratifying amount of agreement with his recent series of letters in the *Commercial Appeal* on the topic of segregation has come in the form of letters and personal calls, Mr. Faulkner said—and mostly from young people, he notes.

On the other hand, there have been the expected bitter denunciations of any change in the South's traditional policy—many of them anonymous—and a number of nuisance phone calls at 2 or 3 a.m. Some of these come from as far away as Florida, he said.

On the touchy racial problem, he said, "It's like living in Alaska and saying you don't like snow; you have to live with it, and you might as well make the best of it."

With Mr. Faulkner here from Oxford for the preview was his wife, his daughter and son-in-law, Mr. And Mrs. Paul Summers, and his step-son Malcolm Franklin, and Mrs. Franklin.

Murry 'Jack' Faulkner, the author's brother, and his wife, of 1336 Harbert, joined Mrs. McLean as the Memphis branch of the family at the event.

Faulkner Steps Out of His "Land of Pharaohs" into Memphis

Edwin Howard / 1955

From Memphis *Press-Scimitar,* June 14, 1955, p. 2. Reprinted by permission.

The little gray-haired man in the gray cotton trousers and the rumpled blue cotton coat stood impassively in the bright light before a poster advertising the CinemaScope spectacle, *Land of the Pharaohs.*

Every now and then he pulled on a Dunhill pipe which he once dropped in the water while fishing. Between flash-bulb flashes, he sipped at a Scotch and soda. Before each picture, he cooperatively relinquished the drink to a Warner Bros. Pictures' representative who thought it might not look nice to some people.

The scene was the Regency Room at Hotel Gayoso. The event was nominally a reception honoring William Faulkner, Nobel and Pulitzer prize author from Oxford, Miss. Actually it was like all such events, a kind of exhibit at which he was to be on display to newspaper, radio and tv people, who would be expected to draw attention, in publicizing him, to *Land of the Pharaohs.* Faulkner's connection with the movie? He wrote it. After the reception he saw it. Early next month, it will open at the Warner Theater in Memphis.

Up from Oxford with the author came his wife, their daughter Jill and her husband, Paul D. Summers Jr., his stepson, Malcolm Franklin, and Mrs. Franklin, Faulkner's brother Jack and his wife, who now live in Memphis, and the Faulkner brothers' aunt, Mrs. Walter B. McLean, also of Memphis. They all put up good-naturedly with the pulling and tugging, the flash bulbs, the just-one-more-pleases, and the you-don't-remember-me-but-I-met-you-at-the-*Intruder in the Dust* premiere gambits.

As at all such affairs, there was no time for sustained conversations. Here, tho, are highlights and sidelights from Faulkner and his family, gleaned by Pres-Scimitar Staff Writers Milton Britten, Roy Hamilton, Edwin Howard, Thomas N. Pappas and Clark Porteous, who were among the pullers and tuggers:

"*Land of the Pharaohs* is nothing new," said Faulkner. "It's the same

117

movie Howard (Producer-Director Howard Hawks) has been making for 35 years. It's *Red River* all over again. The Pharaoh is the cattle baron, his jewels are the cattle, and the Nile is the Red River. But the thing about Howard is, he knows it's the same movie, and he knows how to make it."

Faulkner and Hawks "invented the story" in Italy, Faulkner said. Then Harry Kurnitz and Harold Jack Bloom put it in script form. Faulkner went to Egypt with Hawks to watch some of the filming. "We were there for weeks, tho, without shooting a foot of film. Political trouble. As soon as I could get out, I got."

The famed Mississippian has no more movie work immediately in view, but will turn his world-acclaimed talent to the screen again "whenever Howard wants me." They've been close friends and associates for 25 years. A screen treatment of the novel, *The Left Hand of God,* which Faulkner did for Hawks "has been shelved," Faulkner said. "I understand the Catholic Church objected to it," he added.

Faulkner enjoyed covering the Kentucky Derby for *Sports Illustrated.* (He never got around to mentioning who won, but he wrote a brilliant "color" story of the event.) He said he was a little bit afraid the working newspapermen covering the race would resent his presence in the press box. "After all, I was an outsider." But he said they welcomed him, he liked them, "and we got along fine."

There's another writer in the Faulkner family. Attractive, red-haired daughter Jill, who went with her father to Sweden to receive the Nobel Prize, is a reporter for the Charlottesville, Va., *Daily Progress.* "And I had been working there for two months before they found out—I never did tell them—that I was William Faulkner's daughter." She does rewrite and covers the courts. Once, during a morals case, the judge told her she would have to leave, that she was too young. "He thought I was a teen-ager." she laughed, "but I finally convinced him I was a reporter. Guess I'll have to carry my marriage license around." Her husband, Paul D. Summers Jr., is studying law at the University of Virginia.

Has Jill ever writen an interview with William Faulkner for the Charlottesville *Daily Progress?*

"Ha!," she exclaimed. "I don't even claim him!"

One *Press-Scimitar* staffer told Faulkner a story instead of trying to get one out of him.

"I was with a light tank outfit in France during World War II," our man said. "We were several kilometers from a little town called Chateaubriant in

Brittany. It rained day after day. Two French women walked thru the mud and rain one day to our bivouac, because they had learned there was an officer there from Memphis. They wanted to know: Memphis is near Oxford, Miss., is it not? Yes. Do you know William Faulkner? No. I said, but I had seen his house and read many of his stories. Those women came back several days just to talk about you. There was no one in France, they said, so wonderful to read as Faulkner. The mud and rain were nothing, if they could find out the slightest thing about you."

During the story, Faulkner looked away several times, but always back again. And there was a brief smile and a nice "thank you" when it was over.

Mrs. McLean, Faulkner's aunt, told of his speaking one year in the Women's Building at the Mid-South Fair. "Another year," she said, "they wanted him to come back. I asked him if he would. He said, 'No indeed. Last time I was up there they had me competing with the biggest bull in captivity, and I'm not going back.'"

With Faulkner in Japan

Gay Wilson Allen / 1955

From *American Scholar*, 31 (Autumn 1962), pp. 566–71. Reprinted by
permission. Copyright © 1962 by the Phi Beta Kappa Society.

The sad news of William Faulkner's death brings back to me with nostaligc
poignancy the summer of 1955 when I was closely associated with him for
two weeks in the little mountain resort town of Nagano in Japan. That summer the Exchange of Persons Branch of the United States Department of
State sent two Americans to Japan to lecture, Faulkner and myself. He had
recently won the Nobel Prize in Literature and anything he said or did was
newsworthy in almost every country of the world. I was sent because my
specialty, Walt Whitman, was enjoying (from whatever Valhalla he now in-
habits) a temporary flurry of popular interest on the occasion of the first
centennial of *Leaves of Grass*, and I was the poets' latest biographer. It would
not have been difficult to find eminent critics skeptical of the appropriateness
of representing American culture by either Walt Whitman or William Faulkner, but the reception given Mr. Faulkner left little doubt that he at least was
a happy choice.

As the incomparably less famous, I arrived earlier, stayed longer and followed a more routine schedule than the great novelist, whose presence alone
was a "cultural exchange." But both of us were to participate in the annual
Seminar in American Literature that our Government had begun sponsoring
each summer for about fifty Japanese teachers of the English language and
American literature in the colleges and universities of Japan. These sessions
were then being held in Nagano City, a summer vacation spot near the "Japanese Alps," an overnight trip by rail from Tokyo. Thus it happened that I had
already been at Nagano for a week, lecturing and participating in discussions
with the Japanese professors, when Mr. Faulkner arrived by plane at the
Tokyo International Airport on Monday morning, August 1, which happened
to be a blazing hot day. He was rushed to the American Embassy, where he
promptly collapsed—from "sun stroke," one newspaper reported, from ex-
haustion another stated.

Later I learned that Faulkner had fasted across the Pacific, except for liquid
refreshments, to avoid airsickness, and the ninety-odd degree temperature at

Hanada Field had caused the collapse. The American Ambassador, however, thought otherwise, and provided a bodyguard ostensibly as a guide but actually to keep the distinguished visitor sober. This Faulkner bitterly resented and he never forgave the Ambassador. He did drink a considerable quantity of alcohol every day (he always insisted that it was necessary food), but I never observed him the least tipsy—even after an evening of consuming alternately beer and saki.

A few hours after his arrival in Tokyo Mr. Faulkner had recovered sufficiently to meet the press and to submit to a long radio and television interview conducted by Masami Nishikawa, professor of American literature at Tokyo University, and Miss Shio Sakanishi, a leading social critic. When asked about regionalism in contemporary American writing, Mr. Faulkner replied that he did not know "because I am not really a literary man. I don't know any writing people. I am a farmer, a country man, and I like to write." When not writing, "I breed and train horses." Miss Sakanishi told him that some Japanese writers owned race horses, to which the self-styled Mississippi farmer replied that they must be "pretty successful writers" to own race horses.

Miss Sakanishi remarked that in Japan writers are always asked their opinions on disasters or any extraordinary happening. (Several days before this newspapers had carried accounts of the drowning of several score school children when an excursion boat overturned.) Mr. Faulkner said he wished this were true in his own country, where the artist is not important, not looked up to with respect. "In my country, instead of asking the artist what makes children commit suicide, they go to the Chairman of General Motors and ask him. This is true. If you make a million dollars you know all the answers."

From Nagano the other Americans (four Fulbright scholars) and I eagerly followed Mr. Faulkner's Tokyo activities as reported to the two English-language newspapers. After a short delay to permit him to recover his strength, he was brought quietly to Nagano in a United States Embassy car, but we Americans were not immediately introduced to him. Even after he began his talks (he refused to lecture but consented to answer questions in a very informal manner) we had no chance to get acquainted with him. At first we thought his Embassy bodyguard was trying for some devious reason to keep him from contaminating association with us "eggheads." When we did meet him, he had nothing to say after the perfunctory salutations. We began to wonder if he were not, after all, the Mississippi farmer and not the great novelist we had proclaimed him to the Japanese. Then the realization dawned upon me that he was actually afraid of us. I had heard of his shyness, and knew that he posed as uneducated, but suddenly I could see that he was extremely self-conscious before "university professors," although each of us regarded him as the greatest living American writer.

At the first opportunity I used my own acquaintance with horses (thanks to my boyhood in the Carolina mountains) as a conversational gambit, and it worked like a charm. I found him particularly interested in Japanese rice culture, because, he said, rice was now his main crop on his farm in Mississippi. In fact, he liked to think that we might be eating some of his own rice because the United States had recently exported a considerable quantity of rice to Japan. Everyone thought it a pose when Faulkner, on landing in Stockholm to receive the Nobel Prize, gave his occupation as "farmer." Although he had a sly sense of humor, I decided that he actually did think of himself as a simple country man, whose writing had by some stroke of luck—which still surprised him—won a world audience. It still seemed strange to him that people actually read the books that he wrote in private, and in a real sense for himself alone. His shyness and modesty were not pretended; he was one of the least affected and most genuinely modest men I ever met.

At first the talks at Nagano were disappointing. A Japanese professor would ask a question, Mr. Faulkner would reply briefly—sometimes only with a "yes" or "no"—and then a profound silence would settle upon the room. Maybe for several minutes the novelist would sit quietly at his table, or perhaps busy himself with lighting his pipe, with not a sound from the tatami mats where the Japanese sat gracefully with their legs folded beneath them while we Americans sprawled in uncomfortable postures. But after two or three days Mr. Faulkner began talking in sentences and then whole paragraphs. The embarrassed tension was gone and the colloquy became a great success.

The talk was natural, unaffected, colloquial, at times ungrammatical. The sentences might wander on like one of the famous sentences in a Faulkner novel, but he showed no evasion, no condescension, and occasional flashes of wit without flippancy. Mr. Faulkner did not resent personal questions from the Japanese (he would have from us Americans), and he did not play cat and mouse when asked to explain a difficult passage or the "intention" in one of his novels or short stories. Some of the most interesting replies were on the origin of certain stories. Here is a sample from a tape recording of his talks:

Q. Could you tell me your best story in your own estimation?

F. In my own estimation, none of them are good enough, that's why I have spent thirty years writing another one, hoping that one would be good enough. And so my personal feeling would be a tenderness for the one which caused me the most anguish, just as the mother might feel for the child, and the one that caused me the most anguish and is to me the finest failure is *The Sound and the Fury*. That's the one I feel most tender toward.

Q. Going back to the notes [a previous question], did you make any when you wrote the first section of *The Sound and the Fury*?

F. No.

Q. Would you tell us something about the time you wrote the first section; it seems to me to be so complicated, and I wonder if you wrote it just as you did *The Wild Palms*.

F. That began as a short story, it was a story without plot, of some children being sent away from the house during the grandmother's funeral. They were too young to be told what was going on and they saw things only incidentally to the childish games they were playing, which was the lugubrious matter of removing the corpse from the house, et cetera, and then the idea struck me to see how much more I could have got out of the idea of the blind, self-centeredness of innocence, typified by children, if one of those children had been truly innocent, that is, an idiot. So the idiot was born and then I became interested in the relationship of the idiot to the world that he was in but would never be able to cope with and just where could he get the tenderness, the help, to shield him in his innocence. I mean "innocence" in the sense that God had stricken him blind at birth, that is, mindless at birth, there was nothing he could ever do about it. And so the character of his sister began to emerge, then the brother, who, that Jason (who to me represents complete evil. He's the most vicious character in my opinion I ever thought of), then he appeared. Then it needs the protagonist, someone to tell the story, so Quentin appeared. By that time I found out I couldn't possibly tell that in a short story. And so I told the idiot's experience of that day, and that incomprehensible, even I could not have told what was going on then, so I had to write another chapter. Then I decided to let Quentin tell his version of that same day, or that same occasion, so he told it. Then there had to be the counterpoint, which was the other brother, Jason. By that time it was completely confusing. I knew that it was not anywhere near finished and then I had to write another section from the outside with an outsider, which was the writer, to tell what had happened on that particular day. And that's how that book grew. That is, I wrote that same story four times. None of them was right, but I had anguished so much that I could not throw any of it away and start over, so I printed it in the four sections. That was not a deliberate *tour de force* at all, the book grew that way. That I was still trying to tell one story which moved me very much and each time I failed, but I had put so much anguish into it that I couldn't throw it away, like the mother that had four bad children, that she would have been better off if they had all been eliminated, but she couldn't relinquish any of them. And that's the reason I have the most tenderness for that book, because it failed four times.

One day Mr. Faulkner was asked why his style was so difficult, and he replied, "because of ignorance. . . . If I could write better English I would. . . . I'm not an educated man." This may sound too disingenuous to be accepted as honest, but the story of the growth of *The Sound and the Fury* should caution us against hasty cynicism. On another occasion the novelist was asked how he managed to choose such unusual but appropriate names for his characters. He replied that he did not name them; "they tell me their names." One character in *Pylon* does not have a name: "He never did tell me his name."

After seeing and hearing William Faulkner in these rambling talks every day for two weeks, I came to some conclusions that contradicted a good many critical judgements that I, and other teachers, had been spouting in the classroom. The critics (completely reversing the earliest critics of his works) thought he was a devilishly subtle craftsman who had deliberately contrived intricate plots and involved sentences (and God knows some of them are complicated!), and imbedded in them cunning symbols. That he was the most inventive and original novelist of twentieth-century American literature I still believe, but as I listened to this simple, even naïve, man speaking in Nagano, I asked myself how *he* could have written those novels. I finally came to the conclusion that the talks, for all their frankness and charm and sincerity, came off the top of his mind; not because he was uninterested or not trying, and he was telling the truth so far as he was conscious of it. But artistic creation takes place in solitude, with intense concentration and self-forgetfulness; and it involves all the realms of the artist's being and experience to such an extent that the creation may seem alien and dark to him in his more normal, relaxed hours. Faulkner did not feel that he constructed his plots, but that they "grew"; his characters "told" him their names. And his efforts, as he reiterated with what was often taken as false modesty or "pose," were not always successful. Not all those ten-page sentences are works of art; maybe some of them the author himself just never did get straightened out. To me the structure of *The Sound and the Fury* is a work of genius, but I am willing to believe that it did grow—out of the author's dissatisfaction—as he said it did.

There are, of course, subtleties in Faulkner's art. Perhaps, indeed, he was the most subtle literary artist this country has produced, but the intricate patterns and baroque style were the superabundance of imaginative vitality, not cultivated deliberately. The real man, who sustained the artist within, was the self-effacing "farmer" answering questions in Nagano. He was as simple, unaffected and innately friendly as his Deep South neighbors sitting on the benches in the shade of the great trees beside the Court House in Oxford, Mississippi, the country town where he lived, wrote most of his books, and died.

Faulkner in Massachusetts

Elisabeth Linscott / 1956

From *New England Galaxy*, 10 (Winter 1969), pp. 37–42. Reprinted by permission.

From the kitchen window of our farmhouse, I looked out on the deep snow and saw William Faulkner and my husband plodding through the drifts, each carrying a large suitcase. Bob, who was an editor at Random House, had brought Faulkner from New York for the weekend; our car was stuck in the snow a mile away, there was no place to telephone, so they had to walk more than a mile.

They came in the kitchen door and the first thing Faulkner noticed was the black wood stove in which I had a blazing fire. He stood by it rubbing his cold hands. His shoes and socks were soaking wet; I made him take off his shoes but he was shy about the socks. Finally I pulled them off and put his feet on a towel on the edge of the oven.

And that's how the first weekend began in February 1956.

Random House published Faulkner; he and my husband had become good friends. Bob wasn't his editor; no one was. But he often asked Bob's advice.

The first time I met Bill, he was visiting my husband who was a patient in a New York City hospital. We knew he was coming and my husband had said: "Don't expect him to talk, he simply won't." But he did.

Bill was in New York then about to fly to Egypt and to be an advisor on a movie Zanuck was making. He told us he didn't want to go; he hated to go; he said this several times. "Why not call it off?" I said. He looked shocked and replied. "Oh no, I promised; I couldn't let Zanuck down." And he went.

The next time I met him was at a cocktail party in his honor, also in New York. Everyone else was there when he came in. He had been very ill and we had worried about him. When he arrived, I got up and took both his hands. I was so glad to see him well again. Of course ladies *don't* rise when a man comes into the room, but something about Bill pulled me to my feet that day.

I did not see him again until Bob and I went to live in an old farmhouse in the Berkshire foothills. Bob told me that Bill had never had New England clam chowder. "Let's invite him for a weekend: I have told him about your chowder," said my husband.

126

Faulkner said he would like to come in February because he had never seen snow. (We didn't quite believe this; Bill said many harmless things that one knew were not true.)

He was a perfect guest. He loved to walk in the woods, as we did (many guests never ventured from the house). He praised my cooking and left his room neat as a pin. This first night we had the clam chowder that took me a half day to make from an old recipe that calls for lots of salt pork, butter, milk, and heavy cream. It was served from a big tureen into large, heavy bowls, with common crackers to crumble in it. Bill had three helpings; then we had New England Indian pudding with hard sauce.

With this meal we had a very special wine which had been in the heavy suitcases the men lugged through the snow. Bill was a true connoisseur of wine; my husband said he had taken a great deal of time in our nearest town to select the wine for each meal we were going to have. The liquor store dealer still talks about Mr. Faulkner's call. "He stood *right there*," he tells customers. But during this weekend and the others, Bill did not drink too much.

After dinner, we sat by a big log fire in the study. Again my husband warned me not to try to make Bill talk, but surprisingly he talked a great deal. The newspapers were then full of accounts of a plagiarism suit which we discussed. I asked Bill if he had ever been party to a suit. He said yes and that it had come to trial in Washington, D.C. Before the trial started the judge asked Bill a question about a horse Bill owned, then beckoned him to come to the bench. The judge was a horse fancier and soon they were deep in an animated talk about horses while the lawyers for the two sides tried in vain to get the judge's attention. Bill swore that the judge waved them aside; he leaned over the bench: the heads of the two men were together. Then, Bill said, the judge dismissed the case and asked Bill to continue the horse-talk in his chambers. I don't think a judge *can* do this, but that is the way Bill told it. While the snow continued to fall so hard that by the time we went to bed, the drifts were far up the windows. And the wind blew hard.

The door to the guest room had stuck for a long time; so even when shut, it was open just a crack. Our cat, named Dorcas (for a girl in the old graveyard down the road), slept in the kitchen and was never known to go upstairs.

I heard a noise in the night but didn't get up right away to check it. When I did, I saw that the door to Bill's room was wide open and Dorcas was sleeping close to him. The cat had pushed at the crack until the door swung back and in she went. I was afraid I would awaken Bill if I tried to remove

Dorcas, so I tiptoed back to our room. The next morning Bill told me about Dorcas. He said he liked her. She always slept with him when he visited us, and we teased him about the cat who had fallen in love with him.

Our guest told us that he liked to get up very early so we showed him where the coffee and the other things for his breakfast were kept. When we came downstairs, he had made a big fire in the wood stove and was just taking a piece of toast from the oven. We had forgotten to tell him where we kept the electric toaster. I did not know until then that toast could be made in a wood stove oven but the fire must be very hot.

We had 300 acres of meadow land, pastures, and deep woods and had sold lumber rights that year to a man who was then cutting and "drawing out" the trees. Bill wanted to see this operation, so that morning we bundled up (it was bitter cold) and climbed a 300-foot hill up a path the lumbermen had made by "snaking" the big trees from the top to a big frozen beaver pond below. Snaking was done by attaching one tree at a time by chains to horses who then walked down alone. A man at the bottom unhooked the chains and the well-trained horses walked straight back without a driver.

This fascinated Bill. He ran up and down with the handsome workhorses for so long that I went back to the warm house alone. Then my husband and Bill explored the big beaver pond and examined the beavers' house built by them on the ice with a sluiceway so they could get out if they wanted to. Bill wanted to know all about the beavers and Bob told him we had obtained them from the State Wildlife Department, but not until after a staff memeber had called formally and inspected both of us and all the property. We had hoped the beavers would make a pond, and they did, with a hundred-foot dam.

For luncheon that day we had more of the chowder, which gets better each day. For desert we had pumpkin pie made from our own pumpkins.

In the afternoon we went snowshoeing in the deep woods on crust that sparkled in prisms of red, green, and gold and under trees hung with beautiful icicles, for it had continued to be very cold. Bill said he had never seen snowshoes before but he did very well after a few minutes. (The photograph shows him looking at the snowshoes we loaned him.)

That evening he suggested that we sit in the big kitchen instead of the study, and we all put our feet on the edge of the wood stove. I told him how much I enjoyed his story "The Bear" and that I had read it several times. I asked him whether he was not he young boy in the story. My husband looked alarmed, for that was the kind of question he thought Bill did not like; but after a little hesitation Bill said yes, he had been that boy, going out with the men just as the story tells. And then he talked about hunting in the Mississippi woods and how much it meant to him.

My husband teased me about having been in the publicity business, referring to Faulkner's utter dislike of personal publicity. I said I had met people who pretended not to like it but I believed Faulkner when he said, "This is something I am very serious about. I feel strongly that I have a right to deep privacy. I will do whatever I can in the future, as I have in the past, to impede and frustrate publicity pieces."

We talked about a man who had set himself up as an authority on Faulkner and who writes and lectures about him but had never met him. "He came to Oxford to see me and I wouldn't see him. I have never seen him," said Bill.

The next night I asked other guests for dinner and prepared a roast of beef, cooking it in my wood stove that often became temperamental, in fact downright sullen. My table was set with my best silver, and candles sparkled. The guests were special, to say nothing of Bill, so I was chagrined when, after seating them all formally in the dining room, my husband cut into the meat and said sternly that it wasn't nearly done. Everyone went back to the study while I humbly bore the meat back to the stove. Everyone was hungry and everyone but Bill acted a little miffed. He came out to the kitchen and patted my arm. "Don't let this bother you, honey," he said.

That autumn my husband spent part of each week at Random House where Bill, who said that he could not work at home that year, had a desk in Bob's office. Bob telephoned me that he had told Bill about my baked beans and was bringing him for the weekend. In many recipes I double some of the ingredients to make the dish richer; for the beans I triple the amount of pork. Again Bill brought wine and we had the beans, hot brown bread, and our own frozen raspberries for dessert. Bill had three big helpings of the beans. And an hour after dinner he got sick. "I was a pig." he said.

The autumn foliage was gorgeous that year. We took long walks in our woods, mostly on paths my husband had cut. We sat on a log in a tremendous grove of immense ancient maple sugar trees; the gold leaves fell on our shoulders. We told Bill how sugaring was done in the old days and showed him a broken down "sugar house" with an old iron stove on which former inhabitants had boiled the syrup.

Afterwards we walked through great stretches of ferns that had turned bronze, pale yellow, and white. I picked some of them, and also some vivid red oak leaves, and when we got back to the house I showed Bill how I pressed and sprayed them so they last all winter in table arrangements. He asked if he might have some to take back to New York. I made up a box of them and showed him how to place them in a bowl against the light.

Bill was staying at the Algonquin Hotel in New York City and I sometimes wondered how my ferns and leaves looked in his room.

On our walks we often left the paths to go into deep woods and had to climb over fallen trees and many stone walls. When I was alone with my husband, he went on ahead, never looking back to see whether I made it or not; but Bill waited each time, taking my elbow and helping me over the walls. He was one of the most polite men I have ever met, with really courtly manners.

And for his last luncheon here, we had blueberry pancakes made by my husband and served with hot maple syrup. "Why put cold syrup on hot cakes?" asked my husband. "I will tell this to the head waiter at the Algonquin," said William Faulkner. And he kissed me goodbye.

He wanted to come when the lilacs were in bloom but then he was ill, and then he was dead.

The Last Gentleman

Calvin Israel / 1956

From *Partisan Review*, 35 (Spring 1968), pp. 315–19. Reprinted by permission.

It was in New York in 1956. I saw Faulkner sitting on a bench in Washington Square Park.

At the short distance his face reminded me of Charlie Chaplin, and the way he was inserted rather than seated on the bench had the touch of a Chaplin comedy. He was flanked by people dozing, reading and lounging in the sunshine; he was a quiet center of great activity as strollers passed closely by and children raced, skated and shouted up and down the concrete path. In all the hubbub and movement he sat quietly, pipe in mouth, clasped hands resting on crossed legs, body hunched slightly forward. His gaze seemed fixed upon something far but particular, although only the massive building of NYU lined the outer edge of the park.

Close to where Faulkner was seated several children were teasing a young girl who was learning to skate. As she drew nearer, the skates flew out from under, and she fell heavily on the concrete a few feet from Faulkner's knee. The little girl, who was about ten, and more shocked than hurt by the sudden fall, alternated screams and sobs. Her cheek bled and she clutched one bruised knee as she tried to rise. People rushed toward her; they removed the skates and helped her get up, and one dabbed at her bleeding cheek with a handerchief. A few minutes later, when she became calm and left the scene, the crowd disappeared.

I had, somehow, kept my eyes on Faulkner during the skating accident, and I realized that all through the incident Faulkner had not moved. He had remained immobile in the noise and movement before and about him. He still sat as fixed and uninvolved as he had been when I first noticed him—hands, legs and pipe seemed as detached as some store-window mannequin. All the anecdotes I had read about Faulkner's drinking — the Hollywood episodes — came flooding back as possible explanations. It was because he didn't *look* drunk that I felt compelled to approach him and to try to solve the small mystery. With as much bravado as I could muster, I strolled up casually and spoke to him.

"Hello, Mr. Faulkner."

His eyes flicked up at me quickly and withdrew. He made the barest nod with his head and was silent. Directly in front of me at Faulkner's left was an empty space, and I was hoping that he would ask me to sit down. He didn't. I shifted nervously and was about to say some polite word of goodbye when his eyes snapped up at me again.

"Do you go to college, son? Over there?"

"Yes," I said. "I'm a senior, but not over there — I go to CCNY."

This time his eyes held mine and he repeated the college's name as I had given it. The last letter came out softly and sounded like *wah*.

"I'm an English major," I added. "American literature."

"Oh," Faulkner said softly again. Then, he repeated what I had said last. The word *literature* came out in three syllables and seemed to end *ooh* as he said it to himself. "What's your name?"

"Calvin Israel."

He gave me a puzzled look, repeated my name and smiled. "I'm used to that reaction," I said. "When I get to be a teacher I intend to confuse all my students by telling them my middle name is St. Thomas Aquinas."

Faulkner laughed. He tapped the pipe against his palm and placed it in the lapel pocket of his corduroy jacket. He uncrossed his legs and swung his body toward me. "Sit down, son," he said.

We sat facing each other in bright sunlight through which Faulkner squinted as he talked. As he spoke his eyes moved constantly, resting only now and then upon me, but seeming to take in all that went on about us.

"Are you a New Yorker?" Faulkner asked. New Yorker was two syllables.

"Not much longer," I said. "I'm leaving to go to graduate school."

"Plan to teach?"

"I'd like to write, too." I said.

"That's good," Faulkner replied quickly. "What things?"

"Oh . . . ," I said. "I try poems mostly."

"That's good. " he said again brightly. "I do those all the time."

"I know," I answered. "I read them. There's only one book, isn't there?"

He plucked the pipe out of the jacket pocket and turned slightly away from me. He fondled the pipe and examined the ground in front of us moodily. I had the feeling that I had said something annoying. For a few moments I searched for a way to engage him again, but he came back himself.

"What do you plan to work on?"

"It's a bit hazy right now," I said. "I'd like to try your books. I like *As I Lay Dying* very much, but it's puzzling — the structure, I mean."

Faulkner nodded. "I like *Dying* — do you know *Light*?"

"*Light*? — oh, you mean *Light in August*? I haven't read that yet, but I had a teacher once who thought it was your best."

"What's his name?" he asked.

"Bird Stair."

"No . . . I don't know of him. How about Tom Wolfe?"

"I haven't thought about Wolfe much," I said. "I like his work, but the only problems I've thought about are in Melville and your books."

"What problems do you have with Bill Faulkner?" he asked.

"I think they're similar to the ones in Melville," I said. "If I had to choose a title right now I'd call it something like *William Faulkner and the Problem of Evil*."

He sat straight up and stared at me. "Evil?" he chuckled. "No . . . that seems to fit Melville better than it does Bill Faulkner."

It was clear by now that Faulkners' inaction during the little girl's fall could not be blamed on drinking. I was still puzzled by that detachment, however, and I struggled to find a way to bring it up without bluntness. It was apparent that Faulkner was a very shy and reserved man, and, at that moment at least, preferred many silences to lengthy conversation. His eyes had found the knot of people gathered around a folksinger who was entertaining at the large fountain.

In the previous December, N.B.C. had produced an adaptation of Faulkner's novel, *The Sound and the Fury*. The production had been received poorly by critics, and since I disagreed with their opinions I thought Faulkner might be interested in the reasons.

"By the way, Mr. Faulkner," I began, "I happened to see the TV play of *The Sound and the Fury* a few months ago, and I think the critics were wrong — but they were also right."

His attention returned to me. "Oh," he said, "I've been giving that a lot of thought, too."

"I think," I went on, "if someone who saw the TV play didn't know the book, he would have found the play hard to follow —but if he knew the book, the play was fine."

"I've been thinking some things like that, son," Faulkner said. He lifted the Tyrolean hat and rubbed hard at the hair over his temple. In the sunlight his hair was more iron-grey than the white which appears in such strong contrast to his moustache in photographs. "Durkee's job," he added.

He replaced his hat and watched me light a cigarette. He had shaken his head at my offer of one, and he seemed to be studying the insignificant actions I made in lighting up.

"Well, son," he said, "you seem to be spending too much time thinking about Bill Faulkner. Anything else you want to tell me?"

"There's only one other thing I can think of at this moment, Mr. Faulkner," I answered, "and I'm afraid I disagree with you on that interview in which you made the 'go slow in the South' statement."

"I didn't say *that*," Faulkner said quickly. "You don't — lots of people just don't understand what I said."

He got up suddenly and I stood up also. I was struck by how small he was. "Violence," he said.

"If you mean, Mr. Faulkner, that the danger is violence, then in my opinion it is worth all the chance."

"You don't understand, son," he said again. "You can't understand that *kind* of violence." He offered me his hand and I shook it.

"Good luck, son," he said. He was smiling as he started to move away.

"Mr. Faulkner," I said quickly. "That little girl on skates —who fell — did you see her?"

"Yes, son," he said, "I saw her. Goodbye."

I watched him walk to the fountain and stop to listen to the folksinger. He filled and lighted his pipe and walked around the fountain to cross the street directly in front of the Washington Arch. He stood looking up at the top of the monument, and then, with a playful military bearing, he marched rather than walked throught the arch and disappeared in the crowds along lower Fifth Avenue.

Col. Sartoris and Mr. Snopes

Nancy Hale / 1957

This article originally appeared in *Vogue*.

I first met William Faulkner in 1957 when he had come to Charlottesville, where I live, to be writer in Residence at the University of Virginia, where my husband is professor of English. We met at an afternoon reception the English Department gave for the Faulkners in the Colonnade Club—the faculty club on the Lawn (never called campus) which is housed in one of the original Palladian pavilions Jefferson designed. I had over the years heard some widely varying accounts of Faulkner and I was curious to meet the famous man.

I had seen him out walking alone in the suburban-type streets of Charlottesville, a dapper little figure with a neat moustache, dressed like an actor in a trench coat and fur-felt hat with an Alpine brush, swinging a stick and looking about him with a sightseer's air. He had in fact, become a fairly familiar sight in the months since his daughter had married a law student who soon became a Charlottesville lawyer. It was said to be the familial tie that led him to accept the invitation from the University. He had never acted as Writer in Residence at any other university, was known to be unwilling to lecture, and few people at the University, even on the committee administering the Balch Fund, which supported his appointment, had dared hope he would actually accept.

I passed through the wide hallway of the Colonnade Club back to the ballroom looking over a serpentine-walked wintry garden toward West Range, where, as a student, Poe lived. The receiving line at the door was composed of the chairman of the English Department, his wife, Faulkner, and Mrs. Faulkner, a girlish-looking woman, with the famous Southern waist a man's hands can span. A delightfully dippy hat sat on her head of tiny grey snail-shell curls, and her face was piquant behind a pair of very dark glasses.

The rest of the English Department and the other guests were standing over on the opposite side of the room, talking to each other. It is always difficult to make conversation with a celebrity, and I didn't really blame the English Department for running away from doing it, nevertheless I began to

135

feel increasingly uncomfortable as guest after guest joined the milling crowd, abandoning the guests of honour. Finally I walked over to Mr. Faulkner.

"I think we have some friends in New York in common," I said.

"Is that so, ma'am?" he said.

I mentioned a few people, writers. At each name he would nod, as though giving it his considered attention. When I ran out of names he just stood there, at ease, silent.

There can be nothing quite so awing as complete lack of small talk. I had only encountered it once before, in a notably saintly clergyman beside whom I was placed at a dinner. In the case of the minister I had supposed his attention to be taken up by pressing considerations of Deity; in the case of Faulkner, I could only assume he was thinking about his work.

But the two young English professors who had been deputed to look after Faulkner while he was at the University—get him to his appointments and so on—were going around telling everyone that Faulkner didn't care to discuss books or his own writing, so I knew these topics were out. Small talk is the only real solution to a meeting between strangers, and after a moment more I turned to Mrs. Faulkner, with whom I slipped at once into a flow of conversation.

When I returned to the merry throng on the other side of the room, I looked back at the guest of honour in slight pique. After all, I'd only been trying to be friendly to a fellow writer. As I gazed at the erect little figure, the grey-haired triangle of face with its opposed, wider triangle of grey moustache, it seemed to me he was too simple and unaffected a man to maintain a "creative silence" or to cherish delusions of being too grand for backchat.

A week or so later, my husband and I were asked to dinner one snowy night at the house of one of the young herd-riding professors. The word was that Faulkner would be there. As the wife of a senior professor I knew I would be expected to talk, or try to talk, with the guest of honour, and I rather dreaded it. Books were out, writing was out, joint acquaintances were out, what *should* we talk of? If it was the woman's place to be charming to the man, it was the man's place—surely the Southern gentleman's obligation—to respond. I stood in silence beside Faulkner in the middle of the bay-windowed living room of the little Victorian house, surrounded by chattering friends.

"I hope you're comfortable in your new house," I said. It seemed just too bad to fall back upon such banalities, but I was bound it wouldn't be I who quit the duty to converse. It wasn't, either, as if I myself were such a rattletrap. I remembered how amused I had been when a Southern lady told me her generation was raised never to let a silence fall in a room. It crossed my mind perhaps Faulkner's silence was a rebellion against that very convention.

"Yes, thank you, ma'am," was all he said now.

Our blond hostess passed us the drinks we had asked for, both of them bourbon on the rocks. We lifted our glasses from the silver tray and I said, as I began on mine, "The first sip of whiskey is much the best, isn't it?"

His whole face changed. "Uhh-huuh," he said in that soft, slow voice. "Why, down home, when I come in of an evenin', and walk in by the fire, and sit down there with a drink of whiskey in my hand, I tell you there's nothin' in the world like that first sip runnin' down my throat."

We were off. After that we never had any silences when we met at parties. Simple, sensuous experience was what Faulkner wanted to talk about—the taste of the first sip of whiskey, the sound of tree toads at night in summer, the way it smells when you wake up to fine snow, to mention only things that came up in conversation that night. I remember the only check came when I said, "I've never been to Mississippi. I'd like to go, only I'm scared."

He stiffened. "What of, ma'am?" he said with noticeable coldness. "The Spanish moss hanging off the trees," I said. "It looks so eerie, especially at dusk."

He let his breath out. "Oh," he said, "I thought you meant po*liti*cally."

Faulkner's simplicity was nowhere more conspicuous than in his reaction to being Writer in Residence. The Department had been so sure that the foremost writer in the country would not even bother to come, but now he was here it turned out he was surprised and pleased to find the students really wanted to see him, and liked to talk to him and listen to him.

He would give no formal lectures, but he would answer questions at group conferences of students and staff. At the end of one of these, the presiding instructor said, "I think perhaps we've taken enough of Mr. Faulkner's time—unless, sir, you feel the wish to carry on a bit more?" to which Faulkner replied, "Well, I've told you, this is a dreadful habit to get into, where you can stand up in front of people and nobody can say, 'Shut up and sit down.' "

The readings he gave from his own work were less something to bear than a sight to behold. The audience, including townspeople, would assemble in one or another academic hall, and at last in would march that tiny, set-faced man with the grey moustache, who would proceed to read, face buried in his book, in an almost inaudible tone for fifteen or twenty minutes. I remember that when he read the "Spotted Horses" section from *The Hamlet*, in the McGregor Room of the Alderman Library, it was plain he himself was much amused by what he was reading, but for those of us who couldn't follow his low, slurred deep-South accent, it might almost have been a private joke.

Three of four times during his semester's work he held question-and-answer sessions open to the townspeople. His answers became predictable, if one went to enough of these sessions. It was as if he had worked them out to fit every conceivable question; it was as if he had constructed a carapace for himself out of set phrases. For instance he always referred to writing as "the craft of the human heart" and he always spoke of the writer as one totally without scruples in pursuit of his art. Once, when, as he often did, he spoke of himself as a "failed poet, who had to take up what he could do," the questioner then asked whether a story of his called "Carcassonne" had anything to do with a French poem of the same theme and the same title, Faulkner replied, "I don't know the poem, though if I did know it and I had needed to steal from it I'm sure I would—I wouldn't have hesitated."

Audiences often asked him about a statement he once made to the press, rating Wolfe the greatest of the modern writers precisely because he failed to achieve what he undertook. "For twenty years I've been trying to explain that," Faulkner used to reply, "I meant only that Hemingway had sense enough to find a method he could control, and didn't need or didn't have to, wasn't driven by his private demon to waste himself in trying to do more than that. So, he has done consistently probably the most solid work of us all. But it wasn't the splendid magnificent bust that Wolfe made, in trying to put the whole history of the human heart on the head of a pin, you might say." When he spoke of the human heart, as he so often did, Faulkner nearly always called it "frail and fragyle."

On the whole, however, the townspeople of Charlottesville did not, to use the local phrase, pay the Nobel Prize winner much mind. There was a story current about two young women standing in the window of Timberlake's Drugstore downtown, having a Coke.

"Look there," said one. "Yonder goes Mr. Faulkner."

"Who's he?" the other said.

"You mean you don't know who Mr. *Faulkner* is?" said the first.

"Why, he's Jill Summers's father, of course."

I never seemed to run into Mr. Faulkner anywhere except at semi-official English Department parties, and I wondered who his friends were. One afternoon, on a train returning from a trip to new York, I had a beer in the club car with a Charlottesville broker who is one of those Virginians whose heart is in the hunting field—who gets off from the office at every possible opportunity to ride with the Farmington hounds. Red-faced and portly, he is the spit and image of the men on the horses in fox-hunting Christmas cards.

"We got a fellow comes out with us a lot has something to do with what your husband does. English. Teaching English at the University. Something on that order," my acquaintance said. "Name of Faulkner."

"Oh!—Is he very keen?" I asked, thinking so that's what Faulkner does with his time.

"He's *keen* enough, I reckon. Can't stay away, seems. But naw! He's *terrible*, if that's what you mean. Falls *off*," he added in an incredulous tone.

"You know he's a great writer," I had to tell him.

"Him?" the man said. "That right? How's your husband, by the way? Saw him at the airport the other day."

The Albermarle fox-hunting set, generally known as the county people, are a world to themselves. I suppose they are much like fox-hunting people in Middleburg or Warrenton, or even in Leicestershire, but they are not like Charlottesville townspeople or the University crowd. They live far out on their enormous acres, in houses with lovely names like Castle Hill or Hunting Ridge or Canaan Farm, giving and going to their own lavish parties. They tend not to take an interest in local charities or politics, and they tend not to go to lectures at the University.

I wondered for a moment, in the club car, what the silent Mr. Faulkner found to talk to them about; then I remembered our conversation about the first sip of bourbon. He doubtless talked, just as they talk, about horses. I told myself academic lectures and civic duties are not early as good to write about as simple, sensuous experience is, and that Faulkner's artist's instinct was probably wise to keep him away from the cerebral and worthy and lead him toward the simple and earthy.

I kept thinking of a story about fox hunting I had written myself, years ago. Like many writers I am apt not to know what I think about a subject until I have written about it, and when I got home that night I looked up "The Fox" to find out what my opinion of fox hunting was.

I was struck by one of the characters in the story, a little girl of ten, daughter of some hunting people, who "never got off a horse. When she got off one in the stable, an imaginary one took its place between her legs, and she spent her days trotting, cantering, wheeling, and administering little slaps on the legs with the switch she carried round with her. It was a baby game she had not abandoned. . . . " One reason the child does this, it transpires, is because out in the hunting field she has not yet been allowed to be in at a kill. "Why do you care so much?" her mother asks her. "Because that's the point," the little girl says. "What else do we hunt for? The *point* is catching the fox. . . . You know, sometimes at night I dream that I'm never going to catch the fox. Only in the dreams it's because he always gets away and goes farther."

While I was up North a friend, John Ciardi the poet, asked me to see if I could get Faulkner to autograph Ciardi's copies of Faulkner's two volumes of verse, *The Marble Faun* and *A Green Bough*. Ciardi had heard that Faulkner was reluctant to autograph books, and that he never answered mail. We both hoped that in this case my acquaintance with him would make the difference.

I couldn't find Mr. Faulkner's number in the telephone book, and called up one of the two young professors to ask how best to reach him. He gave me the number, which turned out to be listed in Mrs. Faulkner's name, and told me Faulkner never came to the telephone. All communications, he said, had to be carried on through Miss Estelle—Mrs. Faulkner.

Miss Estelle was charming to me. I told her Mr. Ciardi—"the poet" I said, and she replied "Oh, yes I *know*"—would be most grateful for such a favour; and she said, "I'll ask Bill, and if you'll telephone at lunchtime tomorrow, I'll have his answer for you."

When I called up next day Miss Estelle said, "Bill gave me a message for you. I'll read you what he said."

Here is the message she gave me: "Tell the gentleman I have given up the world of literature for the world of fox hunting, but I'd be delighted to take the gentleman fox hunting."

I felt angry at what seemed a deliberate snub of a fellow artist—a poet of some distinction, after all, and Faulkner was always calling himself a failed poet. It seemed unbelievable that a man whose entire claim to fame was based on his writing should thus dismiss not only another artist but art itself.

I thought of my father, a painter dead these many years, and the way he had felt about art—the highest, the most difficult, the most desirable aim on earth, he would have said, and the noblest. To say one had given up the world of letters for the world of fox hunting seemed to me not only frivolous but ruthless. It was hard to realize Faulkner really said it. What embarrassed me in giving John Ciardi the message was less that I had failed to get his books autographed—though that embarrassed me too—than that Faulkner's refusal was put in such words.

Around that time I went to a party and sat on a sofa with a professor whose field is American literature. I told him about the Ciardi episode, and about the way my father used to feel toward art, and he said, "Oh, Faulkner's ideal isn't art. You must know that. He's always saying in the sessions what stinkers writers are."

"I thought he was just being modest," I said. "What do you suppose he does idealize, then? He's certainly worked hard enough at being a writer."

"It's taken up almost his entire life," the professor said. "But I'd guess his most cherished image is of his grandfather. Old Colonel Faulkner spelt without a u, the one who wrote *The White Rose of Memphis*. Colonel Sartoris is based on him."

"Did you ever read the book?" I said.

He nodded. "As Faulkner might say, it sure ain't art," he said. "The Colonel *wrote*, you see, but he wasn't what Faulkner calls demon-driven. Didn't give it too important a place—didn't give art. A Southern gentleman doesn't. Colonel Faulkner was a gentleman and a horseman. And he had courage."

"I suppose from the aristocratic point of view a writer *is* rather a mean, grasping thing to be," I said.

"Yes. Vulgar," the professor said. "Did you ever hear the story of how the Duchess of Devonshire threw her red wig at Voltaire?"

The following winter, just before Faulkner again served as Writer in Residence at the University, I went to a new Years' Eve cocktail party—very chic, very recherché, neither town, gown, nor county, but international. The hostess had somehow inveigled Faulkner into coming; I learned later that she had known Miss Estelle years before in China.

Faulkner stood, incongruous in the exquisite vast white room with its crimson silk demask sofas and Chinese objets d'art, directly under a blazing crystal chandelier, planted there like a small grey stone wall.

My awe and my desire to accommodate my conversation to his taste had perhaps lessened, or I remember I started—when I walked up to him feeling that I *must* talk to him, because he looked so alone—by asking whether he'd read some book I was in the middle of.

"No, ma'am," he replied. "I don't read much of any. I'm just a country boy from down Mississippi."

I had heard his ignorance act often enough by now that I felt like saying. "Then I can lend you some good books," but I couldn't bring myself to.

"Howsoever, Miss Nancy," he went on. "I did read your new novel the other day. *Dear Beast.* Somebody gave it to me. I thought it was *real* good." I was please to death. "I hear you do a lot of fox hunting." I said, willing to play it his way.

"Well, ma'am, " he said in that very slow, very soft voice, "down home we only hunt foxes on foot, with guns and dogs. Up here's the only place I ever hunted from the back of a horse, and to tell you the truth I spend right much time at it."

"I suppose you love horses," I said, not without wistfulness.

"Well, ma'am, I just can't keep away from them. They scare me to death, that's why. I'm scared to death of a horse, always was. That's why I can't keep away from one."

I seemed all full of unspoken rejoinders that afternoon. What I wanted to say now was, "Why do you waste time on real horses when you've got your inner horses to ride?" But I thought it sounded arty and I didn't say it.

After Faulkner had served as Writer in Residence for the spring semester in each of two successive years, he decided to settle down in a cottage on his daughter's place in Albermarle County and return to his farm in Mississippi only for the planting and the harvesting. The University conferred an honorary professorship on him, and in 1959 Linton Massey, a local collector, lent unique manuscripts, photographs, letters, first editions, and other records of Faulkner's career for an exhibition which was held in the Alderman Library. The books and papers were displayed in glass cases; at the end of the room hung a portrait of Faulkner painted by his mother many years before.

The portrait surprised me. It was like something done, not by some beginning art student, but by a person who had never seen a professional painting. Problems painters solved centuries ago were here unsolved—the greyness of the flesh, the staring eyes, the hard line encircling the head. The picture, which had never been shown before, was brought specially from the house at Oxford, where it hung in the living room. Mr. Massey told me Faulkner thought a great deal of it.

Mr. Massey also told me that Faulkner had given the house in Mississippi its name of Rowan Oak.

"Look it up in *The Golden Bough*," he said. "You'll find it has all sorts of fascinating meanings."

"Do you know whether Mr. Faulkner meant the meanings?" I asked.

"I asked him whether he'd got the name of the house out of Frazer, and he said 'Yes,' " Mr. Massey said. "You know he's a lot better read than he lets on."

When the Faulkners moved out into the country, they left a house which the University had provided for them on Charlottesville's handsomest residential street. A woman whom I have known for thirty years and whom I'll call Edith had been living next door to them with her husband, a distinguished professional man for some years immobilized by an accident, whom I'll call Billy.

Edith told me that when the Faulkners were about to leave, Miss Estelle, with whom she was on the friendliest terms, telephoned to ask if she wouldn't come over for cocktails their last day, and say goodbye.

Edith declined, and she told me she felt she owed it to herself to explain. "I'd like to come," she said, "but I don't think it would be right to. Mr. Faulkner has been living here in the very next house to Billy, and though you know I've asked him, he's never once come over to see him in the whole two years he's been here, when he must have known the pleasure it would give Billy to see him. We were glad to lend Mr. Faulkner our Cephus, when he wanted a driver; and we were glad to do anything else we could to be good neighbours. But no; after the way Mr. Faulkner has ignored Billy I don't think I can come to your house, and I wish you'd tell Mr. Faulkner why."

A day or two later, as the moving van stood outside, Edith saw Miss Estelle across the hedge that separates the two houses and asked her, "Did you give Mr. Faulkner my message?"

Miss Estelle nodded.

"What did he say?" Edith asked.

"He said you were absolutely right," Miss Estelle said.

The following autumn, John F. Kennedy was elected president of the United States. A number of major-prize-winning writers and painters were invited to the inauguration, and a friend of mine who lives in Washington was in charge of inviting them. The program was of course an eminent success—that was the famous occasion when Frost, blinking, recited from memory "The Gift Outright"—but from William Faulkner she was never able to get any answer to the letters and telegrams of invitation that she sent him. (I never did learn how Faulkner handled his mail, whether he threw it all away unopened or what. He must have had some system of discrimination, for during one of his sessions of work at the University he accepted an invitation from the State Department to go on a mission to Greece.)

In April of 1961 I received a letter from my Washington friend, saying, "Our book bearing messages to our brave president is about to go in to him—hopefully—before he leaves for Paris. He needs bucking up before his awesome crises. Every one of the list of one hundred sixty-eight [writers and artists invited to the inauguration] have written something for it except Edmund Wilson and Wm. Faulkner."

"Is there any way of getting from him something handwritten to the President and Mrs. Kennedy, on white paper no larger than this, and a small photograph or snapshot no larger than this sheet of paper? It's getting to be a point of pride with me now to capture [him]."

Mrs. Faulkner must have been away at the time, for I remember I tried to get the message to Mr. Faulkner through his daughter Jill, whom I talked to on several occasions. She was invariably charming, interested, anxious to help, and always said that she would see Pappy got the message. My Washington friend also telephoned to me several times to jack me up.

But nothing ever came of it. I remember thinking I would almost have admired Faulkner's intransigence if it had been based on the pride of an artist who knows art to be higher than politics. But I couldn't believe that was so. (I always meant to ask my Washington friend whether Edmund Wilson, also a Southerner, ever replied to the invitation, if only to decline.)

When Faulkner left the University, he and some friends, including his son-in-law and Mr. Massey, set up the William Faulkner Foundation, which among other benefits to young writers offers an award each year for a "notable first novel." The judges were to be chosen, in order to keep it an award of youth, out of the English Department from men not above the rank of instructor. The first year it was given to John Knowles for *A Separate Peace*.

I met Mr. Knowles at a small dinner after he had been given the award early in 1961, and he was full of the mode of its pesentation. As he told it, Knowles was taken out to meet Faulkner at his house in the country by members of the committee on awards. They were shown into a room where they waited.

Finally Faulkner appeared. Linton Massey made the introductions and said, "Now, Bill, you're supposed to give the award to Mr. Knowles this evening at his lecture. Everyone will be there to see you do it. Miss Hale will be there—everyone."

"Aw," Faulkner was reported to have said. "I can't do that. Can't Miss Hale give it to him?"

"No," Massey said firmly. "You have to. Suppose you just give it to him now."

So, Knowles said, Faulkner took hold of the award—a bronze plaque—walked across the room, and said to him, "Here you are, sir."

Linton Massey felt it necessary to explain. "He's been really feeling quite ill," he said. "And he had a fall out hunting three days ago."

Later Mr. Knowles said to me, "Is Faulkner always like that?"

"No, I don't think so," I found myself saying. "Only when he's being a writer." I had gone away to spend the summer in New England when Faulkner died in 1962—not at his Virginia home but on one of his visits back to Rowan Oak. Besides all the obituaries and editorials I read in the Northern papers, friends sent me clippings from the Southern press about the death of America's foremost writer. One clipping that was a little different was sent to me by my husband a few weeks later.

It is from the Charlottesville *Progress*. At the top is a picture of two men and two women who are sitting, in hunting dress, on a board fence. The caption explains that the riders have just returned from a long hunt last season. Underneath, a headline reads Faulkner Memorial Trophy Established. The story begins as follows:

"A William Faulkner Memorial Trophy Award has been established by the Buck Mountain Riding Club and will be awarded to a junior rider at the club's annual fall horse show.

"The award will go to the junior rider who has exhibited over the past year the keenest interest in riding to hounds, horse shows, and who has shown good sportsmanship at all times.

"Faulkner was a charter member and was director of the riding club since it was founded in 1959. Each year a junior rider will receive the memorial award—an engraved silver trophy."

Reading not from left to right, but from right to left, the riders in the picture are a Mrs. Samuel Wells—large and hearty-looking in black velvet cap, dark coat, and light breeches, her booted legs propped close together on one of the boards of the fence. Next comes the locally famous Grover Vandevender—riding instructor, jobber of horses, and professional huntsman of the Farmington hounds; he is a huge, heavy-faced man who peers into the sun from under his huntsman's cap, wears what is obviously hunting pink, and holds a long huntsman's whip. His black-booted feet, too, are propped side by side. Beside him sits Miss Mary Jordan—a little girl in a bowler hat, black coat, white breeches, and black boots that she has crossed at the ankle because they won't reach down as far as her elders'. She is looking pleased as Punch to be out seeing life in the hunting field.

Down at the far end sits William Faulkner, smaller than the girl, tiny as a child. His legs, unlike all the others', are spread out expansively, his bowler hat sits down low over his eyes, his pipe is in one hand and his whip in the other, and he looks as happy as a clam.

The winter following Faulkner's death, at a party I ran into a friend whom I hadn't seen for some time because her husband had moved from English to another department of the University. She is an intelligent and educated woman who passionately loves horses. I sat down on a sofa with her and asked her what Mr. Faulkner had been like as a person, out hunting.

"His manners are what we all remember about him," she said. "Why, some of those people never even knew who he was—never heard of him—but he'd treat them, treat everybody, with the most exquisite courtesy and consideration. For instance, he used to be the one who always stayed back and closed the gates after the hunt had gone through. Nobody likes that job. Everyone wants to get on.

"And then—it was so charming of him—he used to carry roasted chestnuts in his pockets and, when the hunt checked, he'd bring them out and offer them around. And another thing. You know Grover? Grover Vandevender? Everyone calls him just Grover. Not Will, though. He always called him Mr. Grover."

"How good was Faulkner as a horseman?"

"He was—well, middling. He was always breaking his bones. But we *all* take falls in the hunting field. He was older than most of us, maybe his bones were more brittle. What I remember about Will was how he never pulled his rank. Why, he even gave *me* a signed copy of *The Mansion* one day, because I'd said I liked it. I guess he saw how deeply I meant it.

"But he was perfectly lovely even to the phony people," she went on. "Why, Mrs. C—has a complete set of everything Will wrote, that he signed especially for her. And she is about as phony a woman as I know—so rich, so common, so show-off."

"But she does hunt," I said. "What do you suppose it was he loved so about hunting?"

"I wish I could tell you. It gets us all. I was talking about just that the other morning when I was out with the hounds, and riding along with Ellen and Kate. I said I ought to be home looking after my children and tending to the house, and instead here I was, and just wild to be here, too. I don't know," my friend said. "Hunting's got everything. It uses your pride, and it uses your humility, and it uses you ability to defer to others, and it uses your leadership, and it uses your self-reliance, and your—. Well, I guess it's a microcosm of life. Like skiing. Or sailing."

"Or writing," I said.

Faulkner Talks to Reporters about Integration, Virginians

Ted McKown / 1957

From Charlottesville *Daily Progress*, February 15, 1957. Reprinted by permission.

William Faulkner, Mississippi-born winner of both the Nobel and Pulitzer prizes in literature, told reporters in Charlottesville this morning that he feels racial integration of schools in the South is inevitable.

"As I see it," Faulkner declared, "the white man had better take charge of it (Integration) and control it, rather than have it thrust on him."

Faulkner said he thought the Negro "will have to" achieve equal status in the South, because "the only alternative to progress is death."

"The two races will never live forever separate except by choice. The law can't force it." But he added that he felt it would be folly to "just give" equal rights to the Negro. "He has to be taught that he must earn the responsibility and right to be equal."

Faulkner, who arrived in Charlottesville Tuesday will spend most of the current school semester here working with students at the University of Virginia as the first writer-in-residence under a new University program. He met with reporters this morning after a session with his first class, a graduate class in American literature.

Faulkner told reporters he had accepted the English department's invitation to come to the University "because I like your country, I like Virginia and Virginians." The publicity shy writer added, "Virginians are all snobs, and I like snobs. They spend so much time being snobs, they don't bother you."

Asked what his first reaction to teaching was, Faulkner said, "I'm terrified at first because I'm afraid it (class discussion) won't move." He said his first concern was that everybody might be wasting their time sitting there, "but once it begins to move it's all right."

Any contribution he might hope to make to prospective writers here, Faulkner said, "would come out of my experience as a craftsman in contact with the desire of young people to be craftsmen." Out of 100 students there may be one who would get some value out of his being here, he said, and that if there was one, he thought that would be good.

Questioned on his reaction to the opinion that his picture of the South is "utterly revolting," he said his picture may be revolting, but was not intended to be revolting to anyone. "I am simply using the tools I have to show the fundamental truth of the human heart—man in his eternal conflict in himself—which is the only thing in my opinion worth writing about." He said he was writing about people and not Mississippi or other places.

Faulkner said he considers the measure of a writer's greatness, not the accomplishment of a work, but "the splendor of the failure" to attain his individual dream—"the courage with which they attempted the impossible."

Listing the greatest American novelists on the "most splendid failure" basis, Faulkner placed himself second. Thomas Wolfe, he said, was first, Dos Passos third, Erskine Caldwell fourth, and Hemingway fifth. It was his rating of several years ago, unchanged.

He named as writers he thought may have achieved their goals, Cervantes, Dostoevsky, Marlowe, Shakespeare and possibly Hugo. Asked his opinion of Henry James, Faulkner said he thought James was "a prig" except for this short novel *The Turn of the Screw*.

Moby Dick was one of the greatest single books in American literature, Faulkner said, but he did not name what he thought was the greatest. He also named *Huckleberry Finn*. "While *Huckleberry Finn* was a completely controlled effort," he said, *Moby Dick* was greater because it was "too much for one human being—an attempt that didn't quite come off."

Faulkner said he was not familiar with contemporary young writers, because "like most writers as they get old, I've stopped reading coeval books." He said he preferred to read about people [rather] than ideas.

Asked the importance of a college education for a writer, Faulkner said it would differ with different writers, but he added college "can't make a writer that wouldn't make himself." He said, "no man can write if he's not a humanitarian," and "anyone who spends too much time on style has long since ceased to be a writer."

On his own urge to write, Faulkner said by nature he was a lazy man and that writing is work, but "I do it because it simply won't let me rest in peace." He said that he had written for years "before it ever occurred to me that a stranger might read the stuff," and that he still does not write with a reader in mind.

On critics, "No writer is impervious to criticism, but some may be afraid to listen to it." He said he did not know as he had ever listened to a critic, but that he had been influenced by everything he ever read "from the telephone book on up."

Faulkner in '57

Syed Ali Ashraf / 1957

From *venture*, 1 (March 1960) , p. 13–17. Published by the Department of English, Karachi University, Pakistan.

When the state department informed me that Faulkner had agreed to see me I was thrilled because I had expected a flat refusal. But when I reached the department of English of the University of Virginia where he was an Honoury Fellow the secretary of the department told me that there must have been some mistake. "Faulkner!", she looked up with surprise, "he doesn't see anyone." I didn't budge. I held to my guns, I showed her my itenerary and impressed upon her the fact that I was not following a will o' the wisp but had taken the trouble of coming all the way from a distant land not to be refused like this; could she possibly inquire? "Don't you see! If he has given 10 A. M. as the time, he should have been here? There must be some mistake somewhere."

However, on inquiry it was found that Faulkner was babysitting for his daughter with whom he was living in Charlottesville and who had gone out shopping leaving the grandfather in charge of his fond grandchild. He came at 11:10, a short-statured, shy, reserved man. He walked in very quietly and unostentatiously. I could hardly recognise him, he was much better-looking than his photos and portraits. But there was something cold in him, a touch of aloofness, as if he was afraid that his citadel of defence might be invaded by unforeseen enemies. I was afraid my interview might prove a complete failure and probably I would have to walk out after a few minutes of excruciating boredom for both of us.

I followed him to his room all the time thinking how I should begin. He was an honorary Fellow of the University of Virginia at that time. He had no teaching duty; he could come and go as he pleased; give any lecture he would like to give; meet students and admirers and discuss any literary problem with which he was vitally concerned for the moment. Anything but himself; he was not ready to talk about himself; that was his reputation. I was literally afraid like Prufrock.

However, the ordeal had to be faced and for me, thank God, it was no ordeal. Faulkner did not prove intractable, unsympathetic, irresponsive, rude

or shocking or boring. Edgar was probably right. Professor Edgar Finlay
Shannon, who is at present the President of the University of Virginia, told
me the next day that probably his one year's stay at Virginia had made him
more sociable and ready to talk. Whatever the cause, I didn't find him as
intractable as he was painted to me by others though he was definitely shy
and not so ready to talk or discuss problems as I would have liked him to be.

It was a pleasant day: the 19th of April. The garden week of Virginia
would begin on the 20th: a week of enjoyment for the public who would be
allowed to enjoy the beauty of private parks and gardens. It was rather warm
for the time of the year. Faulkner drew his chair by the wide window which
he had pushed up to let in fresh, wholesome breeze.

I started by thanking him in the usual manner for having granted me this
opportunity of meeting him and talking to him about some of the problems
that a creative writer was facing in our days. The society, for example, was a
confused mass of so many values and standards. Faulkner himself, I pointed
out, appeared to be rather "cynical" (was it the right word?) on occasions.

All the while I was speaking he was looking down at the floor. He suddenly
looked up now and said, "I am an optimist, but I am not an optimist who
thinks that man is a noble and good creature, that he has a bright and glorious
future. No. I feel that sometimes man wants to be better than he fears he will
be. To his surprise he is sometimes better than he thought he would be, more
compassionate than he thought he could be. Man is capable of being better
than he is afraid he will be. Sometimes he thinks he can't be better than what
he is. Sometimes he doesn't want to be better than what he is. But in moments
of crisis he is surprised to find himself doing what he never wanted to do,
what he thought he was incapable of doing."

"That means you believe in the essential good nature of man. That is your
philosophy?"

"No", he replied, "I'm not a philosopher. I'm not a visionary. I've nothing
to preach."

I didn't remind him that he had preached at least once. When he went to
collect his Nobel Prize from Stockholm he told the august gathering which
listened to him surely with rapt attention, "I believe that man will not merely
endure; he will prevail. He is immortal . . .because he has a soul, a spirit
capable of compassion and sacrifice and endurance. The poet's, the writer's
duty is to write about these things. It is his privilege to help man endure by
lifting his heart, by reminding him of the courage and honour and hope and

pride and compassion and pity and sacrifice which have been the glory of his past."

He seemed to be in a different mood now. He again asserted, "I have no philosophy. I write about the human heart in conflict with itself, its fellows, with its environment."

He kept quiet for a few seconds and added, "I write from my observation, experience and imagination, I believe everybody does so. I've no preconceived idea. I think of people. I want to make them live."

His sentences were brief, crisp, painted and emphatic in spite of his quiet monotone and even voice.

"May I get this idea straightened, Mr. Faulkner?" I said. "Is it not true that these experiences have given you a broad, general idea of human life and character and that you adhere to certain values, certain fundamental standards? Actually that is what I meant by 'philosophy' or 'vision'. I don't say that you are a 'visionary', but you have organised your experiences according to certain pattern, certain ideal, haven't you?"

"It is men and women that matter," he replied, "the characters. I don't write the stories. When the characters come alive, they write the stories themselves by behaving as they should."

When I pointed out to him the organising master-mind which the critics have tried to discover in his stories and novels he just dismissed the idea with a slightly contemptuous tone. "They find a lot of things which I never imagined I had put in or which I never thought about when I was writing. The critics may be right. But my duty is to write."

"Why do you write then, Mr. Faulkner, if it is not to express your ideal, your vision of life or your total, organised view of reality?"

He came out with an answer which I had never expected. "I write" he said, "because I want to excel Balzac, Dostoevsky and Shakespeare."

"Which is the most favourite of your novels?"

"None because none is as good as Dostoevsky's or Balzac's novels or Shakespeare's dramas. I don't want to write as good as they wrote. I want to excel 'me. I've no favourite. I'm not satisfied with any of 'em, None of 'em is good enough to suit me. But I go on writing because I hope some day I may produce something which will excel their works."

"I'm definite then that you enjoy writing."

"No, " he said with emphasis, "I don't like writing, I like thinking 'em out. There's no machine to record thoughts, that's the trouble. Writing is a tiresome job."

"What do you like doing then!"

He stopped for a few seconds and slowly said, "Farming, I suppose. I'm a farmer by profession. I've bullocks, horses, farmhouses—all sorts. I like moving in the field."

"But you don't do the ploughing, do you?"

"I've some people to work for me. But I go to the fields and I like doing manual labour."

"You said you've some people. Negroes?"

"Oh, yes."

"May I know then, Mr. Faulkner, what you think of this segregation problem? Do you think the whites are justified in supporting segregation?"

He avoided giving a direct reply. "It is our fault," he said. "We've always been generous to individual negroes who have reared us up but we've never thought well of the negro community. I had a negro mammy who taught me manners, who taught me courtesy. How can I forget that? If they are backward it's because we did not teach them to go ahead. It's our fault. We shall have to suffer for that."

His voice was charged with feeling therefore I did not like to continue this discussion. I did not know at that time that he had to suffer from severe attacks from a large number of people because a few months earlier he had asked the negroes to stop fighting for the abolition of segregation in schools and had identified himself with the conventional southerner. However, as he appeared to be deeply conscious of the fault of the whites I did not like to ask any more questions on that topic. I requested him to autograph a few of his books which I had with me.

He demurred and then said, "You've come from such a long distance that I don't like to refuse you. I'll autograph only one. My publisher doesn't want me to autograph books because he sells some autographed copies at a very high price. However, I'll surely autograph one of these for you. Which one shall I autograph?"

"Any one of these or rather whichever you prefer."

"I've no preference."

He hesitated for such a long time that I chose *A Fable* and he autographed it.

People had warned me that Faulkner would not like me to take his snaps but when I asked his permission he readily allowed me to take his photo. When we went downstairs, Edgar Shannon came down with us and he took our group photo. I told Faulkner of the pleasant surprise I had when I came to know that he was the same Edgar whom I had met at Oxford seven years ago. Faulkner then wanted to take our group photo. I settled everything and handed the camera to him. He just clicked it and immediately handed it over to me as if he disliked it.

"What's the matter?" I asked.

"Nothing. It's the machine. I hate machines. I'm afraid of 'em."

He smiled, the first time during the hour and invited me to visit him at his residence in the evening. But as I had some other programme which I had to attend to I had to forgo this visit though I know I would have enjoyed this evening with him.

I returned to my hotel and when I reached my room I suddenly became conscious that all the while I was thinking of his smile. It was so sincere, sudden and unexpected. I was always trying to imagine something which had made a similar impression upon me. As I entered my room I realized what I was seeking. It was the smile of an innocent village-farmer.

Hard, Fast Rules for Writers: Truthfulness, William Faulkner Tells High School Students

Daily Progress / 1957

From Charlottesville *Daily Progress*, May 8, 1957, p. 17. Reprinted by permission.

Novelist William Faulkner told prospective journalists and writers at Albermarle High School this morning that the one "hard and fast rule" every writer must follow is truthfulness.

"I will never put on paper and release something that I do not believe is true," the Nobel Prize winner in literature said.

Faulkner spoke to two groups of about 60 to 80 students each at the high school's annual Careers Day program. The program brought representatives of about 30 fields to speak to the students.

Asked what the most important things to a journalist are, Faulkner said "Take it you have the grounding in grammar, what you need is the practice in people."

He said students should train themselves in "insight into people, to know why people do what they do," and "to catch people in action at the interesting point."

"People are capable of infinite change. That's what makes anyone want to be a journalist or writer, to write about people, because of the infinite variety," Faulkner said.

"Don't ever get over being curious, wanting to know what you didn't know yesterday," the novelist warned his audience. He listed things important for a writer as "never to judge people, to listen, to watch, to probe, wonder what is the truth behind this action . . . patience, compassion," He later added "One quality a writer has got to have is a demon. He's got to be demon-driven."

Faulkner said he had done newspaper work in New Orleans in his earlier writing days, but never with the intention of taking up journalism as a profession.

Asked how he got into newspaper work, Faulkner said "I like to write, and

I lived in the French quarter there, and I would see strange things . . . and I began to write those pieces and I sent them to the editor."

Other Faulkner commentary:

On his education: "I didn't like school and I quit in the sixth grade. School in those days moved too slow for me . . . and I would have liked to have gone to a good college."

On style: "Any writer who has a lot to say, hasn't got time to bother with style."

On his own long sentence structure: "It comes from the constant sense that one has that he only has a short time before he is going to die."

On his own opinion of his best novel: *The Sound and the Fury* caused him "the most anguish and trouble" and was "the most beautiful failure."

On life: "It's best always to have something a little beyond our reach to work for; then you can always be happy."

Faulkner Meets His Local Readers

Magdalen Andrews / 1957

From Charlottesville *Daily Progress*, May 16, 1957, p. 17. Reprinted by permission.

William Faulkner met his local reading public for the first time yesterday as Charlottesville residents crowded into Rouss Hall at the University of Virginia to hear him read one of his stories and answer their questions.

Faulkner told those present that they were his "best readers." He said that the nicest thing that can happen to an author is to meet and talk with his readers. This is the first time that the general public has been invited to hear Faulkner, who is at the University this semester as writer-in-residence.

Those who missed yesterday's program will have a second chance when the novelist repeats the program May 30.

The author's comments about his audience stemmed from a question about critics. Faulkner said he didn't know the critics and he didn't read what they write. However, he said the critics may find some symbolism in the author's works which the less erudite author did not intend, because both write from the same cultural background.

The professional writer can call his "own shots," at least in his own case, Faulkner said. He said he never did any serious work for television or films because "either one is a compromise" with others involved in the production. "It's just a pleasant way you could get a pay check every Saturday night."

Commenting on other contemporary authors, Faulkner opined that *The Old Man and the Sea* is Hemingway's best work because "he found God . . . Before, he was working in a vacuum." Faulkner predicted that Hemingway's work will get better if he continues writing, "something not all writers can say."

Steinbeck's best work is still to come, Faulkner said.

As he gets older, he reads less and less, Faulkner told his audience, and he has not kept up with the younger generation of writers. But since "they come to see me," he is acquainted with many of them.

Listing some of his favorite reading as *Don Quixote, Madame Bovary, Brothers Karamazov, Anna Karenina*, some of Conrad, all of Dickens and the Old Testament, Faulkner said he had about 50 books "I go in and out of" like seeing old friends. The writer, he continued, is influenced by everything he reads, including the telephone book. He is "immoral" in that he takes what he finds in books, but he is willing to reciprocate to others.

The writer of fiction is not too interested in ideas, the novelist said, any more than he is in facts. His interest lies in people. The author who is satisfied with his work faces the writer's worst possible fate, he said. "Then nothing remains to the writer but to cut his throat."

"I'm lazy," he told his audience, and "I don't like to write." He said when the "demon" won't let him rest, he writes 12 to 14 hours a day for a time and then doesn't write again for months. He said he starts with an anecdote, actions or characters. "Then they take charge of the story. All I have to do is trot along behind with a notebook." He reported that he never did any research or outlining.

Asked about his "brooding concern for humanity" mentioned by a recent critic, Faulkner told the questioner to ask the man who wrote the article. He said people "are the most interesting thing on earth" and man must be concerned if he is to advance.

"A writer is a writer from the time he begins to observe, long before he begins to spell," according to Faulkner, who said that each story commands its own method of telling.

Faulkner reported that he never saw the Greek production of *Requiem for a Nun* because he did so much "running around" and talking to people.

The writer is as pained as the reader over man's injustice as portrayed in his novels, Faulkner told a questioner. He admitted that there are "not as many idiots in Mississippi as in my books, probably" when he was asked about the mental imbalance so often found in his work.

Leaving the topic of writing for the Negro in the South, Faulkner said the "white southerner loves Negroes as individuals but not in the mass." He said the Northern white loves Negroes in the mass, but is terrified of him individually. He said the present situation must change because "you can't have 17 million second-class citizens." He said the Negro wants political, economic and educational equality and won't want to mix with "white folk."

"I don't think anything scientists cook up in a laboratory is going to do away with man" Faulkner said in answer to a question about the present dim view of the future of the human race.

The 40-minute question period followed his reading of "Two Soldiers," a short story published in 1942.

Faulkner Says Negro Must Learn Responsibility

Ted McKown / 1958

From Charlottesville *Daily Progress*, February 21, 1958, p. 15. Reprinted by permission.

Mississippi-born author William Faulkner told a University of Virginia audience last night that the Southern white man must teach the Negro the responsibilities of first class citizenship—and the place for this to begin is Virginia.

The Negro must be taught, he said, "that in order to be free and equal he must first be worthy of it, and then forever afterward work to hold and keep and defend it."

The Negro's status as a second class citizen may come from an inability or unwillingness to accept first class responsibilities, Faulkner said.

"He must learn to cease forevermore thinking like a Negro and acting like a Negro. This will not be easy. His burden will be that, because of his race and color, it will not suffice for him to think and act like just any white man; he must think and act like the best among white men . . . Where the white man, because of his race and color, can practice morality and rectitude just on Sunday and let the rest of the week go hang, the Negro can never let up nor deviate."

The Nobel Prize winning author, who is beginning his second period as writer-in-residence at the University, read a prepared address before about 350 members and guests of three student societies packed in Peabody Hall.

His address, entitled "A Word for Virginians," is to be published in full in the *University of Virginia Magazine*. It has been copyrighted by Faulkner. Portions of it were released to the press last night with his permission.

The meeting was sponsored by the Raven Society, Jefferson Society, and Omicron Delta Kappa honorary society.

Faulkner said Southerners must teach the Negro responsibilities "either by taking him into our white schools, or by giving him white teachers in his own schools until we have taught the teachers of his own race to teach and train him in these hard and unpleasant habits."

"And the place for this to begin is Virginia, the mother of all the rest of the South," the Mississippian concluded.

"A hundred years ago the hotheads of Mississippi and Georgia and North Carolina would not listen when the mother of us all tried to check the reckless and headlong course. We ignored you then, to all our grief, yours more than any since you bore most of the battles. But this time we will heed you."

Faulkner told his audience, "It is easy for the North to blame on us, the South, the fact that the problem is still unsolved. Nor will it help us any to remind the North that, by ratio of Negro to white population, there is probably more of inequality and injustice there than with us."

"Instead we should accept that gambit. Let us say to the North: All right, it is our problem; we will still solve it."

"For the sake of argument let us agree that as yet the Negro is incapable of equality for the reason that he could not hold and keep it even if it were forced on him with bayonets; that once the bayonets were removed, the first smart and ruthless man, black or white, who came along would take it away from him because he, the Negro, is not yet capable of, or refuses to accept, the responsibilities of equality."

Faulkner said, "Whether or not (the Negro) ever learns his A-B-C's or what to do with common reactions won't matter. What he must learn are the hard things— self-restraint, honesty, dependability, purity; to act not even as well as any white man, but to act as well as the best white man."

"If we don't . . . we will look forward each year to another Clinton or Little Rock, not only further and further to wreck what we have so far created of peaceful relations between the two races, but to be international monuments and milestones to our ridicule and shame."

After reading his address, Faulkner spent nearly an hour answering questions from the audience.

Asked what program of education he recommended, he said he believes that "schools for all should raise their standards and become so tough that the boys and girls in them won't have time to care about who sits next to them."

The student who fails in school should be given a test, he said. "If he fails the test he goes to a trade school. If he fails there he goes to the Army."

"I mean by that that education should be a privilege. People should be willing to walk four or five miles to go to school. Nobody should be forced to go to school who doesn't want to," Faulkner said.

"It seems to me to improve education we got to get some folks out of the schools, not get more in them."

Faulkner told the gathering, "It is too late to curse the day when the first slave was sold in the South. It is equally futile to continue to go against the law and the courts which say that the Negro must have equality . . . That's like living in Alaska and being against snow."

Faulkner said he does not expect changes in the status of the Negro in the South to come quickly. "It will be 50 years at least, before (there is) the kind of integration that the NAACP talks about—if it ever does come." He said the Negro is impatient for equality, not integration.

"All the laws of the world won't make the white and Negro mix if they don't want to mix, just as all the laws of the world won't keep them apart if they don't want to be kept apart . . . The Negro doesn't want to mix with the white people anymore than the white people want to mix with him. He just wants the right to decide not to mix."

At the beginning of his talk, Faulkner invited questions and criticism. In his English Department office at the University he is a writer-in-residence, he said, but outside the office "I'm just a Mississippi citizen that admires Virginia and Virginia people, even when they may not like what I'm going to say."

"I'm free game. But flush me first; don't shoot me sitting."

Through Faulkner's View-Finder

Howard Thompson / 1958

From New York *Times*, March 16, 1958, Section II, p. 7. Copyright ©
1958 by The New York Times. Reprinted by permission.

A surprisingly slender man, he sat in the campus restaurant fingering an incongruous martini. For behind William Faulkner, all the sound and fury of Yoknapatawpha County seemed to tower in silent, ghostly guard. Farther back, crouched a gallery of Hollywood ghosts, for the Nobel Prize Winner from the Deep South also has a rather quiet but impressive record as a scenarist.

"I'm always glad to do anything I can to help Jerry Wald," he said after rising gallantly for a courteous handshake. Mr. Faulkner was referring to a West Coast friend, whose new Twentieth Century Fox production, *The Long Hot Summer*, was derived (not by the author, however) from *The Hamlet*. The world-renowned writer is currently a guest seminarist at the university here [Princeton].

How many scripts had the author himself penned? "I reckon about a dozen in all. I first went to Hollywood right after *Sanctuary* was published back in 1934, because I knew Howard Hawks (the producer)—a huntin' man and a broken down aviator like me. He sent for me—called me at home in Oxford. I said to him, 'Now why the hell should I go out there? Here I am—I had $6,000 from the book—with more money than any man in the state o' Mississippi.' Later on I went, though. He'd bought one of my short stories, 'Turnabout' and I helped make it into my first picture. 'Today We Live' with Gary Cooper, Joan Crawford and Franchot Tone. That was Tone's first picture too—and I still think he owes me a good 5-cent cig-ah."

The bemused expression and the brisk clip of his rather high-pitched, softspoken voice suggested that Mr. Faulkner might yet collect that debt.

"Most of my pictures were done for Hawks. He sent for me later on to help adapt what Ernest Hemingway said was the worst book he ever wrote, *To Have and Have Not*. Then I did another one, from the book by Raymond Chandler, *The Big Sleep*. I also did a war picture, one I liked doing, *The Road To Glory*, with Fredric March and Lionel Barrymore. Then there was the one about the Pharaohs, three years ago. (*Land of the Pharaohs* featured probably the most staggeringly spectacular construction of the Pyramids ever filmed.) Hawks and my self and Harry Kurnitz (a fellow scenarist) cooked that one up—mostly Kurnitz."

Was cash the principal inducement? "Well, I made me some money," he said presently, pulling out a pipe and lighting it, "and I had me some fun. Those were the pictures I enjoyed doing the most, probably my best ones." Another pause. "Bogart was a fellow I always liked out there; I did several of his. All told, let's see—I worked at Fox, M-G-M, Warners. And Columbia—that's where I knew Wald."

He was asked for his reaction to Metro's version of his *Intruder in the Dust*, made at Oxford, which this newspaper deemed great. "I'm not much of a moviegoer," he said quietly, "but I did see that one. I thought it was a fine job. That Juano Hernandez is a fine actor—and man, too."

Yet it hadn't made money. "I know. The industry don't know how to sell what the public doesn't want. Wald has that—he seems able to balance the not-want with the does-want. *Peyton Place* might be a good example of that, as a moneymaker—no, I haven't seen it. One I did see recently was my *Pylon* (*The Tarnished Angels* generally shellacked by reviewers). Thought it was pretty good, quite honest. But I'll have to admit I didn't recognize anything I put into it." (The book, not the script.)

Noting that Mr.Wald owned screen rights to his *The Sound and the Fury*, Mr. Faulkner said he had always thought "a story I wrote about a marooned woman and an old convict" might also make a good film. "A kind of involuntary adventure story. That's right—'The Old Man.' "

What about the recent, drastic box office slump? "Could be that the industry had conditioned the public and now has to pay for it. Some good pictures come from out there—God knows how, but they do. One of my favorites was *Citizen Kane* and *The Magnificent Ambersons*—and *High Noon*, whatever became of that? Television? You don't say. There's all you need for a good story: a man doin' something he has to do, against himself and against his environment. Not courage necessarily."

Asked to predict the screen's future as an American art form, Mr. Faulkner just looked—one of the calmest, most penetrating gazes south, or north, of the Mason-Dixon Line. "That's a foolish question," he chided gently. "Like askin' me about the improvement of punctuation. I can tell you this, though; people will always want to communicate with other people. And will— whether it comes from a camera or words on paper or singin' or dancin' or pantomime. I've never had much confidence in my capacity as a scenarist. It ain't my racket. I can't see things."

Not even Yoknapatawpha County? "Nope, I can't see," he insisted. "I can only hear."

Faulkner: Advice to a Young Writer

Daily Princetonian / 1958

From *Daily Princetonian*, March 19, 1958, p. 2.

(Editor's Note: The following is an excerpted, condensed text of a conversation which author William Faulkner had with a Princeton undergraduate last week. This interview was one of a dozen or so talks the Mississippi author had with students interested in writing.)

Keep it amateur. You're not writing for money but for pleasure. It should be fun. And it should be exciting. Maybe not as you write, but after it's done you should feel an excitement, a passion. That doesn't mean feeling proud, sitting there and gloating over what you've done. It means you know you've done your best. Next time it's going to be better.

Remember, you're writing about people. Not about Princeton University or the clubs, but about people. About man as he faces the eternal truths of love, compassion, cowardice, protection of the weak. Not facts, but truths. You're going to write about truth: man as he comes into conflict with his heart.

Don't make writing your work. Get another job so you'll have money to buy the things you want in life. It doesn't matter what you do as long as you don't count on money and a deadline for your writing. You'll be able to find plenty of time for writing, no matter how much time your job takes. I've never met anyone who couldn't find enough time to write what he wanted.

Don't be "a writer" but instead be *writing*. Being "a writer" means being stagnant. The act of writing shows movement, activity, life. When you stop moving, you're dead. It's never too soon to start writing, as soon as you learn to read.

That's the best way to learn how to write, from reading. Study what other people have written. Watch how they're writing about people, not facts or ideas. The real truths come from human hearts. Don't try to present your ideas to the reader. Instead, try to describe your characters as you see them. Take something from one person you know, something from another, and you yourself create a third person that people can look at and see something they understand.

The best time to stop writing is when you're hot. When you know you've got it and it looks the way you want it to, that's the time to stop. Leave it when its hot and then come back to it the next day.

Don't worry about symbolism or style or plot. There are only three plots anyway: money, sex and death. Never forget you're writing about people. Maybe they're not in such a new situation, but maybe you can see them in a different light. Maybe the way you describe them will help other people see the truth that way.

If you enjoy it, if it comes out the way you wanted it to, then you've got a chance. If you don't enjoy it, if it doesn't come easy, if you get tired and don't think it's worth it, then you know you better not write.

Better not spend too much time thinking about what you're going to write. Start in writing now or you may never get started.

It's all right to have a simple plot. Just make sure you say everything you want to say. And don't tell merely what happens to people. Show how the events affect their lives later on. That doesn't mean describing what happens later, but just making the present action an experience which is part of them and which is going to make them into the kind of people they later turn out to be.

I usually build around one quick action that is sharp and definite. Then I show how it affects people and how they react to it. Write about man's conflict with himself and with his fellows.

Remember you're writing about people. Do the best you can and try again the next time. Write because it's fun. Don't write for money. Then if it's fun and if what you write about people can be seen by others as truth, maybe you'll wind up making money.

Faulkner Answers Student Questions at University of Virginia Session

M. Thomas Inge / 1958

From Randolph-Macon College *Yellow Jacket*, May 23, 1958, pp. 2, 4.
Reprinted by permission of the author.

A smiling, complacent man, followed by a quiet, unassuming white-haired gentleman, entered room 202 of Rouss Hall of the University of Virginia on May 12, 1958, at 4:05 p.m.

A large group of students, gathered from all over the state, became quiet and centered their attention on the elderly gentleman. With proud air, his companion briefly introduced the gentleman as "the world's greatest living novelist."

After a period of silence the audience began a question and answer session with William Faulkner, and the following are his answers to the questions asked:

Q: Throughout our education we are taught to adhere to certain rules of punctuation and sentence structure in formal writing. Do you believe that adhering to these rules in any way restricts the style of the writer?

A: I would not say it restricts the style. The writer must adopt the best method for saying what he wishes to say. Any work to be good must be alive and fluid and if this can be done within rules, fine.

Q: What authors influenced the humor in your writing?

A: Humor is not influenced by anything that we read. Humor is an attitude of optimism toward man's predicament, a point of view toward man and his dilemma. Taking man's predicament too seriously is not good for anyone.

Q: What is your attitude toward the Negro?

A: He is only looking for the chance to be equal. The Negroes' position to change must be for the better. The Southern attitude toward him has changed since I wrote *Intruder in the Dust*, but the only alternative to change is death.

165

Q: What do you think of the movie's treatments of good books?

A: I do not believe that the movies can change or harm the novel if the author has done his best. If the book is good, nothing will hurt its reputation.

Q: What are your main sources of information?

A: Personal experience (which includes the books I have read), observation, and imagination.

Q: To what factors do you think the success of your work is due?

A: I always keep to myself an amateur. Success to me was not important; I wrote only because it was fun. I didn't care whether anybody bought it or not. Success is peculiar. If you beg and plead she scorns you. If you show her the back of your hand, she will cling to your knees.

Q: Do you deliberately use symbolism in your works?

A: The writer does not purposely use symbolism but does it instinctively. The writer is like a carpenter. When he needs a tool, he just leans back and gets a tool he thinks will work. He does not sit and think of which to use.

Q: What is man's predicament?

A: He wishes to live in a world where he can do the things he wants. He wants to live in peace and simplicity with little or no suffering, but unfortunately the world has tragic elements.

Q: How will the South be able to pull up her boot-straps?

A: Education. We should try to arrange it so that the best get the best education.

Q: Do you think a young writer's work is of any value?

A: The young writer is under pressure to try to belong to something. But by the time he reaches thirty he will overcome that. He will or should use that previous age as experience. I think that talent is important, but the writer should have three things: ruthlessness, insight, and industry. And he must always be curious as to why man does what he does.

Q: Why are you not as well read in the South as in the North?

A: Everyone in the South has no time for reading because they are all too busy writing.

Q: Do you think that your last book is the best?

A: None of them are good enough to suit me, but I will keep on trying. Perhaps if I live another hundred years I may yet do it.

Q: What do you think of the movies and plays based on your books?

A: I have only seen one, *Intruder in the Dust*, and I thought it was pretty much like the book. I seldom get to the movies.

Faulkner Looks Back on Happy Year at University of Virginia

Beverly Orndorff / 1958

From Richmond *Times-Dispatch*, May 24, 1958, p. 4. Reprinted by permission.

"If you were the last man on earth, would you still write?" a reporter asked novelist William Faulkner at a press conference here Friday.

"Yes, I would," the Nobel prize winner replied dryly. "When a writer passes through the wall of oblivion, he will even then stop long enough to write something on the wall like 'Kilroy was here.' "

He added that a writer would write "even if he had to pay for the privilege of writing . . . even if it was burned up as soon as he wrote it. A writer isn't interested in communication. He wants to make something that wasn't there yesterday."

The press conference followed Faulkner's last public appearance at the University of Virginia as writer-in-residence. He read a selection from *The Sound and the Fury* and answered questions from the audience.

If he takes up permanent residence in Charlottesville, "it'll take a certain amount of doing," he said in reply to a question. "I would have to sell out in Mississippi. It's so far in the future it couldn't be called a plan but more of a hope."

"Both Mrs. Faulkner and I like it here and have been very happy here, and it's not a bad place to spend the next 60 years," he said.

"I could use this last hour to thank all the people of Albemarle county and Charlottesville, but I won't," Faulkner said. "I won't even say goodby. Every individual is the sum total of his past . . . I leave something here—where Faulkner was happy—and I'll take something of Albemarle county with me. But I will come back from time to time so those two separates can be joined together again."

Last year at his first press conference, Faulkner described Virginians as snobs. Asked whether he still thought this of Virginians after living among them for about a year, he replied, smiling:

"That was sort of thrown off in a moment of relaxation, but I do mean it as a certain kind of snobbery. They don't meddle, and this is an admirable quality. They know they're all right and when they accept me, it's because I'm all right, too."

One person asked if he minded Hollywood's treatment of his books when they are turned into movies.

"When I've finished a book, I've done the best I could," Faulkner replied, "and every now and then, I like a little money myself, so they're welcome to do what they want because they can't harm it."

Asked what he predicted for the South, he said: "I imagine that someday man will outlive the South."

Visit with the Author

Newsweek / 1959

From *Newsweek*, 53 (February 9, 1959), p. 6. © 1959 Newsweek, Inc.
All Rights Reserved. Reprinted by permission.

It had taken Faulkner's play [*Requiem for a Nun*] seven years to reach Broadway, and on hand for the opening last week were his daughter, Jill, and her lawyer husband, Paul D. Summers, Jr., but not Faulkner. The world's most reticent author was busy shooting quail back home in the sage-deep meadows piney woods of the tiny college town of Oxford, Mississippi.

To a visitor who dropped in for a friendly drink at the author's Southern mansion set in a grove of pine trees, Faulkner refused to talk about his play, which he has never seen performed (or even rehearsed) in English.

Faulkner was very dressed up for a man who likes to consider himself a farmer: a soft brown tweed sports jacket with leather patches on the elbows, slacks, vest, white sweat socks and rubber-soled shoes, and—unexpectedly—a necktie. He confessed that of late he has been wearing a black derby hat, which he regards as "part of my hunting costume," and which he wears also when he goes out to dinner.

As he sipped bourbon, Faulkner talked of many things, nearly all deeply personal: Mississippi politics, daughter Jill, hunting, Virginia, segregationists, and the rumor that he planned to sell his house. *About that real-estate rumor:* "I wish whoever circulated that story would find me a place in Charlottesville. I'd like to have a farm up there." *About hunting:* "I still get birds, of course, but one thing I've noticed—I can't shoot as fast as I used to. Right now I'm looking forward to the fox-hunting in Virginia." *About the "massive resistance" movement in Virginia:* "I think it is about to crumble. When the time comes to choose between integrated schools and no schools at all, the South will have to choose schools."

Why didn't Faulkner attend *Requiem*'s Broadway debut? "After all, I wrote it," was the author's reply. "I've seen it twice, in German and in Greek. I'm not going to interrupt the bird season to see it again."

Faulkner fashioned the play expressly for actress Ruth Ford, whom he had first known back in the '30's when she was a student at the nearby University of Mississippi. "Bill wrote the play for me," explained Miss Ford in New

York last week, "because I asked him to. Perhaps one reason a Broadway production was delayed is because I went with it, and I'm not a star name.

"And then they read the reviews and the box-office statistics of some fourteen foreign-language productions. I think our play is the *clean* version- I mean, it's stripped down to the real meat of Faulkner. After all, this is the play as he worked on it himself. And he'll come up to see the play, too, when he's ready," the actress added confidently.

It was a complete surprise to Ruth Ford when the first published version of the play came out last week with the following Faulkner inscription: "A play from the novel by William Faulkner, adapted to the stage by Ruth Ford."

William Faulkner—Visitors Not Welcomed

Joe Hyams / 1959

From New York *Herald Tribune*, April 28, 1959, p. 18. Copyright ©
1959 by The New York Times. Reprinted by permission.

Almost every town has its celebrity, but in Oxford, Mississippi, the town
celebrity is also a world-renowned figure. He is William Faulkner, the Nobel
Prize winning novelist, and I am told, every visitor to Oxford tries to see
him, despite Mr. Faulkner's well-deserved reputation for being unavailable.
Although I was here to cover the location filming of M-G-M's *Home From
the Hill*, I felt, like all visitors, that it would be a shame to be in Mr. Faulkner's home town and not talk with him. So I began to ask townspeople working in and around the film how I could get to see Mr. Faulkner.

For the benefit of any other journalists or tourists who may come to Oxford, I have assembled all the information I received under the heading,
"How to Meet William Faulkner."

First, almost everyone in Oxford claims to know him, but actual closeness
of "friends" can be determined by their nicknames for him. Intimate friends
call Mr. Faulkner "Pappy." Just plain friends call him "Bill," and people
who have met him only casually refer to him as "Mr. Faulkner."

Every one in Oxford knows his phone number. Every taxi driver knows
where he lives, but, according to people who refer to Mr. Faulkner as
"Pappy," it's a waste of time to call on the phone for an interview or go to
the house because Mrs. Faulkner will say he's out. "Pappy doesn't like the
phone," I was told. "The boys even have a hard time getting him for poker."

It is also a waste of time to write for an interview because "Pappy" holds
mail up to the light and if there's no check in it, he throws the letter away.

The easiest way to meet Mr. Faulkner, I was told, is to stand across the
street from the Cathcart Reed drugstore in the heart of Oxford from 2:30 to
3:30 any afternoon. Mr. Faulkner usually comes to town at that time. After
shopping, he stands outside looking into space and puffing on his pipe.
"Leave Pappy be for about fifteen minutes, then go up and introduce yourself," I was told.

If I missed him at the drugstore I was told to ask any taxi driver to take me to "Miz Maude." "Miz Maude" is Mr. Faulkner's ninety-two-year-old mother who is an excellent painter and I could tell her I wanted to buy a painting. Mr. Faulkner usually visits his mother in the afternoon and I could "just happen to be there." I was told if I turned left the instant I entered Miss Maude's door, I would be in the living room where I was to quickly admire the paintings on the wall, one of which is of Mr. Faulkner. Perhaps that would spur Miss Maude into talking of her son.

In the event that I actually confronted Mr. Faulkner I was told not to expect him to say anything. "If he does talk to you—by some miracle—just know he talks soft and don't dare ask him to repeat anything," I was told. I also was warned that Mr. Faulkner won't discuss his "works," his private life, and under no circumstances was I to mention his play, *Requiem for a Nun*.

"Pappy might talk about his early days in Hollywood. He will certainly talk to you about segragation, that is, if he'll talk at all."

"Thank You" Is Remembered, and the Simple: "I Write"
Christopher Paddock / 1961

From *Faulkner Newsletter & Yoknapatawpha Review*, 4 (April–June 1984), pp. 1, 4. Reprinted by permission.

I met Faulkner with not too much advance notice, in the spring of 1961, when I was serving as Spanish-English interpreter for a group of Bolivian law students who had been invited to participate in a six-week seminar at the University of Virginia.

One evening, the organizer of the seminar, Professor Marion Kellogg, announced that the group would have the opportunity to meet William Faulkner the next morning. I was to do the interpreting for this session.

The next morning, Faulkner and I were seated at a small table at one end of a large lounge. I still remember some of the questions the group asked him:

Who are your favorite contemporary authors?
Faulkner: I do not have any. I only read the classics. However, there is one Latin American work that I read every year: *Doña Bárbará*, by Rómulo Gallegos.

Of your own works, which is your favorite? Faulkner: Authors are always fondest of the work they are writing or have just finished. But your books are like your children. Just as a parent has a special relationship and affection for a sick child, the one that he has stayed up with and suffered with, so it is that a writer has a special love for the book which, though it is weak, cost him a lot of work and suffering. For me, that work is *The Sound and the Fury.*

Mr. Faulkner, what did you think when they told you that you had won the Nobel Prize?
Faulkner: I was very surprised. I never imagined that things that I had written in the fury of my solitude would find an echo in so many human hearts.

At about this point, Professor Kellogg cut the session short. The professor was a very large man. Faulkner was a small, almost bird-like figure, with a ruddy face, a finely-shaped, somewhat aquiline nose, and penetrating eyes. Professor Kellogg lifted Faulkner out of his chair and, with his heavy hand on his arm, marched him through the crowd toward a door at the other end of the long lounge. Everyone got up and followed behind them. I remained, awed, at the little table where we had been sitting. Just before going through the door, Faulkner stopped, removed the professor's hand from his arm, and returned alone all the distance to where I stood. "Thank you," he told me. "What you do is very difficult, and you did an excellent job."

That night, I was invited with the group to the home of a wealthy Charlottesville hostess. Faulkner was announced by the butler at the head of the stairs descending into the salon. He entered and walked over to where I stood in a small circle of people that included the hostess.

Politely, she turned to him and said, "Mr. Faulkner, how very nice, and what do you do?"

I looked at Faulkner and felt my heart sink.

He glanced at me quickly and unflinching, turned to the hostess, and replied simply, "I write."

Visit to Two-Finger Typist

Elliott Chaze / 1961

From *Life*, 51 (July 14, 1961, pp. 11–12.

For a long time I'd hoped to write a story about a fellow Mississippian, William Faulkner. I wanted to do a plain and unpretentious little piece on Faulkner the man. I'd read a number of magazine yarns about the 63-year-old Nobel Prize winner, and in each of these the interviewer sounded awe-struck, almost frightened, and full of literary soul-searching. My account would be light and rather humorous. After all, here was a man who, despite his stature as a writer, must bicker with his children, get his thumb caught in the sink, cope with an aging gall bladder. Or so I had thought before actually laying eyes on him.

I tried half a dozen times to arrange an interview while Faulkner was at his home in Oxford, but one of his daughters told me he wouldn't talk on the phone to a stranger. In the summer and fall, however, he is a resident writer at the University of Virginia in Charlottesville, and that is where I finally found him.

I caught up first with another of his daughters, who also lives in Charlottesville. She directed me to her father's home but said, "I can't guarantee you success. I can only tell you where to find him and you'll have to tackle him and take your chances. It will depend on his mood, whether he liked his breakfast, you know."

I followed directions and arrived at a two-story brick Georgian house. There was a dusty little red Rambler station wagon with a Mississippi tag parked in the driveway. The front door of the house was open, and I could hear the clack of a typewriter, a steady two-fingered whacking. It occurred to me as I pressed the bell that I hadn't expected William Faulkner's typewriter to sound so commonplace. In fact, I'd never thought of it making any kind of noise at all. It seemed shocking that any manual labor, no matter how mild, should be involved in his transfer of thought to paper.

I thumbed the button again, a cool sweat tickling my ribs as the typing faltered, then ceased. He materialized quietly in the doorway, absolutely composed and motionless as a photograph. I had the feeling I was staring at a picture on the dust jacket of one of his books.

"I'm sorry," I said. "I'm sorry to interrupt you this way."

He inclined the fine gray, almost white, head, as if he agreed that I should be sorry. He spoke in a soft, patient voice, the words barely moving the gray mustache: "Whom did you wish to see, sir?"

"Ah, you, sir," I said foolishly, feeling flustered. "I drove a thousand miles to see you."

This seemed to make him almost sick at his stomach. He winced. Just a flicker of a wince. I explained that I was from Hattiesburg, a fellow Mississippian, and that I had tried to telephone him but had been told he wouldn't answer the phone.

"That's right, sir." He stood now unblinking in the doorway. "What is it you want from me?"

I tried to explain, but the sun was beating down on my head and I was tired and my eyes burned from the long trip and I'm afraid I jabbered. I said that I'd always admired him and suspected that some of his short stories were the best of the very best and that one of them, a piece about a little boy who followed his big brother to an Army induction center, was the most moving thing I had ever read. I said another one which was mostly an account of two women chasing a mule out of a yard was more exciting to me than Hemingway's bridge-dynamiting stuff and how could a writer do so much with a mule and two women?

He sighed, studying me thoughtfully. "You come on in and we'll see what we can do to help you."

In the living room he sighed again and sat on a couch. He began stuffing his pipe, very slowly. He motioned me to a chair. "I have no patience with a certain kind of interview," he said. "The kind where a man comes to me and asks me to say something that will interest his readers. That kind of thing is grotesque, you must realize it."

As I sat opposite him I realized why so many writers had failed. You interview Faulkner on his own terms, if at all, and you would no more ask him about his gall bladder than you would pinch the tip of his elegant nose. He is a tiny man of enormous dignity. He radiates a kind of quiet strength. The feeling of quiet is the primary impression, it is in the voice, the movement of the hands, the way he walks, the controlled glitter of his almost black and hooded eyes.

"So," he said, sipping at the stem of his pipe, "just what, specifically, do you want?"

I cackled uncertainly, abandoning once and for all the brash business of

178 Conversations with William Faulkner

sink and gall bladder, casting around for any plausible excuse to extend the interview. "I just want to write about the way you work," I said. "You know, your working schedule, the tools . . ."

He uncrossed his legs and sat up straighter on the couch, growing and growing. "Why no, no sir," he said, "I wouldn't tolerate that at all. I figure it's nobody's business but my own. You mean, sir, you wish to follow me around and write down everything I do?"

"Oh, no," I cried out in anguish. "Not that, not exactly that." Watching him grow, seeing how he sprouted from that couch, I felt hopelessly impaled on the moment, like a bug beneath glass.

"I could not tolerate that," he said calmly.

I waggled my head. "Of course not."

I asked him about his job as resident writer. What did it mean to be a resident writer?

"There ain't much to it," he said. "There really ain't much to it. You just live here some of the time and you walk around and people see you and say, well, there he is, there he goes. I don't have any kind of an office at the University and I give no lectures. Once in a while I meet with a large group and answer questions about writing. If a man has a problem, some specific question about writing I will try to help him. But like I say, I will not talk just to be talking."

He said that the idea of living part of the time here in the rolling foothills of Virginia appealed to him because he loves horses and dogs and likes fox hunting. Every morning around 6 o'clock he arises and drives to his stables on the edge of town, rides for an hour or more before returning to the house for a shower, breakfast and work. "There is something about jumping a horse over a fence, something that makes you feel good. Perhaps it's the risk, the gamble. In any event it's a thing I need."

He sets himself no regular work schedule at the typewriter. "If you feel you have to write 10 pages a day, it takes the fun out of it and the work suffers. Writing is hard work but it should be fun, it always has been to me. I've never felt any other way about it. I'm an amateur writer, I'm not a literary man."

What, then, is a literary man?

Faulkner considers that a literary man is someone who is preoccupied with the idea of writing for "the benefit of literature, a thing I've not done."

This, of course, is subject to argument, but you don't argue it with Faulkner in his own living room. It is plainly no pose with him. He believes a literary man must select carefully everything that he writes or says. He says that people know how he himself feels in this regard and every time he opens his mouth they don't expect him to come out with something magnificent. He can say, for instance, "Pass the potatoes," and no one is unduly disappointed.

"Your writing life and your regular life are separate things and should remain separate," Faulkner said. "Because writing is a thing born of the imagination and confined largely to the imagination. Of course a writer is going to write, that goes without saying, and the only thing he can do when the demon's on his back is to write it off.

"In the beginning, before a writer has made his stake, he must have another job to sustain him, or he must be a tramp who doesn't give a damn how he lives.

"I don't believe there's anything to this idea that a writer does better if he can go off in the woods somewhere and hole up away from the world. I think that if his stuff is any good it will be good in a hole in the woods, but it would have been just as good anywhere else. And if it's bad, it will be as bad in a hole in the woods."

What about the writer who claims he can't sell anything because his stuff is too uncommon to appeal to the masses?

"I've known a few writers and never have seen one whose stories were too *good* to be published. This, of course, is a very comfortable attitude and no doubt serves its purpose. But you may be certain that with all the bad stuff being published these days, the really good things are bound to sell. It is inevitable. You can't fail with truly good writing, it will surely reach the public. There's nothing to the mute, inglorious Milton business."

As Faulkner spoke in low tones, the voice almost inaudible at times, a few decibels above a whisper, but not weak, only quiet, he paused occasionally to stare into the glowing bowl of his pipe. The pipe seemed a part of his hand. "Financial success is not likely to hurt a writer who is a writer, because you see he never produces the perfect story of his dreams. He may satisfy other people but not himself. And every morning he has something to wake up to, every morning of his life, another chance to try for that perfect story. A carpenter may build the flawless house and a bricklayer may raise the perfect wall, but with a writer it never happens and he must keep on with it."

I told him that many citizens of my town claimed to know him and that a remarkable number professed genuine palship with him. They even recalled exchanging profound truths with him while attending Ole Miss back in the days when he fired boilers and studied there.

Faulkner smiled, the mustache not smiling with him because it is a full one and does not join in a smile. "I don't believe the good people of Mississippi ever will understand how a man can sit in the shade and make $30,000 for defacing a few scraps of paper (the Nobel Prize paid that amount). In Mississippi the people work for their money and you can understand how they feel about writing, why it puzzles them. In Mississippi a man goes out in the sun and sweats for his dollars."

Is Faulkner now working on a novel?

"I always say no in answer to that question. I never say yes."

"But are you?"

"No."

"I heard you typing a while ago, it sounded like two fingers."

"It was, it always is."

"Index fingers?"

"Yes."

"Would you mind if I took a look at your typewriter, you know, just looked at it so I can say I've seen the machine you use?"

"No use to look, it's my youngest daughter's. I don't like to lug my old portable back and forth between Charlottesville and Oxford. She lets me use hers when I'm here." He said his typewriter at Oxford probably is one of the oldest in the country, about 40 years of age and still in working order. "I don't need anything fancy for these two fingers. It will last as long as I need it, I guess."

In the light of the opening moments of his receiving me, I should judge that he had not liked his breakfast worth a damn but was not one to bear the meal a lasting grudge. He had obviously softened when convinced of my sincerity, stupidity and appalling optimism. Mr. Faulkner, by any standards a fine-looking creature, can look colder and kinder than any living human in my experience, and it may be said accurately that I saw both sides of the coin.

Before leaving him I remembered suddenly the pipe I'd brought as a gift. I explained that I'd broken it in some time ago, then quit smoking and there was no use wasting it if he didn't mind a secondhand pipe. I said that any germs on it must have perished months ago, and he reviewed this information without evidence of revulsion. "I thank you, sir," he said. "It's a fine pipe, indeed, and I appreciate it."

"Will you smoke it?"

"Certainly."

He held the pipe in his hand and suddenly it looked quite different, very dark and quiet and right, as if it had found the kind of home all good pipes deserve. I had the feeling the pipe was impatient for me to be gone with my unimportant red face and jittery questions.

"I hope you've gotten what you came a thousand miles to get," Faulkner said as I departed. "That's a long way."

As I moved across the driveway past the little red car with the Mississippi tag, he called out. "Good luck to you." It was the only time I heard him raise his voice.

Faulkner at West Point

Joseph L. Fant, III, and Robert Ashley / 1962

From *Faulkner at West Point*, ed. Joseph L. Fant, III, and Robert Ashley (New York: Random House, 1964), pp. 48–122. Reprinted by permission.

Transcript of questions and answers following a reading from *The Reivers,* April 19, 1962.

Q: Sir, in your address upon receiving the Nobel Prize you said it was the writer's "privilege to help man endure by lifting his heart. . . ." How do you believe that you have fulfilled this task in your work?

A: It's possible that I haven't. I think that that is the writer's dedication. It's his privilege, his dedication too, to uplift man's heart by showing man the record of the experiences of the human heart, the travail of man within his environment, with his fellows, with himself, in such moving terms that the lessons of honesty and courage are evident and obvious. I think that that's the reason, possibly, the poet, the writer, writes. Whether he's successful or not is something else. Probably the only reason the poet ever writes another poem is that the one he just finished didn't quite serve that purpose—wasn't good enough—so he'll write another one.

Q: Sir, I'd like to know, out of all the works you've written in your time of writing, which one do you personally consider to be your best, and what leads you to this decision?

A: That goes back to the answer I just gave. I think that no writer is ever quite satisfied with the work he has done, which is why he writes another one. If he ever wrote one which suited him completely, nothing remains but to cut the throat and quit. And in my own case, the one that is closest to me would be the one that failed the most, that gave me the most trouble. So no writer can judge what he thinks is the best. It's like the mother with the child who is an idiot or born crippled—that that child has a place in the heart which the hale, strong child never has. That may be true of any writer, that the one that's closest to him is the one he worked the hardest at—the failure which was the most painful failure. So I'd have to answer that question in the—which is the one that cost me the most anguish and that I still don't like the most, which is one called *The Sound and the Fury.*

Q: Sir, you said that, if you had fulfilled your ambitions as a writer, the only thing would be to cut your throat and quit. Do you believe this is the reason that Mr. Hemingway died? Sir, do you believe that he killed himself for this reason, or do you believe that his death was an accidental death?

A: No, I don't. I think that Hemingway was too good a man to be the victim of accidents; only the weak are victims of accidents unless a house falls on them. I think that that was a deliberate pattern which he followed just as all his work was a deliberate pattern. I think that every man wants to be at least as good as what he writes. And I'm inclined to think that Ernest felt that at this time, this was the right thing, in grace and dignity, to do. I don't agree with him. I think that no man can say until the end of his life whether he's written out or not. Probably that occurs to almost everybody at some time, that he has done his best, that this is when he would like to write *finis* to his life. I think that Hemingway was wrong.

Q: Sir, in your novel *Absalom, Absalom!*, what is your purpose in relating Colonel Sutpen's story through Quentin Compson—to reveal the character of Quentin, to portray merely Sutpen, or to just portray the South?

A: The primary job that any writer faces is to tell you a story, a story out of human experience—I mean by that, universal mutual experience, the anguishes and troubles and griefs of the human heart, which is universal, without regard to race or time or condition. He wants to tell you something which has seemed to him so true, so moving, either comic or tragic, that it's worth repeating. He's using his own poor means, which is the clumsy method of speech, of writing, to tell you that story. And that's why he invents involved style, or he invents the different techniques—he's simply trying to tell you a story which is familiar to everyone in some very moving way, a way so moving and so true that anyone would say, "Why yes—that's so. That happens to me, can happen to anybody." I think that no writer's got time to be drawing a picture of a region, or preaching anything—if he's trying to preach you a sermon, then he's really not a writer, he's a propagandist, which is another horse. But the writer is simply trying to tell a story of the human heart in conflict with itself, or with others, or with environment in a moving way. Does that answer?

Q: Sir, what is your opinion of the value of modern literature, of the writing about woman's suffrage and confusion of roles as present in modern literature?

A: I look on them as the tools, the material of the trade; that is, they are the conditions which the writer can use in order to portray the human heart in some simple struggle with itself, with others, or with its environment. The sociological qualities are only, in my opinion, coincidental to the story—the story is still the story of the human being, the human heart struggling. To be braver than it is afraid it might be, to be more honest, to be more compassionate, to be nearer the figure that we mean when we say God than it thinks it might be. This integration, segregation, or the sociological conditions are simply tools which the writer uses in order to show the human heart in the struggle of that dilemma—in the battle which is any story. It's the—the individual meets a crisis, does he lick it or does it lick him? That's all any story comes to.

Q: Sir, once again in your Nobel Prize speech, you stated, "Our tragedy today is a general and universal physical fear so long sustained by now that we can even bear it. There are no longer problems of the spirit. There is only the question: 'When will I be blown up?' " And I wonder, sir do you feel that our generation today, the generation we're living in right now, is getting out of this feeling of "When will I be blown up?" less than we were, say, in 1950, when you gave this speech? Do you feel our literature is showing this?

A: I think that the young people have really never believed in that statement, that that was the condition of—a universal condition which is supported more by the older people, that the young people who have felt the same toward the beauty and passion of being alive that I felt when I was twenty-one years old, still feel it. But when I was twenty-one years old, we didn't have that general pessimistic, middle-aged feeling of "When shall I be blown up?" which seems to be in the world today. I don't think it's going to stop anybody from being poets; it's just too bad you've got to carry that load. And that didn't refer to the young people—the young people don't care what the old folks think.

Q: Sir, based on what you just said, do you consider that the present world situation is likely to infuse a new spirit of nationalism into American literature?

A: If a spirit of nationalism gets into literature, it stops being literature. Let me elaborate that. I mean that the problems which the poet writes about which are worth writing about, or composing the music, or painting the pictures are the problems of the human heart which have nothing to do with what race you belong to, what color you are—they're the anguishes, the passions, of love, of hope, of the capacity, the doom of the fragile web of flesh and bone and mostly water, of which we are in articulation, must suffer, stuck together by a little electricity and a world of mostly coincidence, that we can endure it all. Yet there's something in us that makes the individual say, "My anguish is beautiful, it's meaningful," so he writes the poem, he composes the music, he paints the picture not to prove anything, not to defy his fate nor his circumstance, but simply because there is something that is so true and so moving in breathing that he has got to put it down, got to make a record of it. You might say that what drives every poet and writer—he knows that in a short time, three score and ten years, he must pass through the last and final oblivion into nothing, that he is at least going to leave on that wall the scrawl "Kilroy was here." His belief is that his own passions are important, and we must all agree with him. If our own passions, our own problems are not important, then there is no reason to be here. What do we get out of being here?

Q: Sir, I would like to know who your favorite author is.

A: Well, that's a question that really don't make much sense to a writer because the writer is not concerned with who wrote, but what he wrote. To me, anyway, the character, the book is the thing, and who wrote it is not important; and the people that I know and love are Don Quixote, and Sarah Gamp and some of Conrad's people, a lot of Dickens' people, Balzac's people, but not Balzac especially, because I think some of Balzac's writing is bad writing. Some of Conrad's writing is bad writing, but some of Conrad's people that he created are marvelous and endured. So I think that—true of any writer—that he looks on the book and not who wrote it, not who made it.

Q: Sir, in many of your works you deal with perversion and corruption of men. How do you feel this uplifts your readers, exemplified in courage and honor?

A: Well, the easy answer is, it may show them what I don't think they should do, which is easy and glib and meaningless. I think that the reason is that one must show man; the writer, the painter, the musician wants to show man not in his—not when he's dressed up for Sunday, but in all his phases, his conditions; then the very fact that to see man in his base attitudes, his base conditions, and still show that he goes on, he continues, he has outlived the dinosaur, he will outlive the atom bomb, and I'm convinced in time he will even outlive the wheel. He still has partaken of immortality, that the aberrations are part of his history, are part of himself, maybe. But within all that is the same thing that makes him want to endure, that makes him believe that war should be eradicated, that injustice should not exist, that little children shouldn't suffer.

Q: Sir, you say that all works of literature arise from a passion and an agony of the heart. Let's say that you start your life on a river with passion and beauty and agony and, as you go through your life, you are trying to find some goal. What is the path that you find easiest—to withdraw from the river and watch it course by, or to succumb to it, stay with it? Should you withdraw from your emotions or stay with your emotions?

A: I would say by all means to stay with it, to be a part of it. To never be afraid of dirt or filth, or baseness or cowardice, but try always to be better than that, to be braver, to be compassionate, but not to be afraid of it, not to avoid it. I think that the worst perversion of all is to retire to the ivory tower. Get down in the market place and stay there. Certainly, if you want to be a painter or a writer, maybe if you want to be a philosopher, a mathematician, you can get off in a tower, but if you want to be a painter, or a writer, or a poet, you can't be afraid or ashamed—ashamed of your own behavior, not of other people's.

Q: Sir, at the present time, you seem to have great optimism for the human race, but in some of your earlier writings during the period around the 1920's, this optimism was not too prevalent. Was there any period of life that changed your attitude toward the human race?

A: No, I wouldn't think so. I would say that this part of the human race which is going steadily on toward a continuation, toward that sort of immortality, are pretty dull folks. The ones that kick up and misbehave and are comic or tragic to me are interesting. But they are not the sum total of the human race. No one lives long enough in three score and ten years to be the human race; he just entered it for a little while—he was a tenant.

Q: Sir, in the light of the answers you have to some previous questions, that you believe it's the right and duty of an author to show a character in all its phases in any way that is feasible, what is your stand on present-day censorship?

A: Well, there should be no such thing as censorship. If the mind has got to be protected by the law from what will harm it, then it can't be very much of a mind to begin with. The first part of your question, can I have that again, please, sir?

Q: You stated, sir, that you thought it was the right and duty of an author to tell the story of the human heart and its problems. I wonder if you do this and if you do it as *you* see it. You may not see it as others do.

A: I didn't say it was the right and duty. I think primarily the writer, the artist, works because it's fun. He hadn't found anything that is that much pleasure. He is simply telling a story in the most moving and dramatic way that he can think to do it. He's not following any right nor any duty to improve you; he simply has seen something in the magic and passion of breathing which seems so funny or so tragic that he wants to tell you. And he is trying to tell you in the most moving and economical way he can, so that you will be moved, will laugh or cry, as he did. It's no special right and duty—when he gets involved with right and duty, he's on the verge of becoming a propagandist, and he stops being an artist then. He's doing something simply because he likes it, it's his cup of tea. He'd rather do that than anything else he knows.

Q: Sir, just where did you get the basis for your characterization of the Snopes and Sartoris families?

A: That's a difficult question to answer. The writer has three sources: one is observation; one is experience, which includes reading; the other is imagination, and the Lord only knows where that comes from. It's like having three tanks on a collector—you open the collector valve, you don't know exactly how much comes from any one tank, so no one can say just where anything comes from—whether he imagined it, whether he saw it or read it or heard it, but you can count on one thing, that the reason they call it fiction is it *is* fiction—that any writer is a congenital liar incapable of telling the truth, and so even he can never say how much he embroidered, imagined anything because he simply could not take any fact he saw and let it alone. He's convinced he can do much better than God could, so he's going to improve it—change it.

Q: Sir, it's been said that literature today tends toward atheism. What's your opinion of this?

A: I don't think so. I think that the literature of today is too much like the literature of all times, which has been the struggle, the history, the record of the struggle of the human heart. What it's struggling toward, a condition, an esoteric condition like atheism or Puritanism or integration or segregation, is not important—it's the battle the heart goes through in trying to be better than it is, to be less cowardly than it is afraid it might be.

Q: Sir, you're described, I believe, as a naturalistic writer. In America, we've progressed quite a ways in naturalism. What work, if you care not to speak about authors, would you describe as furthering naturalism most in America?

A: To begin with, I don't know what naturalism means. Can you be a little more specific?

Q: I would say, sir, that we've come a long way since before the 1900's. One of the books that I had in mind was *Sister Carrie* by Theodore Dreiser. And also, works by Sinclair Lewis, I believe, would be described as naturalistic, or naturalistic as opposed to romantic.

A: Yes, I see what you mean. I still think that the job which the writer is doing is to tell you a moving story of the human heart in conflict. I would say that Dreiser used the best material he had, the best method, the best skill he had, which wasn't very much. He was a bad writer. But he had a tremendous drive to tell you of the conflict of the human spirit. And that's what I meant by saying that I didn't know what a naturalist writer was. That to me, the writer is simply trying to use the best method he possibly can find to tell you a true and moving and familiar old, old story of the human heart in conflict with itself for the old, old human verities and truth, which are love, hope, fear, compassion, greed, lust. He uses naturalism, romanticism as the tools to his hand just as the carpenter uses the hammer or the saw which fits his hand best to trim the board, but he's simply trying to tell you the same story of the human heart in conflict with itself for the eternal verities which haven't changed too much since man first found how to record them.

Transcript of Questions and Answers during Press Conference

Q: Mr. Faulkner, now that you have completed your question-and-answer session with the West Point cadets, what are your impressions?

A: I am surprised and pleasantly astonished at the things I've found that I didn't expect to find here. I had the layman's notion that this was a stiff, regimented place where robots move to numbers, and I've found it's a little different since I've been here this time.

Q: Didn't you think they seemed very responsive in their questions?

A: I don't know whether I had a selected parade of them, but what I have found here was a—well forward of what I've found at the other schools I have seen. They were in top gear and they knew that they would need to be in top gear and they were. I don't mean racing or running ends, but they were in top gear. In Princeton and Virginia there is something a little sloppy which is not here.

Q: Are you advocating a military background, sir?

A: I'm inclined to think that a military background wouldn't hurt anybody.

Q: I am interested in and was surprised by the cadet reaction to your comment, "If a spirit of nationalism gets into literature, it stops being literature." What made their reaction rather surprising was the fact that their predecessors from this institution, in certain cases, behave as though they think nationalism is a great virtue. Apparently the present student body doesn't.

A: Well, they didn't believe nationalism was a great virtue while they were here. It's only after they got out that they became Edwin Walkers—years after here.

Q: About the young people today compared to your life when you were a youth, do you feel that there's any significant difference?

A: No.

Q: Do you despair of juvenile delinquency?

A: No, there are just more juveniles than there were in my time; they are not more delinquent.

Q: Did you say more juveniles, sir, or more juvenile?

A: There's more juveniles, but they're not any more delinquent.

Q: One of the questions asked was about the younger generation's feeling of getting blown up and whether that feeling had changed since you commented on it when you made your address on winning the Nobel Prize.

A: Well, I still feel that people wonder when I'm going to be blown up, but I still think that ain't very important.

Q: You've advised getting down out of the ivory tower and into the market place. In moving about the market place these days, what distresses you most about contemporary life?

A: You'll have to explain that. I don't know exactly what you mean.

Q: Just generally about contemporary life. Or perhaps what do you despair of most in contemporary life, in moving about the market place?

A: I don't despair of any of it.

Q: What delights you most?

A: What I like best is fox hunting.

Q: The cadets asked also about the perversion and corruption in your novels and how, by this means, you feel that you're uplifting your readers. How is that possible, Mr. Faulkner?

A: Only in—that seems to be a part of the knowledge of human behavior which the artist uses in order to tell you a moving and tragic story of the human heart in conflict with itself, and we assume that the purpose of that conflict is to win even if you have to die with your head still bloody but unbowed.

Q: You repeat that over and over with no embarrassment whatsoever. Is that the one credo that you state over and over again?

A: I would say so, yes. I am convinced that man in time will abolish diseases. It may take a long time, but in time he will abolish war. But I still think he will endure. I think that the last sound on this worthless, fleeting earth will be two people arguing about where they are going next.

Q: Do you find as a writer who has by all means "arrived" that you read as much as you used to?

A: No.

Q: What do you read now?

A: I read the books that I knew and loved when I was twenty-one years old.

Q: Can you tell us some of them?

A: Yes, I go back to the people, not the books—but the people. I like Sarah Gamp—she's one of my favorite people—and Don Quixote. I read in and out of the Old Testament every year. Shakespeare—I have a portable Shakespeare I'm never too far from.

Q: Is this a form of criticism of contemporary writing or writers?

A: No, it's the glands—the mind has slowed down a little and it don't like new things. It likes the old things just like the old man wants his old shoes, his old pipe. He don't want a new one—the new one's better, he realizes that, but he don't want it. He wants the old one.

Q: And you're simply not interested in contemporary literature, is that it?

A: Not enough to keep up with it. When somebody says, "Here's something you ought to read," I read it. And quite often it's good.

Q: Do you think there are any "up and coming" writers?

A: What do you mean by "up and coming" ones?

Q: Well, are there any good young ones?

A: I am sure there are, that they are still writing. They still must be writing, in Russia and behind all the bamboo and iron curtains.

Q: In our country?

A: I'm sure they are, yes.

Q: Are there any you would recommend?

A: Not until I've read what they write, and I haven't read a—I can't think of a contemporary book I have read in the last, well, since Salinger's *Catcher in the Rye.*

Q: Did you enjoy that?

A: Yes, it was a good book. It was a tragic story of a young man that tried to enter the human race and every time he tried it, it wasn't there. It was a very sad and tragic story.

Q: Was *The Reivers* something that you had wanted to write for a long time?

A: Only the story of the human heart in conflict. Until you have written a perfect one and cut your throat, you keep on trying to write that story.

Q: It's very funny!

A: I think so too. It's one of the funniest books I ever read.

Q: Did you have a good time doing it?

A: Yes, delightful. I wish I hadn't written it so I could do it again.

Q: Mr. Faulkner, do you especially like the scene where they were caught on the road and had to be pulled out by the two mules?

A: Yes, ma'am.

Q: Do you find that writing gets any easier as time goes on? Your writing?

A: I can't answer that question. If you know what you want to say, it's easy to put it down, so I don't know how to answer your question. You mean does it get easy to know what to say? No! No easier, no harder. Some days you know exactly what you want to put down and you put it down—other days you don't.

EN 152: The Evolution of American Ideals as Reflected in American Literature 7:55 A.M.–8:50 A.M., April 20, 1962

Captain James R. Kintz, Assistant Professor of English, USMA: Perhaps I should mention, Mr. Faulkner, that this course is not a survey of American literature; it is a course which explores American ideals as they are reflected in our literature. Recently we have been discussing how the Depression influenced the writers of the early thirties.

Mr. Faulkner: Just so none of the gentlemen expect any conclusions, definite conclusions, about American literature from me—I'm not a very literary man. But I remember the Depression.

Q: Sir, we've read your work "Turnabout." In it you added an additional part to the end. We noticed in your novel, from which you read last night, that you employed this same technique. Is this technique done to emphasize a certain part, or to summarize, or simply to express a new idea in addition to the work?

A: No, it's done simply through a need. The writer feels that he has got to do this much more in order to underline, emphasize the story he's telling, which, in essence, is simply the story of people in the battles which you constantly face to get through being alive. That's a matter of style, and I am convinced that the story you tell invents its own style, compels its style. That these are not really tricks; they look like tricks and the writer can use the same trick again, but he's not using it because it is a trick—he uses it because it works.

Q: Sir, I was wondering, in the story "Turnabout," there is the young British boy, Midshipman Hope, who actually played World War I as sort of a game—he and his colleagues would count "beavers" every time they'd see a net on a mast, while the American, Captain Bogard, was actually quite conscientious about the war and realized war for what it was, at least he seemed to. Yet the young English boy was killed and the American was not. I wonder if there were actually any conclusions we were to draw from this as to the attitudes that we should have toward the subject of war.

A: No, only the Englishman was only about eighteen or nineteen years old; he should, in normal times, still be in school. The American captain was a mature man—twenty-five or twenty-six. It was not a different attitude—national attitude—toward war; it was a different attitude because of age—of youth and something of maturity. If it showed anything, it showed that possibly the man who was mature might know more how to survive war than a child might. I don't think the story set off to postulate that, but that might be a possible definition of it.

Q: Well, sir, going back to one of the questions that was asked last night, in your acceptance speech of the Nobel Prize you said, "Our tragedy today is a general and universal physical fear so long sustained by now that we can even bear it." And going a step further, in your short story "Turnabout," you picture the American captain in one of the last scenes dive-bombing on a German target, and he wished that all the kings and all the presidents—in effect, all the leaders of the world—were there so that he could wipe them out. Do you feel that this universal fear of this problem in the world today is a cause of our leaders?

A: I don't believe you quite finished—that this universal fear is a cause of our leaders—now finish that. I don't think I understood quite what you meant. That the universal condition has produced the leaders we have, or has compelled the leaders to be not good leaders—which do you mean?

Q: Well, sir, that's what I wondered, actually what you meant. You brought out the fact that we have this universal fear, and then in the story "Turnabout" you create a war situation and you have this American captain, who in effect had everything to live for—he had had a good life in America—and you have him dive-bombing on a German target and hoping in his own mind that he could wipe out, or wishing in his own mind that he could wipe out, all the kings and generals and presidents. In other words, sir, are the leaders responsible for war?

A: Well, I wouldn't say that, but the leaders are responsible for the clumsiness and the ineptitude with which wars are conducted. War is a shabby, really impractical thing anyway, and it takes a genius to conduct it with any sort of economy and efficiency. I think this man at that moment was—had done the thing that all soldiers in battle at some time have done—to have cursed all the high echelons that got all of us into this to kill some of us. That was something that at that moment he could feel, but it would not be a conviction of his that he would keep always—just at that moment.

Q: Then sir, this was a universal feeling of the heart that you were bringing out.

A: Yes, that's right. Any soldier would feel that toward the brass safe back in the dugouts and the chateaux that didn't have to run those little boats, or didn't have to ride the aircraft low enough to bomb the chateau.

Q: Sir, last night you stated that the basic goal of an author was to portray the conflict of the human heart. Now, just what do you feel today is the chief trouble with which people are concerned, or should be, and how much has this changed since, let's say in particular, the time of the Depression?

A: I don't think it has changed at all basically. Only the ephemeral symptoms alter—they are not too important. But basically the drives of the heart are the same. It's the verities, for the verities have been the same ever since Socrates, which are courage and pride and honor—compassion. It's man's knowledge that at bottom he is not very brave, that he is not very compassionate, but he wants to be—his conscience—call it what you will, call it God, but he wants to be better than he is afraid that he might be—that he might fail, yet he still tries. I think that is shown in the people that portray incredible

courage in battle; that man is fighting too, yet something—we don't know
what it is—drove him to do what he himself didn't believe he could; that
people show pity—they are the verities which all the writing is about. The
temporary conditional things of the time are not too important. At this time,
in my country, the South, there is a problem of segregation and integration—
racial trouble. But they are not really important in the long view of man's
record. At other times, unemployment; at other times, women's rights—they
were important ephemerally at the moment, but not important as measured
against the passions and hopes of man's heart.

Q: Sir, you said that man's desire to be braver than he really is, more
honest and better than he is, has always been the same, and the conflicts of
the human heart remain the same. Do you think, sir, that the problems of this
age, the increased problems, will have any effect on men's ability to cope
with the conflicts within this sort of feeling, and that this will change?

A: It will, I am convinced, to this extent, that man can learn from experience. It takes a lot of it, it takes a long time, but man alone has learned from
experience to cope with environment. He's a frail, fragile collection of
nerves, and yet he has endured climate, change of temperature. He has sur-
vived all the bigger forms of life, and I think that he, in time, he will solve
his problems. I think in time he will solve the problem of atomic warfare, of
the dread we all live under of being blown up by someone who can buy an
installment-plan bomb from some Swiss manufacturer and drop it on somebody he don't like. It will take time, but I am convinced that man is the most
durable of all, that he will outlast even his evil.

Q: Sir, I am interested in this hope of man. Hemingway in his early work,
especially I'm thinking of his "Snows of Kilimanjaro," pictures man as
someone who is disillusioned, who has no real hope, no life to him. Yet in
his later work—I'm thinking of *The Old Man and the Sea*—he pictures man
as someone with life, with faith, with hope, and with resolution. It seems
strange to me that he would kill himself after he seems to have regained a
faith in man. I was wondering if you know any possible reason why, after he
seems to have regained his faith, he would then decide to take his life.

A: The only reason I would undertake to guess would be that every writer
wishes to reduce the sum of all experience, of all the passion and beauty of
being alive, into something that will last after him. If he's the first-rate poet,
he tries to do it in a quatrain. If he's not a first-rate poet, then he tries to do

it in ten pages—he's a short-story writer. If he can't be a short-story writer, then he resorts to eighty thousand words and becomes a third-stage novelist. But he is trying to reduce the passion and beauty that he saw of being alive into something concrete that can be held in the hand, and he fails, and he tries again. I would say that there was a certain point that Ernest reached where he said, "I can't do it, no man can do it, and there's nothing remains worth staying alive for." Or he could have been sick and in pain, and I think that that had something to do with it because he had spent a lot of time in the hospital. The last time I saw him he was a sick man. But I prefer to believe that he had reached that point that the writer must reach—Shakespeare reached it in *The Tempest*—he said, "I don't know the answer either," and wrote *The Tempest* and broke the pencil. But he didn't commit suicide. Hemingway broke the pencil and shot himself.

Q: Sir, you said that the verities haven't changed since the time of Socrates. This seems to be about what you said in your acceptance speech of the Nobel Prize when you said that people are always worrying about the bomb falling on them. It seems now that people are no longer planning far ahead into the future. They think about the pleasure that they can have now because they don't think they can count on what tomorrow will bring. Do you think that this will cause any change in the basic things that we feel are moral and just?

A: Not really. That is sad and tragic for the generation that had to spend all its time, its waking time, wondering shall I still be alive tomorrow. That is ephemeral—it's too bad for them, but not too bad for the human race because the human race will survive that too. I think that in a few more years there'll be less and less worry about someone dropping that bomb, that in fifty years people will have forgotten—they won't forget the bomb, but they will have forgotten what it felt like to wonder every night when you went to sleep would it fall, would the balloon go up before you could wake?

Q: Sir, you made a lot of mention that man will survive these physical features—his environment and the atom age. Do you think that he will also survive himself and his society with respect to psychological breakdown? It seems as though there has been an awful lot of emphasis on man's mental breakdown—the people in the insane asylums, the number of divorces and suicides, and things of that nature.

A: That is, in my opinion, an ephemeral symptom of the fear which has come about through the new pressures man has invented for himself in this century. There are more nervous breakdowns because there are more things for man to worry about. Also there are more nervous breakdowns because there are more people to break down. That would have something to do with it. But man in his essence in the long view doesn't change. I like to think that he improves gradually—very slowly. The individuals enter the human race and they may break down, collapse, they may make trouble, and they are gone—their tenure is ephemeral. But man himself, in that continuation, I'm convinced, improves. In time, he will get rid of all the evils that he can't cope with—he will get rid of war and disease and ignorance and poverty in time. It may be a long time, and we won't be here to know it, but I'm convinced he will.

Q: Sir, when you feel moved by something so that you want to write about it and make a story out of it, do you write immediately and spontaneously and completely write out the whole story, or is it a gradual process? I'm interested in how you go about writing.

A: There's no rule for that in my case. I'm very disorderly. I never did make notes nor set myself a stint of work. I write while the idea is hot, and the only rule I have is to stop while it's still hot—never to write myself out—to leave something to be anxious to get at tomorrow. Since I have no order, I know nothing about plots. The stories with me begin with an anecdote or a sentence or an expression, and I'll start from there and sometimes I write the thing backwards—I myself don't know exactly where any story is going. I write—I'm dealing simply with people who suddenly have got up and have gotten into motion—men and women who are moving, who are involved in the universal dilemmas of the human heart. Then when I have got a lot of it down, the policeman has got to come in and say, "Now look here, you've got to give this some sort of unity and coherence and emphasis," the old grammatical rules—and then the hard work begins. But it's a pleasure— it's just like you get pleasure out of a hard, fast tennis game—with me, only at some moment the policeman has got to compel the unity and coherence and emphasis to make it a readable story.

Q: Sir, do you ever feel tempted to get your characters out of trouble? Once their characteristics have gotten them into some sort of trouble, do you feel tempted to help them out?

A: I don't have time—by that time, I'm running along behind them with a pencil trying to put down what they say and do.

Q: Sir, thinking of a definition that Tolstoy once had of literature—that good literature was something which taught a good lesson, bad literature was something which taught a bad lesson, and that great literature was something that taught a good lesson that was applicable to all mankind, what is your idea of such a definition?

A: I agree with him absolutely. Only I do think that the writer has not got time to say, "Now, I'm going to teach you a lesson." The writer is saying, "I'm going to tell you a story that is funny or tragic." The lesson is coincidental, even accidental, but all the good books do fall into those categories— he's quite right, I agree with him. But he himself didn't set down to write a book to teach anyone a lesson, I think. He was simply writing about people involved in the passion and hope of the human dilemma.

Q: Sir, in answer to one of the questions last night—I believe it was, "How your portraying more or less perverted characters would help uplift the human heart"—you said that if nothing else it would show that it would be a good idea not to be like these people. I wonder if you ever do portray people who are more or less perverted with the idea of presenting them as unfavorable, or do you just present them just as they are—just as a story about them in the struggle of their heart. Do you ever try to present them as either unfavorable or favorable?

A: Not really. The first thing that a writer has is compassion for all his characters—any other writer's characters. He himself does not feel that he has the power to judge, and these characters, these evils are there. In the story he's telling, it seems to him necessary and good and the best way to tell his story to use this. He doesn't advocate it, he's not condemning it, it's there, and in his clumsy way the first thing he must do is to love all mankind, even when he hates individual ones. Some of the characters I've created, I hate very much, but it's not for me to judge them, to condemn them; they are there, they are part of the scene that we all live in. We can't abolish evil by refusing to mention these people.

Q: Sir, may I ask you one more question along that line? Did you see or do you see Popeye and Joe Christmas as being similar people?

A: Not at all. Popeye was the monster. Joe Christmas, to me, is one of the most tragic figures I can think of because he himself didn't know who he was—didn't know whether he was part Negro or not and would never know.

Q: Sir, did Popeye have the same problem of not having a society to belong to?

A: Now I don't understand Popeye. He, to me, was a monster. He was just there.

Q: Sir, recently in the newspapers and national magazines, there have been several articles about government aid to the artist. I was wondering how do you feel about this?

A: Why, I would think that the artist ought to get whatever help he can get from any source. All he really needs is a little whiskey and a little tobacco and a little fun. And it don't do him any harm to have to do a little hard work for it, too, but I don't think that a little help is going to ruin the good artist. I don't think that the good artist has got to come from the gutter, either. So whatever he can get from his government, let him take it.

Q: Sir, then you don't feel that government aid might lead to, say, control of the artist?

A: Not to the good one. The good one, nobody can control him because he can't control himself. The second-rate one might be turned into a machine, a propagandist, but the first-rate one can't be—nobody can control him, not even himself.

Q: You spoke just now, sir, of first- and second-rate artists. Now how, exactly, would you separate first- and second-rate authors? Would it be by the trueness or the accuracy of the story which they are telling or just by their style—which one, or both?

A: It would, in my opinion, be absolutely by the trueness that they are telling, and I don't mean the sticking to fact because facts and truth don't really have much to do with each other. It's to stick to the fundamental truth of man's struggle within the human dilemma. He can be a bad writer, he can—I mean by that he could be a bad punctuator or grammarian—but he's still a first-rate writer if the people that he's portraying follow the universal patterns of man's behavior inside the human condition.

Q: Quite a few of the writers back in about 1900—when they would write a story such as about the meat packers in Chicago—would try to tell the story of individuals, but with a thought in mind that they saw an evil in society which should be corrected. Do you think, sir, that a writer has an obligation to try to point out through his stories an evil that he sees in a society or should he just tell a story of individuals and not try to make any generalization about society?

A: Let him stick to his story. If he feels that evil enough, he can't keep it out of the story. He don't have to make an effort to bring it in to show anyone. Let him stick to his story dealing with men and women in the human dilemma. If he feels that social evil enough, it will be there. That was the case of Sherwood Anderson and Sandburg and Dreiser and the other people writing in Chicago about that time—they were not propagandists on social evils. They couldn't keep the evil, the awareness of it, out, because it moved them as people. That was a part of their own dilemma.

Q: Sir, what do you think was the reason for the exodus of the artists of America to Europe during the time of the Expatriates?

A: Probably a restlessness or itching feet as a result of the first war. That was the first time Americans in any quantity moved around much, went anywhere. And it was the legacy from the soldiers who had gone to strange lands, seen strange customs—an unrest, an upset. I think that's all that it was.

Q: Sir, last night you said that the youth of today have the same passions and desires that youth have always had. What is your opinion of the college student of today and the trouble he seems to get into in riots and this sort of thing? In your opinion, is this just an attempt to express himself, or just what do you believe it is?

A: Well, it could be. It could be a perfectly normal impulse to revolt. The riots and the troubles that students get into nowadays are not too different from the ones they were getting into back in 1900. There are just more of them. But the riots, the desires to protest, are still the same, and I think it's a force of youth that is misdirected. Now I won't say that, because I am not too sure it does any harm. Maybe it's a good safety valve. But it's a force that, if it could be directed into another channel, it could do something a little more—well, I don't like the word productive either.

Q: Sir, along the same line, do you feel that this reaction of youth, the juveniles of today, could be a result of not living what our hearts would have us live? In other words, the conformity of today? We are expected to react to certain pressures and to lead our lives in a certain way and go through high school, get our diplomas, go through college, dress the proper way, behave in the proper way. Do you feel that the outbursts of youth are the result of this sort of constriction or restrictions?

A: I think that a great deal of it is a direct result of that. The trouble is that man is not to be pitied, but the generations of men have—can be born into an unfortunate time. I think that the pressure, the need to order the mass of humanity is a result of too many people and not enough room. If people are not more or less regimented, there won't be room for anyone to lift his elbow. And I think the young man and the young woman resents that. I would. Rightly. But, because there are too many people and less and less room, that is a condition which must obtain, and the young man and young woman must be tough enough to not let that make too much difference to him.

Q: Sir, how serious do you think the problem of world over-population is?

A: I think it is very serious.

Q: Do you have any suggestions for a solution—anything that can be done now for this?

A: Well, unless a law is passed that woman can't have but one child just like she can't have but one husband. That may come.

Q: Sir, referring back to a question a moment ago, how would you redirect the energy of youth today? Would you attempt to do it as there has been an attempt to do it?

A: I wouldn't like to see anyone attempt to direct the energies of youth. That's what Hitler did. That's what people like Hitler do. I think that there should be room for youth itself to decide where that energy wants to go instead of having to blow it off in a safety valve.

Q: Sir, what about President Kennedy's Peace Corps? Do you think that this is a Hitler-type move? I mean it is voluntary now, but they are trying to direct the energies of youth.

A: I don't believe that. I am not convinced that it will do a great deal of good, but I don't believe it will do the sort of harm that Hitler accomplished when he got hold of young people in Germany. I think that the difference is in the temperament of the German and the mixture of Anglo-Saxon and Latin and German which are us now.

Q: Sir, concerning the South and the problem of segregation—you said that you thought the human being was always improving. Do you think that in the South there is a growing feeling that a man who has the ability despite whether he is black or white should have the same opportunity to compete and to excel in a job?

A: I am inclined to think that with most people in the South that belief has been there all the time, but it's befogged by so much old, emotional inheritance that it is very difficult. It's hard for the Southerner to recognize that as simply and primarily a moral problem that has but one answer. It's very difficult to do that. It's a condition that will take a great deal of trying and trimming and fitting. It will cause a great deal more trouble and anguish. And I, myself, I wouldn't undertake to guess how many years it will be before the Negro has equality in my country, anything approaching equality. But I am convinced that the Negro is the one that will have to do it, not by getting enough white people on his side to pass laws and bayonets, but to make himself—to improve himself to where the white men in Mississippi say, will say, "Please join me." There is too much talk of right and not enough talk of responsibility in the whole thing.

Q: Sir, on the same subject of the South, what do you feel that the modern South is coming to in respect to industrialization—the movement of business from the North to the South? I would think that the tempo of life would have been speeded up somewhat.

A: Yes, it has, but then that change from the land to the town and the city is general through this country. It's not particularly unique to the South. It's only that the South is a little behind the rest of the country. But the same change is going on everywhere. In the South it will run into the old racial problems. But the same change is something that we have got to live with, to cope with. It's not Southern.

Q: How much are religion and sexual fear the basis of racial hatreds?

A: Well, there are some. But I think that basically what the people in the South are afraid of is the Negro vote. That if enough of him can vote, he will elect his own people or his own kind to office until some blackguard white man comes along and uses him again through his, the Negro's, ignorance.

The Negro must—education is actually the solution, the only one which I can see. The Negro must be taught the principles of responsibility. In effect, for the next few years the Negro has got to be better than the white man. He has got to be more honest, more moral, because his color is against him. He's got to be the one that compels the white man to say, "Please join us."

Q: Sir, we have talked today a great deal about the attitude of the American people towards war. This question is one we quite often hear around here. The question is simply, what do you feel should be the basic attitude of the American people towards the professional soldier? Do you feel that the professional soldier and a mighty army, such as President Kennedy seems to be advocating, are justified in view of the word situation, or are they merely a necessary evil or an outright evil.

A: I would say that right now and until we know better, until conditions change, they are justified and damn necessary. But all life is in a constant flux. The only alternative to motion is stasis—death. And these conditions must change. It would be nice if we had a constant new crop of leaders trained for leadership coming up as a constant new crop of military officers coming up all the time, instead of using government as a refuge for your indigent kinfolks as we are prone to do in this country. A man can't make a living any other way, we elect him to something.

Q: Sir, I was wondering about the type of government we have here in the United States. We seem to be working toward an objective we have stated in our Constitution, and we feel that this is the best form of government. We have tried to put this into other countries in Asia and in Europe, and yet they seem to fail in a great many instances. Do you think that possibly this form of government is unique to countries of western and northern Europe and the Americas and cannot be applied to countries in Southeast Asia and the Middle East?

A: I would hate to believe that. I think that our mistake is that we don't try to educate the people in the foreign countries to know enough about the sort of government that we attempt to force on them. I would not like to believe that certain people are ethnologically incapable of democracy. I would like to believe that all people are, but I do think that people have got to be educated to it. I think that we got educated to it through the hardship that we went through in the early times of our Revolution. I think that at that time we were fortunate in the leaders that came to the top were not the people like the Chinese and the Russian peoples. I don't believe that we are any wiser or more sensible than Russians or Chinese. I would hate to think that only the Anglo-Saxon is competent for democracy. It looks like it, but that's only the ephemeral condition of today, which will pass.

Q: Sir, in view of our world situation, in view of what you said about the fact that man will straighten himself out, do you feel that it should be the role of the United States to initiate a move towards a lessening of international tensions by unilateral disarmament or maybe a little closer cooperation? Do you feel that this is part of the answer?

A: I am not too sure that all the summit talks and the foreign ministers' talks ever do much good, but I don't think they do any harm. And certainly as long as people talk, they don't fight.

EN 152: The Evolution of American Ideals as Reflected in American Literature 9:30 A.M.–10:25 A.M., April 20, 1962

Q: Could you tell us, Mr. Faulkner, exactly what qualities Don Quixote has that make him one of your favorite characters?

A: It's admiration and pity and amusement—that's what I get from him—and the reason is that he is a man trying to do the best he can in this ramshackle universe he's compelled to live in. He has ideals which are by our—the pharisaical standards are nonsensical. But by my standards they are not nonsensical. His method of trying to put them into practice is tragic and comic. I can see myself in Don Quixote by reading a page or two now and then, and I would like to think that my behavior is better for having read *Don Quixote*.

Q: Mr. Faulkner, there have been several comments recently concerning your style. I am thinking specifically of your sentence structure, in which you seem to have run-on sentences consisting possibly of twenty-six or twenty-seven lines, and also of your vague pronoun references. By vague pronoun reference I am thinking of the first five or six pages of *Intruder in the Dust.* When you speak of a "he" and do not refer to the subject of this "he," I wonder if you have any special purpose in doing this, or is this just the result of the thoughts in your mind as you are trying to express your thoughts?

A: The germ of it was a special purpose—not at all to be obscure. I think that any artist, musician, writer, painter would like to take all of the experience which he has seen, observed, felt and reduce that to one single color or tone or word, which is impossible. In fact, he would like to reduce all human experience onto the head of the pin as the man engraved the Lord's Prayer on the head of a pin once. He can't do that, but he is still going to try. And the obscurity, the prolixity which you find in writers is simply that desire to put all that experience into one word. Then he has got to add another word, another word becomes a sentence, but he's still trying to get it into one unstopping whole—paragraph or a page—before he finds a place to put a full stop. The style—I think the story the writer is trying to tell invents, compels its style. That no writer has got the time to be obscure for the sake of obscurity. It's because at that moment he couldn't think of any better way to tell the story he was trying to tell.

Q: Sir, do you believe that the events in an author's life have any significant effect upon his writing?

A: I think that every experience of the author affects his writing. That he is amoral or thief, he will rob and steal from any and every source; he will use everything; everything is grist to his mill from the telephone book up or down, and naturally all his own experience is stored away. He has a sort of a lumber room in his subconscious that all this goes into, and none of it is ever lost. Some day he may need some experience that he experienced or saw, observed or read about, and so he digs it out and uses it. I don't think he gets off to suffer experience just to use it. But everything that happens to him he remembers. And it will be grist to his mill.

Q: Sir, I just finished reading *As I Lay Dying*. You stated last night that there are three things that a person, a writer, may draw upon in order to get his ideas for a story. One was imagination, another was experience, and the third was observation. I would like to know where you got the idea for *As I Lay Dying*.

A: They are people that I have known all my life in the country I was born in. The actions, the separate actions, I may have seen, remembered. It was the imagination probably that tied the whole thing together into a story. It's difficult to say just what part of any story comes specifically from imagination, what part from experience, what part from observation. It's like having—as I said last night—three tanks with a collector valve. And you don't know just how much comes from which tank. All you know is a stream of water runs from the valve when you open it, drawn from the three tanks—observation, experience, imagination.

Q: Sir, I would like to know if at present you have any ideas concerning what you are going to write in the future. Do you have any feelings that you feel you would like to put down on paper sometime in the future or that you are working on right now?

A: No, a disorderly writer like me is incapable of making plans and plots. He writes simply about people, and the story begins with a phrase, an anecdote, or a gesture, and it goes from there and he tries to stop it as soon as he can. If he can stop it in ten pages, he does. If it needs a hundred pages, it demands a hundred pages. But it's not done with any plan or schedule of work tomorrow. I am simply writing about people, man in his comic or tragic human condition, in motion, to tell a story—give it some order and unity and coherence—that to me seems tragic or funny.

Q: Sir, I would like to know if you could tell us where and when you first learned to give these stories of yours this unity and coherence and meaning. Was there some definite time of your life in which this was taught to you or you learned it?

A: I learned it by what seems to me necessity. I was the oldest of four brothers, and we had certain chores—milking and feeding and things like that to do at home—and I found pretty soon that if I told stories the others did the work. That was when I begun to dabble in fiction. And I could get boys from the neighborhood in when there was a lot of work to be done, get that done too—I sort of contracted out, you see.

Q: Do you think an American author, Mr. Faulkner, has to have another job besides writing?

A: Yes, I do. I think any author should because, if your are not careful, you'll begin to think of the work you do in terms of how much you can make. And everybody likes a little money for tobacco and whiskey and a little fun occasionally besides something to eat. And it's best to have a job so that the writer can remain an amateur all the time; never let the writing get involved with earning the daily bread. So I think that any writer should have another job, unless he is rich.

Q: Sir, in regard to the racial incidents in the last few years, such as freedom riders and school integrationists, do you believe that they have any day-to-day effect on Southern institutions, or are the Southern institutions just going to change in gradual evolution?

A: It's part of the change, and I think that any condition, situation, human living situation will have to change because life is motion and the only alternative to motion is stasis—death. It's bound to change whether we like it or not. It will change. These are the ephemeral symptoms of the unrest which take unhappy—bring about unhappy, unfortunate situations, but I don't think that they either help or impede the progress of change, which is inevitable and will occur.

Q: Sir, when you are actually putting something on paper, do you let yourself flow out freely until you, say, feel temporarily empty, or do you have to force yourself to write for an extended period of time?

A: I have, myself, one simple rule, which is to write it only when it is hot, and always stop before it cools off so I will have something to go back to; never to write myself out. But there is somewhere, whether you realize it or not, there is the policeman that insists on some order, some unity in the work. But I would say to never force yourself to write anything. Once you do that you begin to think, "Well, I might as well force myself to write something and make a little money out of it." And then you are sunk—you are gone, you have stopped being a writer. You must be an amateur writer always. You must do it because it's fun, just like you play a hard set of tennis because it's fun, not for profit—because it's your cup of tea.

Q: Sir, do you consider such controversial works as *Tropic of Cancer* and *Lolita* good literature, or do you consider them just a collection of sordid incidents written for money?

A: I wouldn't undertake a judgment until I read the book. I haven't read that book yet. I would like to read it before I decide. I would give anyone the benefit of the doubt and assume that he is primarily trying to tell me a story rather than to titillate me.

Q: Sir, right after the First World War there was a group of American writers who went to France, the Expatriates. I'd like to know if you, at the time, had any opinion about their journey to France from America—why they went and what they did.

A: That came up this morning in the other class. I think in the War, 1917–18, is the first time that Americans ever really did much traveling to any extent in great numbers. And the exodus to Europe among writers afterwards was still a part of the same unrest. They had—some of them had been soldiers and found out that life in Europe was different and was pleasant and they went back to it. But I think it was part of the whole seethe, that unrest that suddenly got us involved in a war that many miles away which is still going on. I don't mean the war but the seethe, the unrest, the movement. And they—the writer, the artist is quite often the venturesome one, and he was the vanguard of the exodus, the trek back and forth to Europe.

Instructor: Perhaps, sir, you would comment to this class, as you did to the last, on the difference in the attitudes toward war of Midshipman Hope and Captain Bogard in "Turnabout"—the young British midshipman who treated war as a game as opposed to the very serious American captain.

A: Yes, I believe what I said was that it was a contrast not of nationalities so much as age. The British midshipman was only seventeen or eighteen years old—should still have been in school. The American captain was a mature man, and the American captain survives where the seventeen-year-old midshipman didn't, possibly because maturity will help a man to survive in a crisis. That the soldier who has a little maturity—a little—not so much experience but the discipline to stop and weigh what he's doing, where he is, may survive where the younger man who is no less brave or no more brave will lose his life—if that story did prove anything like that—I think that was. . . .

Instructor: Of course, I am sure most of the cadets now realize that we taught the story, or we discussed it, from the standpoint of attempting to infer about national characteristics or national attitudes from these two people and were completely wrong.

A: Yes, I don't think that national characteristics, attitudes, are important, and I am inclined to think now that they are dangerous if you pay too much attention to them. That people have got to be people first, whether they like it or not.

Q: Sir, would you say that the bravado the young midshipman had is better in a way than the courage which the captain possessed in a mature manner, and that actually the older man was influenced by the young man?

Later on in the story the captain does dive his plane toward a house almost to the point of collision.

A: Well, they were national traits. The swagger and the *insouciance* of the midshipman were British traits; the captain's colder, considering courage was typical of a Yale Skull and Bones man, which he was. I think that when he dove his bomber down on the roofs of that chateau, it was a gesture of revolt against all the brassbound stupidity of the generals and admirals that sit safe in the dugouts and tell the young men to go there and do that. That that was something that probably every soldier in war has felt. They have cursed the whole lot of them—that my brother is the man I am trying to kill. But you people safe at home—curse all of them. I am sure every soldier has felt that.

Q: Sir, in your short story "Beyond," I was wondering what the young child with the wounds in his hands and feet represented.

A: That was probably allegorical, symbolical, out of the background of religion which we all have and which is a part of the experience the writer draws from without deliberately trying to draw a parallel between this child and Christ—it's there, and if it seems good at the moment, he uses it with all gratitude—with all circumspection he will use it.

Q: Sir, what is your purpose in the revision of "The Bear," the short story about the boy and the large outlaw bear?

A: It was not really revised. It was a necessary portion of what to me was not a collection of short stories, but a novel, a book [*Go Down, Moses*]. And it seemed to me that it was necessary to break the story of the bear at one point and put something else in for the same reason that the musician says, "Now at this point I will need counterpoint. I will need discord. Or I will suspend this theme for another." It seems right for him to do. That was the reason. The story, if you drop out the—I think it's the third or fourth section, is just as I wrote it.

Q: Mr. Faulkner, I was just wondering if there was any personal experience involved in the inspiration of the events that transpired between the boy and the bear in that story.

A: Well, that was a part of my youth, my childhood, too. My father and his friends owned leases on the land similar to that. And I was taken there as soon as I was big enough to go into the woods with a gun, and I don't remember now just how much of that might have been actual, how much I invented. The three-toed bear was an actual bear. But I don't know that anyone killed him with a knife. And the dog was an actual dog, but I don't remember that they ever came into juxtaposition. It's difficult to say. That's the case of the three tanks with the collector. The writer's too busy to know whether he is stealing or lying. He's simply telling a story.

Q: Sir, last night you made a statement that you yourself write to tell a story, primarily. And you write it the best way possible and as vividly and as descriptively as possible. Do you believe that most authors are bound by this rule or that they do have some motive such as teaching a lesson or, to put it tritely, that they have a phrase, "The moral of the story is . . ."?

A: I am inclined to believe that we all write for the same reason. There can be a writer who has been so harried and so outraged by a social condition that he can't keep that social condition out of his story. But he is primarily telling a story of man struggling in the human condition—not a sociological condition but the condition of the heart's dilemma. I don't believe that he realizes until after that he has preached a sermon too. I think that he was primarily telling a story.

Q: Sir, along this same line, would you say that books such as *Uncle Tom's Cabin* would be written because of sociological conditions?

A: I would say that *Uncle Tom's Cabin* was written out of violent and misdirected compassion and ignorance of the author toward a situation which she knew only by hearsay. But it was not an intellectual process, it was hotter than that; it was out of her heart. It just happened that she was telling a story of Uncle Tom and the little girl, not telling the story—not writing a treatise on the impressions of slavery, because everybody knows that slaves have always had a hard time of it, not just Negro slaves in America, but the whole history back in Biblical times. She was simply writing a story which moved her, seemed so terrible and so hot to her that it had to be told. But I think she was writing about Uncle Tom as a human being—and Legree and Eliza as human beings, not as puppets.

Q: Sir, I would like to know exactly what it was that inspired you to become a writer.

A: Well, I probably was born with the liking for inventing stories. I took it up in 1920. I lived in New Orleans, I was working for a bootlegger. He had a launch that I would take down the Pontchartrain into the Gulf to an island where the rum, the green rum, would be brought up from Cuba and buried, and we would dig it up and bring it back to New Orleans, and he would make scotch or gin or whatever he wanted. He had the bottles labeled and everything. And I would get a hundred dollars a trip for that, and I didn't need much money, so I would get along until I ran out of money again. And I met Sherwood Anderson by chance, and we took to each other from the first. I'd meet him in the afternoon, we would walk and he would talk and I would listen. In the evening we would go somewhere to a speakeasy and drink, and he would talk and I would listen. The next morning he would say, "Well I have to work in the morning," so I wouldn't see him until the next afternoon. And I thought if that's the sort of life writers lead, that's the life for me. So I wrote a book and, as soon as I started, I found out it was fun. And I hadn't seen him and Mrs. Anderson for some time until I met her on the street, and she said, "Are you mad at us?" and I said, "No, ma'am, I'm writing a book," and she said, "Good Lord!" I saw her again, still having fun writing the book, and she said, "Do you want Sherwood to see your book when you finish it?" and I said, "Well, I hadn't thought about it." She said, "Well, he will make a trade with you; if he don't have to read that book, he will tell his publisher to take it." I said, "Done!" So I finished the book and he told Liveright to take it and Liveright took it. And that was how I became a writer—that was the mechanics of it.

Instructor: Would you recommend any specific works for these aspiring soldiers to read, sir, or would you recommend a particular sequence of your works that might help them in an approach to your novels?

A: To my notion, literature is such a pleasant thing, having kept it amateur, that I wouldn't advise anyone to read or write either as a job or duty. But I would say that, read everything. It don't matter what it is. Trash, the best, the worst, read everything. And if anyone does want to be a writer, he certainly must learn his craft, and the best way to learn it is from the people who can do it well. But I would read for pleasure and I would write for pleasure—not for money, not as a duty.

Q: Sir, do you have any particular reason for making some of your books a collection of short stories and another book a novel?

A: Yes, there must be some reason. In some cases the short stories, though they fall into the form of short stories, are to me continuous chapters in what is actually a novel. In other cases they are simply a collection of short stories in order to collect [them] into a book. As I said, I think that any writer wants to put down the magic of breathing in one word if he can, in a sonnet if he can, in a short story if he can, then in a novel if he must. But he is not too interested in the form it finally takes as a book. He is simply trying to get it down and get it said, and he would like to say it in one word if he could, which is impossible. It's like a jewel.

Q: Sir, did you have any particular reason for choosing the work that you read last night?

A: Yes, I had spoken to my son-in-law, Summers, who was here, class of '51, and I asked him what he would like to hear a middle-aged writer read when he was here, and he said he thought it should be from the current work, the one I just finished. I asked Major Fant about it, and Major Fant agreed. So that was sort of a unanimous opinion that's what we would read.

Q: Sir, I understand during your stay here you have been observing cadet life a little bit, especially at reveille. What is your opinion of the freshman or Fourth Class System?

A: Now, I don't know enough about it to be—to express opinions like that. But I have a different idea of the sort of men that are here from what I had when I came. I had expected a certain rigidity of—not thinking—but of the sort of questions I would get. And I was pleasantly astonished to find that the questions I got came from human beings, not from third classmen or second classmen or first classmen, but from human beings, from young men that had an idea that maybe a gray-headed bloke like me knew answers, and [could] answer the question. But I assume that your system—Fourth Class System—is a good one or they wouldn't have it.

Q: Sir, some of the remarks you made last night when you were reading showed a knowledge of the terms used around a race track. Do you ever research any of your topics?

A: No, that's out of observation, all the horse business more or less from experience. My father was a horseman, I have lived among horses all my life and still own horses and hunt in Virginia. And I have lost enough money at race tracks to know something about the jargon.

Q: Sir, could you tell us something about your grandfather? I understand that he was an interesting man and may have had some influence on your writing.

A: Yes, he was. He came into Mississippi on foot when he was fourteen years old. Ran away from home in Virginia looking for a distant relation—found him. At the moment his uncle was in jail for having shot a man. He—well, the story is that he saw a young girl in a yard that he passed and said, "When I get big I am going to marry her." And he did. That is, all this is the sort of thing that any hack writer might invent, you see, as a character. But later he got into politics. He went to the Mexican War as a friend of Jefferson Davis. In 1860 he organized, raised, and paid most of the expenses for the Second Mississippi Infantry and came to Virginia as its colonel. He commanded, as senior colonel, the brigade with Jackson until Bee arrived and took command before First Manassas. He went back after the—in the election of officers the next year at Opequon Creek—he was a martinet, and his men elected his lieutenant colonel to command the regiment, and my grandfather got mad and went back to Mississippi, and got bored after a while and raised a company of partisan cavalry that was finally brigaded into Forrest, and he finished the war there as a cavalry-man. And later got in politics and made some money. He built a railroad there—the first railroad in the country. He made the grand tour in Europe, and then he took to writing books, and I may have inherited the ink stain from him. He was killed in a duel before I was born.

Q: Sir, there has been a lot of talk recently about goals for America, and the President has appointed a commission to study this. Do you believe that it is necessary for a nation to have a certain set of defined goals, or do you feel that an individual should go along by himself?

A: I think if the individual takes care of himself and his own goals and his own conscience, that his nation will be in pretty good shape.

Q: Sir, in your book *The Sound and the Fury*, in the first part things are seen through the eyes of the idiot Benjy. Why did you do this?

A: That was that same hope that I tried to express that the artist feels to condense all experiences onto the head of the pin. That began as the story of a funeral. It's first—the first thing I thought of was the picture of the muddy seat of that little girl's drawers climbing the pear tree to look in the parlor window to see what in the world the grown people were doing that the children couldn't see, and I decided that the most effective way to tell that would be through the eyes of the idiot child who didn't even know, couldn't understand what was going on. And that went on for a while, and I thought it was going to be a ten-page short story. The first thing I knew I had about a hundred pages. I finished, and I still hadn't told that story. So I chose another one of the children, let him try. That went for a hundred pages, and I still hadn't told that story. So I picked out the other one, the one that was the nearest to what we call sane to see if maybe he could unravel the thing. He talked for a hundred pages, he hadn't told it, then I let Faulkner try it for a hundred pages. And when I got done, it still wasn't finished, and so twenty years later I wrote an appendix to it, tried to tell that story. That's all I was doing on the first page, was trying to tell what to me seemed a beautiful and tragic story of that doomed little girl climbing the pear tree to see the funeral.

Q: Sir, along these lines, when you first begin to write a story, do you have sort of an outline in your mind of what the whole story is going to consist of or do you sort of develop it as you write?

A: I would say it develops itself. It begins with a character, usually, and once he stands up on his feet and begins to move, all I do is to trot along behind him with a paper and pencil trying to keep up long enough to put down what he says and does, that he is taking charge of it. I have very little to do except the policeman in the back of the head which insists on unity and coherence and emphasis in telling it. But the characters themselves, they do what they do, not me.

Q: Why did you have so much trouble trying to end *The Sound and the Fury?* If an author has something in his heart that he has to get down on paper, why is it such a struggle to bring it about?

A: He wants to make it on paper as startling, as comic, anyway as moving, as true, as important as it seems in the imagination. And in the process of getting it into cold words on the paper, something escapes from it. It's still not as good as when he dreamed it. Which is the reason that when he finishes that to the best of his ability, he writes, tries again—he writes another one. He is still trying to capture that dream, that image of man, either victorious or defeated, in some splendid, beautiful gesture inside the dilemma of the human heart.

Q: Sir, I was wondering if you read much of the criticism that is written about your own work.

A: Don't read any of it. I'd rather read my fiction at firsthand, I think.

Q: Sir, have ever desired to be anything besides a writer?

A: Why sure, I'd like to be a brave, courageous soldier; I have thought of all sorts of things I'd like to be. I'd like to be a beautiful woman. I'd like to be a millionaire.

Q: Sir, we have a paper downstairs in an English display which comments on Robert Frost's impression of Mr. Khrushchev. Mr. Frost has a rather favorable impression of this man. What is your opinion of such a personality as Mr. Khrushchev?

A: Probably my opinion of Mr. Khrushchev is the same one the newspapers and what I read have given me. I know too little about him. I have my doubts of that whole system and I—and since I doubt, that whole system, I would doubt anyone it spewed up to the top, no matter who he was. But I know too little to have an opinion that's worth expressing—that is, any opinion I express would have to be, how to say it, from up here [pointing to his head], not from here [pointing to his heart].

Q: Sir, you place your stories against a whole host of different backgrounds, and I was wondering what background you yourself are happiest in, that you feel most at home in.

A: Well, almost anywhere. I am something like a cat probably. One place is the same as another to me. I get along, as far as I know, quite well with all sorts of people. There's a—some reasons that some time of the year I like Virginia because they have the fox hunting that I like there; at other times of the year I like Mississippi because there are things I like there. In the background that the writer uses in his story, he simply uses the one he is most familiar with, so that he won't have to do a lot of research. People behave the same. But you might make little mistakes or dialect or custom that someone from Cape Cod would say, "Uh-uh, us folks don't act like that up here," but if you are located in the country you are familiar with nobody can check you on it. You don't have to be careful.

Q: Sir, you stated last night that one of the primary sources that a writer gets his ideas from is someone else's books—reading. Do you just pick something up as you go along, something that interests you, or do you have a schedule of reading?

A: No, I never have. When I was young I was an omniverous reader with no judgment, no discretion—I read everything. As I have gotten along in years, I don't read with the same voracity, and I go to the book as you go to spend a few minutes with a friend you like. I will open the book to a particular chapter or to read about a particular character in it. Not to read the book just to spend a little while with a human being that I think is funny or tragic or anyway interesting.

Q: Last night you said, sir it was a writer's duty to portray the feelings and emotions of the human heart. Well, what books, other than some of your own works, do you feel best do this?

A: Well, almost all do, except the ones that are untruthful and shabby and are simply written to titillate and to make money. Almost any book you open will do that—anything in Shakespeare, Tolstoy, Dostoevsky, Balzac, Gautier, Dreiser, Lewis, Anderson. There are problems which you recognize at once as being familiar problems, that is so familiar, or familiar enough to—where you say, "Yes, I believe that's so, I believe that's true, that this is what I felt or what I imagine myself feeling. I would know this anguish. Anyway, I believe this anguish is so."

Q: Sir, what do you think are the outstanding traits of the South as a region?

A: Do you mean the ones that are the most noticeable or the ones that you would like the best?

Q: Well, both of them, sir.

A: Well, the most noticeable trait is belief that we can repeal 1962. I would think that the trait I like best is of courtesy, of automatic courtesy. That is, you say, "Thank you," and "Sir," and "Ma'am," to anyone—everyone—regardless whether—hospitality. I don't like the emotionalism, the propensity to depend on the emotions instead of on the gray matter. I don't like the hot summers. I have said for sixty-five years I'd never spend another summer there, and yet I am going back in June.

Q: Sir, what is your attitude to having motion pictures made of your works?

A: Well, it's a good way to make a little money. I have in the contract that I don't have to see the picture, so it never confuses me, and I spend the money, sometimes wisely—but anyway it's nice to have a little money now and then.

Q: Sir, do you reread your old works?

A: Yes, just as I will reread into certain pages of Dickens to spend time with people that I like or are funny. I like my sewing machine agent Ratliff, I will go back to read about him, to laugh again quite often, just as I read about Sarah Gamp, just as I read into *Don Quixote*.

Q: Mr. Faulkner, in *Knight's Gambit* there is a character named Monk, who was an imbecile. Exactly how did you create him?

A: I can remember a country man in my county that looked like him, who was half-witted, and possibly the story came from that. This man, a half-wit, harmless, but with no future, nothing to be done—and so possibly I tried to invent a future, even a tragic one for him, something to leave his mark on the world instead of living and dying a harmless half-imbecile. That's a case—it's difficult to say just where you get the idea, it may be from something you saw—then you won't let it alone. Certainly I don't think that any writer ever wrote down or put down anything he actually saw or heard because a writer is congenitally incapable of telling the truth about anything. He has got to change it. He has got to lie. That's why they call it fiction, you see.

Q: Sir, what do you consider to be the qualities that an imbecile or half-wit possesses that enables him to see stories in the way that you are looking for?

A: I wouldn't say that he has those qualities. That is the prerogative of the writer to use his imagination to that extent if it makes something that seems moving and true. Maybe the imbecile should have quality. That's what I mean by truth. He probably hasn't, which is the fact, but maybe he should, which is the truth.

Q: Sir, why were you so apparently anxious to involve yourself in the First World War? You were rejected by the American Army and you joined up with the Canadian. Were you just restless or curious?

A: Sure, something going on. Folks in Mississippi didn't get to travel much. There was a chance to travel free. Of course, when you are seventeen or eighteen you don't have any more sense that that, you know.

Q: A lot of people, sir, have commented on the present state of American morals and say that we are going to the dogs in certain ways. Do you believe that our morals have actually been diluted that much from what they were years ago?

A: The first thing I can remember hearing my Grandmother and my maiden aunt say is, that young people are going to the dogs. That was back in about 1904 or '05 and probably young people always will be going to the dogs; there will always be somebody seventy or eighty years old to notice it and tell you about it. I was going to say that there is probably more juvenile delinquency today because there are more juveniles.

Q: Do you think the period of the Depression has had very much effect on literature, on the stories people wanted to tell?

A: Only—it has changed the outside pattern of what they want. It hasn't changed what they did. It hasn't changed the passions and hopes that drove them to the actions. It would appear in the story as the coincidence of the environment, not as any alteration in the hope, the striving of the particular human heart, because the dilemma is the same one. It has nothing to do with depression or segregation. The dilemmas are a little more eternal than that.

Q: As a general rule, sir, can someone find your attitude towards a subject by examining the attitude of some of your characters in your stories?

A: Probably a lot of people have tried that. I think that any book should have on the first page, "The author declines to accept responsibility for the behavior or actions or speeches of any of these characters, because he is simply trying to tell you a story." And these people that he uses, they don't necessarily have to believe as he believes. He quite often hates them, disagrees with them. But they seem to him necessary to tell the story which he is trying to tell.

Q: Sir, what is your evaluation of poetry as the means of expressing the human heart?

A: To me, poetry is first. The failed poet becomes a short story writer. The failed short story writer has nothing left but the novel, so he's a novelist. But poetry, to me, is first. That is the nearest approach to condensing all the beauty and passion of the human heart onto the head of the pin.

Q: Sir, do you actually believe it is possible then to communicate the feeling of one person to another person, completely?

A: Yes, you don't necessarily need to depend on words to do it, but, yes, I think people can communicate.

Q: I mean, sir, do you believe it is actually possible to give a completely accurate communication?

A: Yes, possible, But it is not always deliberately possible—that is, you can't sit down—I am going to communicate a thought to you, so here it is. I think that that is by accident, the communication comes across a long distance and maybe years later through something that neither party believed was going to carry the message.

Q: Sir, during your writing do you ever become discouraged with your work, or have you always felt that you were enjoying this to the utmost and that you would always write throughout the rest of your life? In other words, have you ever become discouraged in your work at any time?

A: Yes, constantly. That's why writing is such a matchless vocation to follow. It never gives you any peace. The discouragement is because it ain't quite as good as that dream, it ain't quite as good as you want it to be—you are frustrated, your are enraged at it. You tear it up, burn it, but you don't quit. As soon as you cool off a little, then you try it again, because there is nothing that can match the pleasure of creation—of creating some form of art, because only that way can you affirm your immortality. That all any artist is trying to do is, he knows that after a few years he will pass through the final gate into oblivion. He is simply going to leave on that wall "Kilroy was here." Not for power, not for money, but simply to say "I was here for a little while, I left this mark."

Q: Sir, many times in their works, authors include characters which are said to be either autobiographical or to represent a close relative or friend. Are these characters ever put in there purposely to represent these people or is it just telling a story and they just happen to coincide with real people?

A: As I said a while ago, the writer is incapable of telling the truth. He couldn't take an actual human being and translate him onto paper and stick to the facts. He has got to change and embroider. And he will—he is completely ruthless about that. He will alter the known human being out of all recognition if it suits his purpose, because he is simply not trying to portray that human being but to tell you a story of that human being moving—in motion.

Q: You speak, sir, of human immorality and at the same time you say that man will pass into oblivion. Now, I don't quite understand what you mean by that.

A: Well, the individual—you and I know that after a certain time we will be no more. Where we will be then we don't know yet. But we do know that at a certain time we will be no more. That's what I meant by the mortality of the individual. The immortality is the fact that frail, fragile man, a web of bone and nerves, mostly water, in a ramshackle universe has outlasted most other forms of mammalian life. He has outlasted his own disasters, and I think that he will continue—that, for the reason I believe I said this morning, that the species which has created the fine picture, the music, the statues, the books, is too valuable for omnipotence, God whoever he is, to let perish. That is the immortality of the race, not of the individual.

Q: Sir, then you feel that evolution, the mammalian evolution, ceases with the human being, that we couldn't possibly die out and something better take our place?

A: I don't know. I wouldn't make a statement like that, nobody would, actually. We don't know what man might evolve into—just how low he is, what flea he is on something that we can't even see, it is so great, so vast.

Q: Sir, if that small child in your short story "Beyond" represented religion, why would you portray him as just a small child who is always crying and dirty and lacking self-control?

A: I didn't say that he represented religion. I said that, if I had put holes in his hands and feet, it was very likely a symbolism out of my religious background from the image of the Christ—that I wasn't trying to show up the Christ at all. I simply, at that moment, felt that my story needed the symbolism which I could borrow from the history of the crucifixion or the marks of the crucifixion on this child. I would have to read the story again to probably answer you more, because I don't remember the story. That was a long time ago.

Q: Sir, the essay seems to be entirely foreign to your style of writing and thinking as a form of literature. Have you ever had any experience at essay writing, or what's your opinion of yourself writing an essay?

A: Well, my opinion is that that's not for me, that I don't have enough education, I don't know anything about ideas, to write an essay. All I know about are people in the seethe and fury of the human condition, in motion. Like all uneducated people, I have a certain distrust of ideas. I think that, if I had to depend on something, I would depend on what my heart tells me, not on what my mind tells me, because I have no confidence in my brain.

Q: Sir, a little while back you made the statement that you rank poetry as the first form of literature, then short stories, then the novel. Around here, sir, in our English Department, we find that we are to write clearly and concisely in as few words as possible. Is this why perhaps you rank the short story ahead of the novel?

A: It's not why, but they go along with each other. What you are taught about preciseness and brevity is exactly what the poet has learned to practice, only the poet can cast over it such a magic that you can see the picture of all human passion in the fourteen lines of the sonnet. That's the magic of his talent, but the conciseness is exactly what you are trained [in] here. It's to say it in one word, if possible, which is what the poet wants to do. It can't be done, so he takes fourteen lines.

Index